MA

SUPER
PLONK
2006

ABOUT THE AUTHOR

Malcolm Gluck, having left the *Guardian* after 15 years, is devoting himself to writing books and taking photographs. *The Simple Art of Marrying Food and Wine* (with Mark Hix) was published in 2005. His book on the winemakers of the New World, with his own photographs, is being published in 2006.

MALCOLM GLUCK
SUPER PLONK 2006

THE TOP 1000

Collins

First published in 2005 by
Collins, an imprint of
HarperCollins*Publishers*
77–85 Fulham Palace Road
Hammersmith
London W6 8JB

The Collins website address is www.collins.co.uk

Collins is a registered trademark of HarperCollins Publishers Ltd

10	09	08	07	06	05
6	5	4	3	2	1

Editor: Susan Fleming
Design: Bob Vickers
Indexer: Lisa Footitt

A catalogue record for this book is available from the British Library

ISBN 0-00-720774-3

Printed and bound in Great Britain by Clays Ltd, St Ives plc.

To
MATTHEW FORT,
who said 'Yes'!

'Be independent, Malcolm. Don't let anyone get you in his pocket. And another thing – I'd rather you were brought home dead than drunk.'

My father as Polonius, as paraphrased by J. L. Carr (who must have been listening) in *A Season in Sinji* (Quince Tree Press, £6.99).

CONTENTS

SUPERPLONKS OF THE YEAR (AND OTHER INDULGENCES)   xi

INTRODUCTION   xv
How this book works   xxiv
How I rate a wine: what makes a Superplonk a Superplonk   xxv

ASDA   1
BOOTHS   27
BUDGENS   43
CO-OP   57
E-TAILERS   71
MAJESTIC   81
MARKS & SPENCER   109
MORRISON'S   129
ODDBINS   139
SAINSBURY   163
SMALL MERCHANTS   195
SOMERFIELD   223
TESCO   243
THRESHERS   281
WAITROSE   297
YAPP BROTHERS   329

INDEX OF WINE NAMES   335

ACKNOWLEDGEMENTS

I rely upon my own individual judgement where wine is concerned but everything else requires a team. I am, then, grateful to publishing director Denise Bates and my editor Susan Fleming. I thank Jane Hollyman who manages the marketing, Louise Lawson who organises publicity and my book-signing tour, Nick Ford who runs the sales team, and Bob Vickers who does such a great job with the design. Grainne Fox at the Ed Victor agency is also to be thanked. And my debt to my two Sues, Gluck and Bolton, who manage all the data is enormous. I'd also like to say how grateful I have been for the support of my www.superplonk.com editor, Rick Staff, during this past year.

SUPERPLONKS OF THE YEAR (AND OTHER INDULGENCES)

I've long toyed with the idea of singling out certain wines each year in this book. But it seemed an irrelevance. With my rating system such wines stood out anyway. Three things changed my mind and persuaded me I should do it. First, the bad publicity inexpensive wines got at the witless hands of the *Which? Wine Guide* when it attacked under £5 wines. Second, the fact that I was finding more and more terrific wines at bargain prices, contradicting the advice and snobbish views of other wine critics. Third, I felt it might be fun and something different, for this book at least, and allow me to select deserving wines which were not necessarily the highest rating in their categories.

There are many wines, persons, and retailers other than the ones below deserving of a Superplonk of the Year nomination. I acknowledge Tesco's and Oddbins' in-depth conversion to screwcaps and Majestic's wonderful nose for a bargain but Threshers pipped them both to the Retailer of the Year prize on the grounds of the compelling simplicity of its game plan to woo drinkers. I would also dearly liked to have included some wines which vintage changes and other uncertainties forced me to ignore.

Without doubt, Threshers' Vineyard X Garnacha 2003 from Spain, a risible £2.33 (on the basis of buying two bottles and getting a third free), would be a Red Wine of the Year, perhaps *the* Red Wine of the Year. However, the vintage deserving of that accolade is likely to be exhausted by the time this book is in print and a later vintage, the 2004, replace it. This is a good wine, an amazing bargain, but it is not quite as cohesive as the earlier vintage (though it still rates 16 points). I would also have given a prominent place in the Old World Wine of the Year category to Beau Monde 2004, a fluent Burgundy from the dynamic Boisset company of Nuits-St-Georges, which is not only screwcapped but available at Sainsbury, on promotion, for £4.99. Sainsbury told me, however, the wine would be sold out by the time this book was in print.

WINE RETAILER OF THE YEAR

Threshers – for its brave three-bottles-for-the price-of-two offers on all table wines in all its branches all of the time.

WINE PRODUCER OF THE YEAR

Fairview Estate, South Africa – where proprietor Charles Back continues to create not only exciting, meaningful wines but exciting, meaningful changes in the lives of the people who produce them.

RETAILER OWN-LABEL RANGE OF THE YEAR

Morrison's – for the cheeky Cielo de Luz range of Chilean reds and whites.

RED WINE BOX OF THE YEAR

Asda – for the succulent No 2 French Merlot (16 points, £15.98).

WHITE WINE BOX OF THE YEAR

Waitrose – for the elegant Chileño Chardonnay/Sémillon 2004 from Chile (16 points, £15.99).

WHITE WINE OF THE YEAR

Tesco – for the deliciously screwcapped Tesco Chilean White NV (I6 points, £2.86).

RED WINE OF THE YEAR

Asda – for the softly engaging Asda Chilean Merlot NV (16.5 points, £2.98).

ROSÉ WINE OF THE YEAR

Waitrose – for the captivating Cuvée Fleur Rosé, Vin de Pays de l'Hérault 2004 (16 points, £3.55).

SPARKLING WINE OF THE YEAR

Somerfield – for the classy Somerfield Vintage Cava Brut 2000 from Spain (17.5 points, £6.99).

FORTIFIED WINE OF THE YEAR

Tesco – for the tasty Finest Oloroso Sherry NV
(16.5 points, £4.99).

OLD WORLD WINE OF THE YEAR (dead heat)

Sainsbury – for the screwcapped, tangily crisp
Muscadet La Régate 2004 (16 points, £2.99).
Booths – for the shapely Château Pierrail Bordeaux
Supérieur 2002 (16.5 points, £5.99).

NEW WORLD WINE OF THE YEAR (dead heat)

Co-op – for the richly savoury Graffigna Shiraz/
Cabernet Sauvignon 2003 from Argentina
(16.5 points, £3.99).
Majestic – for its brilliant Coldridge Estate Merlot
2003 (16 points, £3.69) from Australia.

SUPERPLONK CHUTZPAH WINE OF THE YEAR*

Waitrose – for Green Point ZD 2001 (16 points,
£12.99) from Australia, the first bottle fermented,
i.e. champagne-style, sparkling wine in the UK to be
sold with a crown seal (aka a beer cap).

* pronounced 'hoots-pa', the incomparable Yiddish term
chutzpah means to exhibit dazzling bare-faced cheek
(like the kid who poisoned his parents and said to the judge:
'Be merciful. I'm an orphan').

INTRODUCTION

In the sixteen years since I became a wine writer, Britain has gone from being a narrow-minded beer island to an all-embracing vinland. This transformation is not simply one of concern to the social scientist or anthropologist but of genuine revelatory interest to any intelligent Briton possessed of an enquiring palate and an inquisitive mind. It has been alleged that this very guide aided and abetted this metamorphosis by leading the way in popularising the wine from supermarkets. But it was the *Guardian* newspaper, in autumn 1988, which triggered that abetting.

Having read an article I had written that same year on *How to Thicken Coq au Vin Using the Blood of Advertising Executives,* the newspaper wondered, on the strength of this piece of tomfoolery, if I would care to write for it. I was invited out to lunch, at a new fusion-food eatery in Charlotte Street in Fitzrovia, by Alan Rusbridger, now editor of the paper, and Matthew Fort, its newly appointed food and drink editor.

'What we want from you,' they said, 'is a wine column. We think you're the man for it.'

'We want something,' added Alan recklessly, 'which approaches the subject totally differently. That no-one has ever written before.'

I replied that this did not present a problem. How about a column based solely on the wine in supermarkets? I pointed out that wine critics seemed never to set foot in such demotic emporia.

Mr Rusbridger took a sharp intake of breath. He and Matthew Fort exchanged glances. 'Well, I suppose supermarkets do sell wine. Do they?' said the future editor-in-charge.

Matthew wasn't sure. But what they were sure about was that they were prepared to take a punt and consider such an outrageous idea. And so a deal was struck. March 1989 saw the first Superplonk column appear under my name and it made me sick to read it as I rushed out on Saturday morning at first light and feverishly opened the *Weekend Guardian* wherein it appeared. Were these words mine? Had I truly concocted a sentence which was utter nonsense and a paragraph introduction which did not follow on from the one before? And where had all these strange infelicities come from?

My name was attached to the column but I did not feel I was its author. It was a travesty of the care and acute consciousness I had put into it. If I remember correctly, one of the wines had its description so curtailed it read as gibberish. I spent a weekend of utter dejection. A lifetime's ambition (well, the lifetime of a mature newspaper reader at any rate) turned to bitter ashes in my mouth.

I faxed a furious letter to Mr Rusbridger first thing on Monday morning describing my disquiet and he replied saying that sub-editors had often to

trim articles to ensure they were the required
wordage and fitted the page. But I had written the
exact words asked for. I had counted each one. It got
no better as the next few years progressed. One
morning I awoke to find my column extolling the
virtues of Danish wines. The sub-editor, whom I
now referred to as Dewhurst (after the chain of
butcher's shops), had for some reason excised the Sp
of the red wines in the column and metamorphosed
them into a D. I ask you: *Danish Rioja?*

Often the column did not appear as promised
and the promotional wines I had written about, once
the column did appear, had only a few days left
before their prices reverted to normal. But by the
time modern computer technology arrived, and with
new sub-editors on my case and the ball, the column
began to appear as I had written it (though even then
my hidden jokes were sometimes ruined by being
spelt out and once my reference to Yasser Arafat was
struck out on the grounds that 'the *Guardian* gets
enough stick about its stance on Israel without you
sticking your oar in').

Computer technology is not the only thing
which has changed the world of the *Guardian* and of
wine over the past decade and a half. In 1988,
Sainsbury's had just six Aussie reds and eleven
Aussie whites in its range. It really wasn't sure about
Australian wines. The then head of wine buying at
this retailer, a few years previously, had confidently
told an Aussie saleswoman that Australian wine
'would never catch on in the UK'.

How wrong he was (he was also the prescient pundit who averred, when he was contacted with the news that a totally unknown writer was going to launch a newspaper column based on supermarket wines, responded with 'Are you sure this is wise?'). Now Sainsbury's has 112 Aussie bottles on its shelves. The cheapest of the bunch sixteen years ago was the own-label non-vintage Shiraz/Cabernet at £2.45 (15 points out of 20). Sainsbury's Australian Cabernet Shiraz 2003 is the nearest equivalent today and, what d'ye know?, it rates 15 points also. I daresay Sainsbury wishes its business was as consistent in other respects.

Australia has surprised everyone. In Julian Maclaren-Ross's quite dreadful 1947 novel *Of Love and Hunger* (recently re-published in Penguin Classics, 5 points out of 20, £8.99) he writes, 'She fetched in a canister of biscuits and a bottle of port. Australian port. Not very good but still better than nothing.' Nowadays the port drinker can trog down to Oddbins and dive into the headily perfumed exuberance of D'Arenberg Fortified Shiraz. It may no longer be allowed, quite rightly, to pass itself off as port, but it can legitimately pass itself off as a staggeringly delicious fortified wine.

Other changes have embraced even stick-in-the-muds like Burgundy. Macon Blanc, for example, has improved out of all recognition in the past fifteen years. New Zealand has also happened on the scene in a big way. Remember Jackson Estate Sauvignon Blanc? The late 1980s and early 1990s vintages were fantastic, tastier than the pioneering Cloudy Bay, and with the 2004 (17.5 points, £8.99) it was back to form with a vengeance. This screwcapped wine offered superb layers of citrus, under-ripe gooseberry, grapefruit and firm pear. An outstanding liquid, it is more beguiling than Cloudy Bay 2004 (£13.00, 14 points) by far. You can find it – if indeed there any bottles left – at Majestic and Waitrose.

Sixteen years ago the latter retailer seemed merely a posh version of Harrods. Now it is a national force. Back in 1988 Waitrose had fifteen wines from Australia, a mere single bottle from South America, four from South Africa (a disgraceful breaking of the boycott), three from California and just two from New Zealand. In contrast, it had thirty German wines which outsold all of the New World wines combined. Today? Germany is struggling and, well, you hardly need statistics to be aware of how much the British palate has taken to New World fruit.

I suppose the biggest change in sixteen years has to be the prevalence of screwcaps. But change has also been thrillingly apparent in previously moribund, rustic wine areas of Europe.

Since 1988, the Languedoc has emerged to become France's most intriguing wine region. It is now producing more thrilling wines in greater abundance than ever before.

In sixteen years the Co-op has also got its act together and become a terrific wine retailer.

Argentina and Chile have become influential exporters on a scale not dreamed possible.

And what of retailer's like Morrison's? It didn't exist for me in 1988 for it was an exclusively northern phenomenon. Dutifully, northern readers told me get off my London backside and go and investigate. Dutifully, I did so. This retailer had never seen a wine journalist before I came knocking. Now it can offer bargains all over the country (having acquired and absorbed Safeway) and its wines appear in several critics' columns.

Majestic is another great growth area. When I first wrote about this retailer it got up *Guardian* readers' noses big time. It only sold, and still sells, wine by the case or mixed case and some readers demanded I bar them, on those grounds, from inclusion in the column and this guide. It is a tribute to the tolerance of both readerships that news of Majestic's vinous coups is now received with equanimity and, if I am to believe Majestic, stampedes of readers whenever a bargain appears in these pages.

However, after all those years together, the unthinkable has happened. The *Guardian* newspaper and I are no longer together. I published my last Superplonk column in the newspaper on December 11 2004. We began seriously to fall out of love a few years back, once the Saturday supplement in which I was published became a frothy colour magazine full of ads for loud motor cars and with articles about flashy gimmicks no-one needs.

Once *Guardian* readers knew I was going, I was
humbled to receive hundreds of e-mails, cards and
letters, protesting my departure. Hopefully, such
stalwarts will buy this book and access the website
and stay in touch with me that way. Several readers
wrote to the newspaper directly (and a list of some of
the readers who wrote to me appears at the back of
this book). One of the most amusing (and pertinent)
correspondents was Mr Ian Evans.

To the Editor, *Weekend Guardian*
Sir,
Some while ago you lost Julie Burchill,
who, even when she was talking nonsense, was
at the very least readable and usually thought
provoking.
More recently you have lost Malcolm
Gluck – always informative, and able to make
the sometimes intimidating world of wine
buying accessible, interesting, affordable and
enjoyable, to anyone with access to a
supermarket.
To paraphrase, 'To lose one is
unfortunate, to lose two seems like
carelessness.'
None of the subsequent writers has filled
the gap left by Ms Burchill and as for your new
wine writer, having read her column, what can
one say!
A quote from her first contribution seems
to sum things up. 'I haven't had a chance to

try...[at £25 a bottle !!!] but "my friend likes it" .'
Just like Simon Hoggart, I made the last bit up,
but you get my drift!

One might also ask if the purpose of
buying wine is to 'impress your friends by
being achingly fashionable'. God save us! What
is the woman playing at ????

A few years ago I bought, on the strength
of Malcolm Gluck's column, a couple of cases
at about £12 a bottle. An internet search
recently quoted a delivery price ex-VAT of
nearly £60 a bottle. That's an example of the
level of knowledge and expertise that you've
lost!

What were you thinking of?
Ian Evans.

Another missive which touched a chord was
this: 'Beat the drum slowly...eyes streaming with
Cabernet-soaked tears I gave my wife the terrible
news....Gluck is going....I could hardly utter the
words...my old friend and mentor for God knows
how long...deepest gloom. "Yippee!" wife yells, "at last
I can get the *Independent*!" I will miss you terribly.
David Armitage.'

Thanks, Ian and David. Needless to say the
Guardian didn't print Ian's letter as written. However,
leaving so respected a newspaper has forced me to
question the basis of my approach to wine writing:
am I right to continue to believe value-for-money is
paramount? Am I past my sell-by date? Having

pioneered the idea of a wine column based on good value wines, were the new young drinkers prowling the shelves indifferent to price?

I did not question these basic precepts of my approach for long. Neither did the publisher of this book. More than ever, we believe the great majority of drinkers want to find wines which deliver excitement and sensuality without having to dig too deeply into their pockets. As proof, this book is still a best-selling wine guide. It is still the only guide which rates wines points out of twenty. It is still the only guide which covers so many wines and so many wine retailers.

And it is still the only wine guide which comes backed up by a state-of-the-art website where subscribers can get in touch with the author, via e-mail, any time and on anything connected with wine. As long as electricity continues to flow and my liver carries on functioning, I will continue to make my living tasting and writing about wine.

HOW THIS BOOK WORKS

I am still the only wine writer who rates wines on the humane basis of value for money, and I suspect I always will be. For me, there is no romance in expensive wine unless the liquid in the bottle is sublime.

The book, you will readily perceive, is divided into retailer sections but not sub-divided by countries of origin. This information is important at point of sale yes, but here you need the information only as part of much else. The most important retailers are represented. The supermarkets are Asda, Booths, Budgens, the Co-op, Marks & Spencer, Morrison's (including Safeway), Sainsbury, Somerfield, Tesco and Waitrose. The wine shops are Majestic, Oddbins, and Threshers, but you will also note e-tailers, smaller merchants and such important regional merchants as Yapp Brothers.

You will note also that I have done away with descriptions of all wines below 16 points. Wines scoring between 14 and 15.5 points are rated but not described. The website, superplonk.com, carries details and ratings of all the wines I taste, the good, the bad and the ugly (even those wines which rate under 10 points), but the book concentrates solely on the top raters, the wines which deserve drinking. These are the ones scoring decent points out of 20 – red, white, rosé, sparkling and fortified.

Nothing could be simpler. But immediately you ask: how does this rating system work? This is how:

HOW I RATE A WINE: WHAT MAKES A SUPERPLONK A SUPERPLONK

It is worth repeating: value for money is my single unwavering focus. I drink with my readers' pockets in my mouth. I do not see the necessity of paying a lot for a bottle of everyday drinking wine and only rarely do I consider it worth paying a high price for, say, a wine for a special occasion or because you want to experience what a so-called 'grand' wine may be like.

I do taste expensive wines regularly. I do not, regularly, find them worth the money. That said, there are some pricey bottles in these pages. They are here because the wines are genuinely worth every penny (which is what the definition of a superplonk is). A wine of magnificent complexity, thrilling fruit, superb aroma, great depth and finesse is worth drinking. Such a wine challenges the intellect as much as the palate and its value lies, like a great theatrical performance or outstanding novel, in its unforgettableness. I will rate it highly. Even though it costs a lot, the lot it costs is justified.

20 points Life rarely throws up perfection. Indeed, some aesthetes regard true beauty as always revealing a small flaw. I do not. There is no flaw in a 20-point wine. It has perfect balance, finesse, flavour and finish – dull terms to describe the sum of an unforgettable experience. A perfect wine is also perfectly affordable. That is not to say (necessarily)

£2.99 or even £4.99, but a sum related to common sense. Even if such a wine costs £100 it is still worth 20 points and the possible pain of acquisition. A 20-point wine is Mitsuko Uchida playing Mozart's piano sonatas, it is the 1962 Spurs football team, it is *Some Like It Hot*, it is Elizabeth David's recipe for mackerel with mustard butter. It is Roger Federer's backhand.

19 points What's a point between friends? Or between one wine and another? 19 points represents a superb wine of towering individuality and impact. Almost perfect and well worth the expense (even if it is an expensive bottle), such a wine will flood the senses with myriad smells, tastes and flavours and provide a tantalising glimpse, whilst it lasts, of the sheer textured genius of great wine. Such a wine is individual, rich, subtle yet potent, and overwhelmingly delicious. It can start, and finish, a conversation. Indeed, a 19 points is like a wonderful conversation – as one between Kenneth Tynan and Bernard Levin might be.

18 points This is an excellent wine but lacking that ineffable sublimity of richness and complexity to achieve the very highest rating. Such a wine offers superb drinking and thundering good value and it must exhibit a remarkably well-textured richness. True, I do emphasise texture above other aspects of complexity (like all those fruits some tasters are determined to find in a wine) and here the texture is so well married to the acids and sugars that it is all of a piece. Such a wine is remarkable, immensely drinkable, complex and compelling. It is the Beatles' *Yesterday*, it is Schubert's *Die Schöne Müllerin*, it is Bill Evans playing *Waltz for Debbie.*

17 points An exciting, well-made wine, almost invariably hugely affordable, which offers real glimpses of multi-layered richness. It will demonstrate individuality and incisiveness and it will offer a seductive mouthfeel and sense of luxury. It may be a more immediate wine than those rating higher, but it will still linger in the memory the day after it is drunk – for it will have given a delightful and impressive performance. A 17-pointer is Jonny Wilkinson, Max Schmelling, Tim Henman, Jimmy Greaves.

16 points This is a very good wine indeed. Good enough for any dinner party and any level of drinker (with the possible exception of those most toffee-nosed of snobs for whom pleasure usually comes associated with a fat price-tag). Not necessarily an expensive wine is implied here but it will be a terrifically drinkable, satisfying and multi-dimensional one. It will be properly balanced and often be excellent with particular kinds of dishes (which it enhances). It is Ry Cooder, Diane Krall, *Guys and Dolls.* It is Phil Larkin's poetry.

15.5, 15, 14.5, 14 points There are some terrific
wines often to be found at these ratings, but they are
more Gilbert and Sullivan, Crosbie, Stills, Nash &
Young, than Mozart or Beethoven. Astute readers
note that many of the under £3 wines, wines ignored
by many other wine writers purely on grounds of
price, rate 14–15 points and so this is a happy
hunting-ground for drinkers who dislike spending
even close to a fiver for a drinkable bottle.

Whilst I cannot, on grounds of lack of complexity
and perhaps texture, rate these wines as I would a
16-pointer and above, they are nevertheless worthy
superplonks.

ASDA

Head Office:
Asda House,
Southbank,
Great Wilson Street,
Leeds LS11 5AD

Tel: (0500) 100055 (230 branches nationwide)
Fax: (0113) 2417732

Website: www.asda.co.uk

For tasting notes of Asda wines scoring less than
16 points, and ratings of wines less than 14 points,
visit www.superplonk.com

16.5

WHITE £6.98

'A' Limoux Chardonnay 2003 FRANCE

Gorgeous apricot and burned crème caramel. Those
seeking an alternative to expensive white Burgundy
could do a lot worse than check out Limoux (the
Chardonnay may be less subtle than those further
north but it can offer more exciting scenery).

16.5

WHITE SPARKLING £2.98

Asda Vintage Cava 2002 SPAIN

Wonderfully elegant, demurely rich and delicious.

16.5

RED £2.98

Asda Chilean Merlot NV CHILE

Dark chocolate-centred fruit with soft furry tannins
which adhere like Velcro track to the deeply berried
texture. It is surprising, to put it mildly, that anyone
can turn out a drinkable wine at this price with the
obscene level of alcohol duty levied by this
government.

16.5

WHITE £5.98

Asda Extra Special Pinot Grigio, Maso Gua 2003 ITALY

Deliciously different: grapefruit, hint of dry peach,
citrus.

16.5

WHITE £6.96

Brown Brothers Pinot Gris 2003 AUSTRALIA

Screwcap. Delightful apricot and lemon with a
genteel smoky undertone.

16.5 (Coleen McLoughlin/Alexandra Gluck) WHITE £4.52
11.5 (the author) USA
Blossom Hill Chardonnay/Viognier NV

Coleen McLoughlin is, so I am reliably informed by
my daughter Alex, the girlfriend of a footballer
called Wayne Rooney. Ms McLoughlin has been
reported as saying that even when she's in a posh
restaurant she always orders Blossom Hill (which
makes you wonder what kind of restaurant can be
deemed posh and have such a wine on its list,
but the mysteries of these things are, I concede,
beyond me). Alex likes the wine too and she said I
was being elitist to dismiss it with a mere 11.5 point
rating and so here it is elevated to premier league
status.

16.5 WHITE £4.99
Casillero del Diablo Concha y Toro CHILE
Sauvignon Blanc 2004
A crisp, classic Sauvignon Blanc of length and
crunchy concentration.
Also at Majestic, Oddbins, Somerfield, Tesco,
Threshers.

16.5 WHITE £4.97
Casillero del Diablo Concha y Toro CHILE
Chardonnay 2004
The buttery touch is burned yet delicate. Terrific
texture and delicacy yet real rich fruit to finish.
Also at Majestic, Oddbins, Threshers.

16.5   WHITE DESSERT (half bottle) £3.99

Cranswick Reserve Selection   AUSTRALIA
Botrytis Sémillon 2002
18.5 points in 2010–15. Superb dessert wine. Has fine
acids, peach and honied passionfruit richness, and
the texture is like cough syrup (well, almost). A
genuine throat charmer.

16.5   RED £6.98

Diemersfontein Pinotage 2004   SOUTH AFRICA
Exciting tobacco-edged blueberries and plums,
slightly charred at the edges, herbs and plump
tannins.
Also at Waitrose.

16.5   RED £5.99

Errazuriz Estate Carmenere 2003   CHILE
A superb cheese wine of great berried depth, soft
plums and blackberries and ripe tannins with a
black olive edge.
Also at E-tailers (Everywine), Small Merchants (D.
Byrne & Co., Fareham Wine Cellar, Luvians, Vicki's of
Chobham, Wimbledon Wine Cellars).

Chile is the elegant strumpet of the wine world: *any style you
like, dearie, anyway you want it.* What great fun the wines are,
and invariably reliable. I always turn first to the Chilean
wines on any restaurant wine list to see just how little I can
get away with and still acquire a first-rate tipple.

16.5   RED £5.99

Errazuriz Estate Cabernet Sauvignon 2003   CHILE

Very gripping, vivid fruit, a combination of chocolate
and burned berries, and the tannins cut a wave of
flavour to finish up kicking their well-shod heels in
the throat before quitting.
Also at E-tailers (Everywine), Oddbins, Somerfield,
Waitrose.

16.5   WHITE £7.98

Jacob's Creek Reserve Chardonnay 2002   AUSTRALIA

Very elegant, well-textured, nicely restrained, dry yet
very purposeful peach, pear and citrus fruit.

16.5   WHITE £4.48

Lindemans Bin 77 Sémillon/Chardonnay 2004   AUSTRALIA

Superb texture and rich fruit of elegance and style.
Offers lemon with melon and a hint of charred apricot.

16.5   RED £5.94

Novas Carmenere/Cabernet Sauvignon 2002   CHILE

A deft blend of Carmenere, Cabernet Sauvignon and
Syrah which combines cocoa, plums and roasted
berries with adult tannins.
Also at E-tailers (Vintage Roots).

16.5   RED £6.98

Peter Lehmann Barossa Shiraz 2002   AUSTRALIA

Quite remarkable persistence for such seemingly
graceful, soft plums and berries. Quite remarkable.

16.5

RED £5.16

SOUTH AFRICA

**Railroad Red Cabernet Sauvignon/
Shiraz 2003**

One of the glugging reds of the year. Has youth,
chutzpah, wit, richness and muscle.
Also at Tesco.

16

RED £5.99

CHILE

Anakena Cabernet Sauvignon Reserve 2002

Wonderful high-class, spicy chicken red wine.

16

WHITE £3.36

SOUTH AFRICA

Asda South African Chenin Blanc 2004

Terrific tipple here. Dry, slow-to-evolve pear and
gooseberry with very understated acids. Classy.

16

RED £6.98

SOUTH AFRICA

**Asda Extra Special Stellenbosch
Pinotage 2003**

And it is extra special. Thick as minestrone yet more
aromatic, rich, and deep – with unguent tannins.

16

WHITE DESSERT £3.21

AUSTRALIA

Asda Moscatel de Valencia NV

Screwcap. The UK's great pud wine bargain. Rich,
sweet, honey-drenched fruit.

16

WHITE SPARKLING £3.72

SPAIN

Asda Cava NV

Dry and crisp, with a hint of melon/raspberry.

16
RED £6.98
Albet I Noya Lignum Negre 2003 SPAIN
Very classy finely charred blackberries with tart
tannins.

16
RED SPARKLING £7.99
Banrock Station Sparkling Shiraz NV AUSTRALIA
Brilliant roasted plum/prune fruit, sweet yet dry and
savoury – all at the same time.
Also at Sainsbury.

16
WHITE £5.99
Blason de Bourgogne Macon Villages 2002 FRANCE
Classy, very classy, dry vegetal – a decent white
Burgundy of steel and freshness.

16
WHITE £4.00
Bin 042 Chardonnay/ FRANCE
Sauvignon Blanc 2003
Organic. Most individual blend combining ripe
melon with dry citrus and pear.

16
RED £5.51
Casillero del Diablo Concha y Toro CHILE
Cabernet Sauvignon 2003
So quaffable it's a sin. And what can be more
satisfying than that kind of indulgence?
Also at Sainsbury, Tesco.

16   RED £4.97

Casillero del Diablo Concha y Toro Merlot 2004   CHILE
Lovely ripe berries coated in thickly armoured
tannins. Fine grilled edge to it. Weight, with finesse.

16   WHITE £4.99

Casillero del Diablo Concha y Toro   CHILE
Gewürztraminer 2004
Screwcap. 18 points in 2008–9. Very restrained and
firm, not typical, genteel – but in time will become
more exciting.

16   RED £14.96

Châteauneuf-du-Pape 'La Bernardine'   FRANCE
Chapoutier 2003
Sweet cherry-edged fruitiness from a hot vintage – so
beware the tannins.

16   WHITE £4.11

Danie de Wet Chardonnay Sur Lie   SOUTH AFRICA
Unoaked 2004
Insouciantly elegant. Words cannot do justice to
wine of such style for this kind of money.

16   RED £5.48

Evans & Tate Langhorne Creek Shiraz 2003   AUSTRALIA
Screwcap. Real thick jammy richness as it stretches
itself like a woolly sock over the taste-buds.
Elongated plums on toast might be another way to
describe this wine.

16

RED £3.98

Funky Llama Cabernet Sauvignon 2004   ARGENTINA

Big juicy red berries, hint of citrus and lychee (yes,
I know it's unlikely but this wine does call itself
funky), to firm granite-edged tannins of chunky
ripeness. Curry red of the year? Certainly a red to
douse out the chilli fires with (and, unlike beer,
enhance the dish in so doing).

16

RED £4.98

Gérard Bertrand Classic Fitou 2002   FRANCE

How to turn a country bumpkin into a polished
townie – though even so, a few earthy traits are evident.

16

RED £6.52

Gérard Bertrand Terroir,   FRANCE
Coteaux du Languedoc 2001

Chunky, soft, ripe and serious-minded – but it has a
twinkle in its eye.

Additives in Wine (1)

Additives in wine enjoy a long history and Argentina has now
contributed an entertaining chapter. Two Britons were arrested
in Buenos Aires last year in possession of 10-million pounds'
worth of cocaine. The local bobbies found 440lb of the drug
along with 10,000 wine bottles, with the idea that 250g of the
former would be dissolved in each bottle of the latter and the
lot exported to Britain. I have, alas, been unable to discover
which brand the wine was (or the price, grape variety, and
vintage, and so I cannot hazard even a potential rating score).

16

RED £6.98

Graham Beck Shiraz 2003 SOUTH AFRICA

Fine grilled edge to cherries and plums. Weighty,
with finesse.

16

WHITE £4.98

JJ McWilliams Sémillon/Chardonnay 2004 AUSTRALIA

Austerity with refinement here. Real classy citrus
and pineapple (under-ripe).

16

WHITE £7.97

Jacob's Creek Reserve Riesling 2003 AUSTRALIA

18 points in 2008. Delicious crisp edge to
petrol-edged melon and citrus. A classic – given
time.

16

RED £5.98

Jaime Rioja 2003 SPAIN

One of the most modern Riojas I've tasted with its
toasty berries and woody ripeness (without the wood
dominating the fruit and creating an effect like
sucking balsa).

16

WHITE £7.98

Jamiesons Run Chardonnay 2002 AUSTRALIA

Superbly oily textured, complex melon/peach/
citrus and gooseberry with a lilting finish of
great class.

16

RED £4.56
FRANCE

**La Chasse du Pape Grande Réserve,
Côtes du Rhône 2003**

The cherries and plums cannot stay the flood of
tannins on the finish.

16

RED £4.48
AUSTRALIA

**Lindemans Bin 55 Shiraz/
Cabernet Sauvignon 2004**

Lovely chunky berries, ripe plums on the side, gently
grilled tannins! A terrific Aussie red.

16

RED £4.51
CHILE

Misiónes de Rengo Merlot 2003

Chunky sweet chocolate with hugely chewy tannins,
very dense wine.

16

WHITE £4.51
CHILE

Misiónes de Rengo Sauvignon Blanc 2004

Ripe oily melon which leads to an expressively nutty
finish.

16

RED (3 litre box) £15.98
FRANCE

No 2 French Merlot NV

Wonderful charred berries with rapacious tannins.
Great rollicking style. Deservedly it's the Red Wine
Box of the Year at 66p a glass.

16

RED £3.99
ROMANIA

Prahova Valley Pinot Noir Reserve 2000

Not typical Pinot but typical Romanian gusto to the
fruit and the tannic edge is nicely judged.

16

Penfolds Thomas Hyland Chardonnay 2003   AUSTRALIA
Elegant, ripe, textured, confidant. A real treat of an
Aussie Chardy.

16

Peter Lehmann Barossa Sémillon 2003   AUSTRALIA
18 points in 2010. Drink it with abandon now. With extra
special care in 5 years.
Also at Booths, Morrison's, Sainsbury.

16

Paul Mas Sauvignon Blanc,   FRANCE
Vin de Pays d'Oc 2003
Screwcap. Firm, elegant, dry, very carefully
constructed and stylishly understated.

16

Petite Ruche Crozes-Hermitage   FRANCE
Chapoutier 2002
Chunky cherries, pert blackberries, dusty tannins.

16

35 South Chardonnay 2004   CHILE
Lovely oily richness and grapefruit edge to the ripe
melon and pear.

16

35 South Cabernet Sauvignon/Merlot 2004   CHILE
It's the texture which makes it so incredibly classy
for the money.

16   RED £5.98

Stormhoek Cabernet Sauvignon 2003   SOUTH AFRICA
Most unusually lengthy blockbuster Cabernet of
great swinging berries, tannins and acids. Superb
with meat and cheese dishes.

16   WHITE £7.98

Tabali Reserva Chardonnay 2003   CHILE
Most unusual sage-edged fatty fruit, buttery and
brilliant with smoked fish.

16   WHITE £7.98

Villa Maria Private Bin Sauvignon   NEW ZEALAND
Blanc 2004
Screwcap. 17.5 points in 2007. Firm gooseberry and
citrus fruit, dry, classy, concentrated.
Also at Budgens, Sainsbury, Somerfield, Tesco.

16   WHITE £7.97

Villa Maria Private Bin   NEW ZEALAND
Gewürztraminer 2004
17.5 points in 2010–12. Spicy, warm but very elegant. An
inspired aperitif – though goes well with complex fish
dishes.
Also at Waitrose.

16   RED £4.98

Vega Barcelona Tempranillo/Shiraz 2003   SPAIN
Lovely vigour yet depth and breadth here. A molten,
soft, warm, generous wine.

16

WHITE £7.98
AUSTRALIA

Zilzie Estate Chardonnay 2004
Screwcap. Very elegant to open, then turns raffish
and unpredictable rich, firm, feral, gently whacky.

16

WHITE £4.97
AUSTRALIA

Brown Brothers Dry Muscat 2004
Screwcap. 16.5 in 2009. One of Oz's best-shrouded
secrets: a floral-edged, grapefruit-toned, subtle spicy
tipple of great charm.
Also at Budgens, Somerfield.

16

WHITE £4.48
AUSTRALIA

Wolf Blass Eagle Hawk Chardonnay 2004
Rich yet far from over-cooked, delicate yet not close
to being a shrinking violet, cosy but not sycophantic.
Also at Sainsbury, Somerfield.

OTHER WINES 15.5 AND UNDER

15.5

WHITE £6.98
NEW ZEALAND

**Asda Extra Special New Zealand
Sauvignon Blanc 2004**
Screwcap.

WHITE £2.97
CHILE

Asda Chilean Chardonnay 2004

RED £4.98
AUSTRALIA

Asda Australian Reserve Shiraz 2003

RED £3.99

Asda Côtes du Rhône-Villages 2003 FRANCE

RED £5.48

Andrew Peace Mighty Murray Malbec 2003 AUSTRALIA

WHITE £5.98

Brown Brothers Sauvignon Blanc 2004 AUSTRALIA
Screwcap.

RED £5.97

Evans & Tate Shiraz/Cabernet 2003 AUSTRALIA
Screwcap.

WHITE £5.97

Evans & Tate Classic White 2004 AUSTRALIA
Screwcap.

ROSÉ £5.98

Fetzer Valley Oaks Syrah Rosé 2004 USA
Screwcap.

RED £6.48

Gérard Bertrand Collection Pinot Noir, FRANCE
Vin de Pays d'Oc 2001

WHITE £3.98

Hardy's Wayfarer Chardonnay 2004 AUSTRALIA

WHITE £5.61

Jacob's Creek Chardonnay 2004 AUSTRALIA

RED £5.56

Lindemans Reserve Merlot 2002 AUSTRALIA

WHITE £6.98

Albet I Noya Lignum 2004 SPAIN
Organic.

RED (3 litre box) £13.48

35 South Cabernet Sauvignon 2004 CHILE
Also at Threshers (16 in bottle).

RED £8.98

Spier Private Collection Malbec 2004 SOUTH AFRICA

WHITE (3 litre box) £12.98

Santerra Dry Muscat 2004 SPAIN

RED £8.98

Serafino Cabernet Sauvignon Reserve 2002 AUSTRALIA

WHITE £5.98

Stormhoek Pinot Grigio 2004 SOUTH AFRICA

WHITE £5.98

Wolf Blass Red Label Chardonnay 2004 AUSTRALIA

15

WHITE £3.56

Asda Argentinian Torrontes 2003 ARGENTINA

WHITE SPARKLING £10.67

Asda Champagne Brut NV FRANCE

FORTIFIED £4.56

Asda Manzanilla Sherry NV SPAIN

FORTIFED £3.74

Asda Fino Sherry NV SPAIN

WHITE £5.00

Anakena Chardonnay 2004   CHILE

RED £6.98

Asda Extra Special Barossa Shiraz 2002   AUSTRALIA

WHITE £4.78

Asda English Regional Wine 2004   UK

WHITE £3.78

Asda South African Chardonnay 2004   SOUTH AFRICA

ROSÉ £4.99

Banrock Station White Shiraz 2003   AUSTRALIA
Screwcap.

WHITE (3 litre box) £12.98

Bear Crossing Sémillon/Chardonnay NV   AUSTRALIA

RED £4.98

Jacob's Creek Shiraz/Cabernet Sauvignon 2003 AUSTRALIA

WHITE £4.78

Greenfield Winery Chardonnay 2003   USA

ROSÉ £7.97

Jacob's Creek Sparkling Rosé NV   AUSTRALIA

WHITE SPARKLING £7.99

Jacob's Creek Sparkling Chardonnay/   AUSTRALIA
Pinot Noir Brut Cuvée NV
Also at Sainsbury, Tesco, Waitrose.

WHITE £5.97

Lizards of Oz Reserve Viognier 2004   AUSTRALIA

WHITE £5.99
Misiónes de Rengo Chardonnay Reserve 2003 CHILE

WHITE £4.51
Misiónes de Rengo Chardonnay 2004 CHILE
Also at Somerfield.

WHITE (3 litre box) £15.98
No 4 Chardonnay NV FRANCE

RED £5.99
RWC Shiraz Reserve 2003 SOUTH AFRICA

RED £5.92
Rock Red Shiraz/Grenache/Pinot Noir 2003 AUSTRALIA

RED £8.99
Serafino Shiraz Reserve 2002 AUSTRALIA

RED £6.94
Tabali Reserva Merlot 2002 CHILE

WHITE £4.98
Wontanella Colombard/Viognier 2004 AUSTRALIA
Screwcap.

14.5

RED £4.26
Asda Premium Claret 2003 FRANCE

RED £4.72
Asda Argentinian Malbec Reserve 2002 ARGENTINA

RED £2.80
Asda Australian Red NV AUSTRALIA
Screwcap.

RED £5.48	
Asda Chianti Classico 2003	ITALY

WHITE £5.98	
Asda Extra Special Barossa Valley Sémillon 2003	AUSTRALIA

WHITE £5.48	
Asda New Zealand Sauvignon Blanc 2004 Screwcap.	NEW ZEALAND

WHITE £2.86	
Asda Chilean White NV	CHILE

RED £2.62	
Asda Claret NV	FRANCE

WHITE £3.32	
Asda Australian Chardonnay NV	AUSTRALIA

RED £3.52	
Asda Chilean Carmenere 2004	CHILE

WHITE £5.02	
Blason de Bourgogne Villages 2003	FRANCE

WHITE (3 litre box) £14.14	
1st Cape Colombard/Chardonnay 2004	SOUTH AFRICA

RED £4.52	
Cape Grace Merlot 2003	SOUTH AFRICA

WHITE £4.96	
Douglas Green Sauvignon Blanc 2004	SOUTH AFRICA

WHITE £4.98

Pasqua Sagramosa Soave 2003 ITALY

RED £4.48

Viña Albali Reserva Valdepeñas 2000 SPAIN
Also at Budgens.

ROSÉ £4.99

Wolf Blass Eagle Hawk Rosé 2004 AUSTRALIA
Screwcap. Also at Sainsbury.

RED £5.98

Wolf Blass Cabernet Sauvignon/ AUSTRALIA
Merlot 2004

WHITE £3.98

Watchpost Bianco di Custoza 2003 ITALY

14

WHITE £3.62

Asda Vin de Pays Sauvignon Blanc NV FRANCE

WHITE (3 litre box) £11.63 (bottle) £2.86
Asda Hungarian Chardonnay NV HUNGARY

WHITE £2.98

Asda Chilean Sauvignon Blanc 2004 CHILE

WHITE £5.36

Asda Extra Special Casablanca CHILE
Sauvignon Blanc 2004

WHITE £10.57

Asda Extra Special Chablis Premier Cru 2002 FRANCE

	RED £10.98
Asda Extra Special Barolo 1999	ITALY

	RED £2.81
Asda Côtes du Rhône NV	FRANCE

	RED £2.86
Asda Chilean Red NV	CHILE

	WHITE £4.52
Andrew Peace Mighty Murray Chardonnay 2004	AUSTRALIA

	RED £2.99
Asda Chilean Cabernet Sauvignon 2004	CHILE

	RED £13.97
Avantegarde Pinot Noir 2002	USA

	RED £3.72
Banrock Station Red 2003	AUSTRALIA

	WHITE (3 litre box) £13.14
Banrock Station White NV	AUSTRALIA

	WHITE £3.72
Banrock Station White 2004	AUSTRALIA

	RED £4.00
Cuvée Picheral Bin 040, Vin de Pays du Gard 2001	FRANCE

	WHITE £3.72
Cape Promise Colombard 2004	SOUTH AFRICA

RED £4.41
Château Prince Noir Bordeaux 2002 FRANCE

WHITE £4.98
Denis Marchais Hand Picked Vouvray 2003 FRANCE
17 points in 2012.

WHITE £3.72
Dumisani Chenin/Chardonnay 2004 SOUTH AFRICA

RED £12.98
Fagus de Loto de Hayas 2002 SPAIN

WHITE £6.99
Graham Beck Sauvignon Blanc 2004 SOUTH AFRICA

WHITE £11.98
Hanging Rock Sauvignon Blanc 2004 AUSTRALIA
Screwcap.

RED £7.98
Hanging Rock 'Amaroo Farm' AUSTRALIA
Mourvèdre 2004

RED £11.98
Heathcote Cambrian Rise Shiraz 2002 AUSTRALIA

WHITE SPARKLING £5.99
Hardy's Stamp of Australia Sparkling AUSTRALIA
Pinot Noir/Chardonnay Brut NV
Also at Sainsbury, Somerfield, Tesco.

WHITE (3 litre box) £13.48
JP Chenet Colombard/Chardonnay NV FRANCE

WHITE £4.99
JJ McWilliams Sémillon/Sauvignon 2004   AUSTRALIA

RED £4.99
JJ McWilliams Shiraz/Cabernet 2004   AUSTRALIA

RED £4.98
Ken Forrester Petit Pinotage 2004   SOUTH AFRICA
NOTE TO THE HAWK-EYED READER: this wine
scores 16.5 points elsewhere but the bottle I tasted at
Asda lacked something (fruit, texture) and so it had
to be rated less. As I was tasting the wine so close to
deadline I could not taste more bottles to arrive at a
definitive judgement. Such, sometimes, are the
irritations of doing this job for a living (and why
wines should be screwcapped instead of relying on
the lottery of cork).
Also at Somerfield.

RED £4.02
Lindemans Cawarra Merlot 2004   AUSTRALIA

RED £5.02
Lindemans Reserve Merlot 2003   AUSTRALIA

RED £6.98
Lizards of Oz Reserve Malbec 2002   AUSTRALIA

RED £4.51
Monkey Puzzle Cabernet Sauvignon/Merlot 2004   CHILE

WHITE £9.98
Matua Paretai Sauvignon Blanc 2004   NEW ZEALAND
Screwcap.

	RED £7.98
Metala Shiraz/Cabernet Sauvignon 2002	AUSTRALIA
	WHITE £4.98
PKNY Chardonnay 2003	CHILE
	RED £4.98
PKNY Carmenere 2003	CHILE
	WHITE £3.98
Riverview Gewürztraminer 2002	HUNGARY
	RED £3.98
Santerra Tempranillo 2003	SPAIN
	RED £10.15
Spier Private Collection Pinotage 2004	SOUTH AFRICA
	RED £4.98
Sagramoso Valpolicella Superiore 2002	ITALY
	WHITE £4.97
Sterling Rocks Sémillon/ Sauvignon Blanc 2004 Screwcap.	AUSTRALIA
	WHITE £4.98
Three Choirs Variations Aromatic 2004 Organic.	UK
	RED £4.98
Wontanella Sangiovese/Petit Verdot 2004	AUSTRALIA

WHITE SPARKLING £7.99

Wolf Blass Red Label Sparkling   AUSTRALIA
Chardonnay/Pinot Noir NV
Also at Sainsbury.

RED £4.98

Wontanella Tempranillo 2004   AUSTRALIA
Screwcap.

RED £4.98

Yellow Tail Cabernet Sauvignon 2004   AUSTRALIA
Also at Waitrose.

BOOTHS

4–6 Fishergate,
Preston,
Lancashire PR1 3LJ

Tel: (01772) 251701
Fax: (01772) 255642

Customer help-line: (08705) 134262

E-mail: admin@booths-supermarkets.co.uk
Website: www.everywine.co.uk

For tasting notes of Booths' wines scoring less than
16 points, and ratings of wines less than 14 points,
visit www.superplonk.com

17.5

RED £12.99

Casa Lapostolle Cuvée Alexandre Merlot 2002   CHILE

One of the most accomplished cultural
achievements on earth. This is the Merlot drunk by
those who find Château Pétrus, the awesomely
expensive Bordeaux red of the same grape,
somewhat less rewarding at ten times the price of
this.

17

RED £8.99

English Oak Minervois La Livinière 2002   FRANCE

Lovely engulfing fruit of dynamic richness and
rampant, roasted berries and spirited plums.

17

RED £5.99

La Remonta Malbec 2003   ARGENTINA

Sheer sybaritic berries in silky liaison with craggy
tannins.

17

WHITE £7.99

Springfield Estate 'Life from Stone'   SOUTH AFRICA
Sauvignon Blanc 2004

One of the sleekest Sauvignon Blancs on UK wine
shelves. Offers high-class under-ripe gooseberry with
elegant acids.

17

WHITE £11.99

Iona Sauvignon Blanc 2003   SOUTH AFRICA

So, Les Sancerrois, having finally got the message
that the Kiwis in Marlborough are turning out
world-class Sauvignon Blanc, now have somewhere

else to visit and grapes to marvel over: here in Elgin in the Cape at the fantastic mountain estate of Andrew Gunn.

16.5   RED £4.99

Casillero del Diablo Concha y Toro Cabernet Sauvignon 2004   CHILE

Superb tannins bring to a fabulous climax a red of chocolate roasted nuts and warm berries. Also at Budgens, Waitrose.

16.5   RED £6.99

Casa Lapostolle Cabernet Sauvignon 2002   CHILE

Gorgeous coffee-edged tannins and genteel, lightly roasted berries.

16.5   RED £5.99

Château Pierrail Bordeaux Supérieur 2002   FRANCE

A stunning mouthful of roasted berries, fat herbs and nuts, and tannins you might only shatter with a road drill.

16.5   WHITE £7.99

D'Arenberg 'The Hermit Crab' Marsanne/ Viognier 2003   AUSTRALIA

Screwcap. Very waxy, genteel, opulent-to-finish lemon, pear and very dry apricot. A truly invigorating mouthful. Also at Waitrose.

16.5 RED £7.99

Rosso di Montepulciano Azienda Agricola
Poliziano 2003 ITALY
Delicious! Utterly crunchily scrumptious! Roasted
black cherries!

What is it about red wine which makes it so eminently suitable
for spilling over and in some cases throwing directly at people? I
am inclined to take the charitable view and regard it as a ritual,
one designed to convey to the victim good wishes for a healthy
life. New research offers some justification for this notion,
finding that resveratrol, a compound in red wine, can 'extend
the life span of every organism' which takes it, according to
David Sinclair of Harvard Medical School in Boston, who led the
study. This bears out the hypothesis that the jars buried with
eminent mummies, identified as the containers of red wine,
were there as symbols of the life-enhancing properties of the
liquid to which ancient upper-caste Egyptians were partial
(Tutankhamun, for example, was devoted to red). Had she
known this, would the angelic Anna Ford have been so happy to
have throw red wine all over the detestable Jonathan Aitken?
Had Bill Clinton been aware of red wine's virile side, would he
have been so embarrassed to have knocked a glass of the stuff
over Indian prime minister Atal Bihari Vajpayee at a reception at
the White House in September 2000? And thus doused, would
Mr Vajpayee, aware of the good wishes soaking his jacket, have
sat there not in stony, tight-lipped silence but heartily thanked
his host for the generous libation? The most recent famous
recipient of red wine was Australia's prime minister John
Howard who, in July 2004, had a cup of red wine hurled in his
direction during a protest in Melbourne.

16

RED £5.99

Alamos Bonarda Catena Zapata 2003 ARGENTINA
Spreads itself over the tongue like toasted strawberry
and blackberry jam.

16

RED £3.99

Château Villerembert-Moureau Minervois 2004 FRANCE
Big berries here, bold and polished, yet the tannins
have a certain cragginess.

16

RED £2.99

Casa Morena Bodega Felix Solis Vino SPAIN
de la Tierra NV
Stunningly ripe yet not OTT berries, hint of malted
chocolate, touch of black olive to the tannins.

16

WHITE SPARKLING £12.99

Champagne Baron-Fuente NV FRANCE
Extremely elegant, dry and very unfussy.

16

RED SPARKLING £6.49

Concerto Lambrusco Reggiano ITALY
Medici Ermete 2003
A red bubbly of authentic individuality and very dry
berried brilliance.

16

WHITE £4.29

Château de Béranger Picpoul de Pinet, FRANCE
Cave Co-op de Pomerols 2004
Stealthy, couth, affirmative – this is a subtle, dry,
crisp-yet-complex white of great charm.

16

WHITE £4.99

Domaine de la Bastide Viognier, FRANCE
Vin de Pays de l'Hautérive 2004

Dry apricot and waxy lemon. Very firm (yet very polite).

16

RED £7.99

Domaine Chaume-Arnaud FRANCE
Côtes du Rhône-Villages Vinsobres 2002

Good smooth berries with a very chewy edge. Has great warmth, a comfort liquid.

16

WHITE £4.99

Firefinch Colombard/Chardonnay, SOUTH AFRICA
Springfield Estate 2004

Provides a wealth of opportunity for table-talk. Is it posh? Isn't it rather vulgar? Is it dry? Isn't it too pert? Hmmm…just shut up and drink.

16

RED £6.99

Gran'Arte Trincadeira 2003 PORTUGAL

Full-on, unambiguous fruitiness of depth and daring.

16

WHITE £4.99

Inycon Fiano 2004 ITALY

Very subtle but extremely attractive. It has a lovely demure peach/pineapple sheen to it with lithe acids. A provocative, sippin' white wine.

16

RED £4.99

Inycon Nero d'Avola 2003 ITALY
Superb tannins coating ripe plums and cute wild
raspberries.

16

RED £13.99

L'Angélique de Montbusquet St-Emilion 2001 FRANCE
Claret in the Aussie Shiraz meets Barolo mould.

What does a man look like after 195 years in jail? This was
the hefty sentence an alleged wine fraudster faced last year
when he was accused by a Colorado court of taking people's
cash for something which, apparently, did not exist. He
dealt in wine futures. Just as he could bank his clients' cash
he could bank on their greed: the expectation that the price
they paid for wine today would go up in value tomorrow.
The ten counts of fraud he faced were nothing new in US
scam circles. We've been here before. But only
comparatively recently with wine. Wine dealers, legitimate
ones let alone the rogues, have only been able to dangle the
carrot of future profit before the avaricious eyes of investors
in the past 40 years or so. Real estate, gold mines, company
shares, even blobs of paint called art, have a longer history
of attracting those with an appetite to speculate but wine,
before the 1960s, was not considered a worthy investment
vehicle. It is now a very glamorous one; underpinning the
further *ignis fatuus* that, if all else fails, the wine can be
drunk (and it will be gorgeous).

16

DESSERT WHITE (half bottle) £4.99

Nivole Moscato d'Asti Michele Chiarlo 2004 ITALY

A lovely end to a meal: a bubbly of honied
raspberry.

16

ROSÉ £3.79

Nagyrede Estate Cabernet Sauvignon HUNGARY
Rosé 2004

A very calm, unhysterically well-tailored rosé of
elegant dryness.
Also at Budgens.

16

RED £7.49

Pica Broca La Sauvageonne, FRANCE
Coteaux de Languedoc 2002

Rusticity taken to great lengths! Most satisfyingly
combative and concentrated.

16

RED £8.99

Quinta de la Rosa 2002 PORTUGAL

One of the Douro's most civilised table wines.

16

RED £14.99

Quintis Amarone della Valpolicella ITALY
Valpantena 2001

A brilliant accompaniment to *The Times'* crossword
puzzle. It solves clues by itself (in spite of being a
mite thick).

16   RED £2.99

Santa Clara Chilean Red Viña
Requinqua NV   CHILE
One of the snazziest red wines around for the
money. Terrific unguent red berries and taffeta-
edged tannins.

16   RED £13.99

Wither Hills Pinot Noir 2003   NEW ZEALAND
Screwcap. 16.5 points in 2007. Beautiful gamy
cherries and raspberries.
Also at Oddbins, Waitrose.

16   WHITE £8.49

Jackson Estate Marlborough   NEW ZEALAND
Sauvignon Blanc 2004
Screwcap. 16.5 points in 2007. Finely modulated
gooseberry/citrus fruit. A fine tipple by any
standards.
Also at Sainsbury, Somerfield.

16   RED £6.99

Clancy's Red Peter Lehmann 2002   AUSTRALIA
Vigorous marriage of several of the mightiest and
orneriest red grapes around (too tiresome to record
here). It makes for provocative tippling and an
excellent case for polygamy.
Screwcap. Also at Budgens.

16

WHITE £5.69

Peter Lehmann Barossa Sémillon 2003   AUSTRALIA
Screwcap. 18 points in 2010. Drink it with abandon
now. With extra special care in 5 years.
Also at Asda, Morrison's, Sainsbury.

OTHER WINES 15.5 AND UNDER

15.5

RED £6.99

Bleasdale Shiraz/   AUSTRALIA
Cabernet Sauvignon 2002

WHITE £3.99

Domaine de Pellehaut Blanc, Vin de Pays   FRANCE
des Côtes de Gascogne 2004

WHITE £6.49

Merloblu Castello di Luzzano 2003   ITALY

WHITE £9.99

Roero Arneis Cantine Ascheri 2003   ITALY

RED £8.99

Springfield Estate   SOUTH AFRICA
Cabernet Sauvignon 2002

15

WHITE £5.99

Brown Brothers Limited Release   AUSTRALIA
Riesling 1999

	RED £8.99
Carmen Reserve Carmenere/	CHILE
Cabernet Sauvignon 2002	

	WHITE £9.99
Cave de Turckheim Alsace Grand Cru	FRANCE
Riesling Ollwiller 2002	

	RED £4.99
Les Ruffes La Sauvageonne,	FRANCE
Coteaux de Languedoc 2003	

	RED £5.49
Chinon Cuvée de Pâques,	FRANCE
Domaine de la Roche Honneur 2003	

	WHITE £5.99
Falasco Garganega Vendemmia	ITALY
Tardiva Valpantena 2004	

	WHITE £7.99
Gavi del Commune di Gavi Masseria	ITALY
dei Carmelitani 2004	

	RED £2.99
Louis Chatel, Vin de Pays d'Oc Listel NV	FRANCE

	WHITE £3.29
Les Deux Colombard/Chardonnay,	FRANCE
Vin de Pays des Côtes de Gascogne 2004	
Screwcap.	

	RED £8.99
Rasteau Prestige Domaine des	FRANCE
Coteaux de Travers 2003	

WHITE £7.99

Mud House Sauvignon Blanc 2004 NEW ZEALAND
Screwcap. Also at Small Merchants (Bentalls,
Harrods, Harvey Nichols, Selfridges).

RED £6.99

Ravenswood Vintners Blend Zinfandel 2002 USA
Also at Budgens, Tesco, Waitrose.

14·5

RED £4.99

Château Le Pin Bordeaux Rouge 2003 FRANCE

WHITE £3.99

Castillo de Almansa Colección Blanco SPAIN
Bodegas Piqueras 2004

WHITE £3.99

Peaks View Sauvignon Blanc 2004 SOUTH AFRICA

RED £7.99

Sablet Côtes du Rhône-Villages, FRANCE
Château de Rignon 2003

14

RED £6.99

Archiodamo Primitivo di Manduria ITALY
Pervini 2003

RED £5.99

Beaujolais-Villages, Domaine des Côtes FRANCE
de la Molière 2002

RED £8.99

Barbera d'Asti Superiore La Luna ITALY
e I Falo Terre da Vino 2002

Rosé sparkling £13.99	
Champagne Baron-Fuente Rosé Dolores NV	France

White £4.99	
Château Pierrail Bordeaux Blanc 2004	France

Red £9.99	
Château Jupille Carillon St-Emilion 1999	France

Red £5.99	
Chianti Cantine Leonardo 2003	Italy

Red £3.99	
Domaine St-Laurent St-Chinian 2003	France

Rosé £4.49	
Domaine de Pellehaut Rosé, Vin de Pays des Côtes de Gascogne 2004 Screwcap. Also at Waitrose.	France

Red £3.29	
Les Deux Grenache/Syrah, Vin de Pays de Vaucluse 2004 Screwcap.	France

White £6.99	
Nepenthe 'Tryst' White 2004 Screwcap.	Australia

Red £6.99	
Nepenthe 'Tryst' 2003 Screwcap.	Australia

RED £3.99

Rapido Rosso Beneventano 2004   ITALY
Screwcap.

WHITE £7.49

Riesling Kabinett Josef Leitz 2003   GERMANY
16.5 points in 2011–12.

WHITE £8.99

Shaw & Smith Sauvignon Blanc 2004   AUSTRALIA

WHITE £7.99

Steenberg Sémillon 2003   SOUTH AFRICA

WHITE £9.99

Skillogalee Riesling 2003   AUSTRALIA
Screwcap. 17 points in 2010–12.

WHITE £8.99

**Sweet Chestnut Chardonnay
Limoux 2002**   FRANCE

WHITE £5.29

**Selva d'Oro Falchini Bianco di
Toscana 2004**   ITALY

RED £4.29

**Syrah Domaine du Petit Roubie,
Vin de Pays de l'Hérault 2003**   FRANCE
Organic.

WHITE £5.99

Trio Sauvignon Blanc 2004   CHILE
Screwcap.

Viña Sardasol Merlot Bodega Virgen Blanca Navarra 2003

RED £3.99
SPAIN

Vavasour Sauvignon Blanc 2004
Screwcap.

WHITE £9.99
NEW ZEALAND

BUDGENS

Stonefield Way,
Ruislip,
Middlesex HA4 0JR

Tel: (020) 8422 9511
Fax: (020) 8864 2800

E-mail: info@budgens.co.uk
Website: www.budgens.com

For tasting notes of Budgens' wines scoring less than
16 points, and ratings of wines less than 14 points,
visit www.superplonk.com

17.5

Errazuriz Estate Max Reserva CHILE
Cabernet Sauvignon 2002

The best red in the store? Nine quid is a lot of
money but this is a lot of wine – seriously
impressive, tastily complex yet not demanding, and
it finishes with the aplomb and deadly accuracy of
Roger Federer's backhand.

16.5

Leasingham Bin 61 Shiraz 2002 AUSTRALIA

Most impressively cultured yet gently raunchy –
lovely roasted berries, herbs, and fantastic warm
tannins. As cuddly as a Wendy Cope poem, as
forthright as a gripping one from Heaney.

16.5

Casillero del Diablo Concha y Toro CHILE
Cabernet Sauvignon 2004

Class from nose to throat is on offer here. The
tailoring, uniting taffeta and silk, is immediately
striking yet provocatively enduring (which may be
the essence of style in this context).
Also at Booths, Waitrose.

16.5

Errazuriz Estate Chardonnay 2004 CHILE

Screwcap. Deliciously well-textured (oily), ripe yet
not inelegant. A very confident, chic white wine.
Also at E-tailers (Everywine), Oddbins, Sainsbury,
Somerfield, Tesco.

16.5

WHITE £6.49

McWilliams Hanwood Estate AUSTRALIA
Chardonnay 2003

Very subtle re-working of *Pride and Prejudice*. Surely
this is the Chardonnay Jane Austen sipped on her
honeymoon? Feminist scholars may dispute this
conclusion, but if the wine has this effect I would be
dishonest to dismiss it.
Also at Threshers.

16

RED £5.03

Argento Malbec 2004 ARGENTINA

Coal-dust-edged plums, ripe yet most charmingly
serious (without being po-faced).
Also at Majestic, Sainsbury, Tesco.

16

RED £6.99

Bonterra Shiraz/Carignan/Sangiovese 2003 USA

Has an international Spanish/Italian stylishness with
just a hint of Californian sunshine.

16

RED £7.03

Château de Respide Graves 2002 FRANCE

A really classy claret – best served lightly chilled (to
bring out the spice, the brisk berries, and the
chocolate-edged tannins).

16

RED £7.03

Durius Tempranillo 2003 SPAIN

Classy, firm, very lip-smackingly agreeable.

16 RED £4.99

FRANCE

Herrick Merlot, Vin de Pays d'Oc 2003
Lovely burned berries. The hint of cocoa to the
tannins is only one attribute which makes this wine
very firmly in charge of itself.

16 RED £4.99

FRANCE

Herrick Syrah, Vin de Pays d'Oc 2002
Hint of spice to ripe blackberries and plums give
this red backbone and class.

One of the major differences between the Old World,
European approach to winemaking and the New World,
southern hemisphere approach is in the obsession the latter
producers have about the single grape variety. Before
Australia and California made Chardonnay known as a grape,
many drinkers of, for example, Chablis (which is exclusively
Chardonnay) would not have had this grape top of mind;
indeed, many people who say they like Chablis are surprised
to learn it is a Chardonnay. In the same way, before Shiraz
came along, the grape called Syrah could stay comfortably in
the background even in areas like the northern Rhône where
it is a 100% constituent of the local red wines. The words
Chardonnay and Syrah used never to appear on French wine
labels (indeed, it was against regulations, on the elegantly
preposterous grounds that a grape is merely the scaffolding
of a wine, the architect is the vineyard and therefore it is the
vineyard which should be honoured on the label). These
regulations have now been relaxed as a result of the success
of New World wines in export markets.

16

WHITE £7.03

Louis Jadot Macon Blanc Villages 2004 FRANCE
A very well-crafted, subtle, demure white Burgundy –
has some charming creamy touches to the crisp
lemonosity (I'm getting bored with the term citrus
and its parsings).

16

WHITE SPARKLING £32.99

Moët & Chandon 1999 FRANCE
Difficult not to give this 16 as it is impressively
mature. Chic, beautifully flavoursome, and very
finely tailored. True, thirty-three quid is a lot of
dosh, but this wine is a great deal of posh.

16

ROSÉ £4.03

Nagyrede Estate Cabernet Sauvignon HUNGARY
Rosé 2004
Lovely dry cherries with a fine hint of excitement
from the blackberried pepperiness.
Also at Booths.

16

WHITE £5.03

Peter Lehmann Wildcard Chardonnay 2004 AUSTRALIA
It has this sly self-awareness as it flirts with dryness
yet, thankfully, doesn't quite succeed.

16

WHITE £5.99

Peter Lehmann Chenin Blanc 2004 AUSTRALIA
18 in 2008–10. Lovely subtle tangy fruit which will
deepen most interestingly over time.

16

RED £7.03

Clancy's Red Peter Lehmann 2002 AUSTRALIA
Vigorous marriage of several of the mightiest and
orneriest red grapes around (too tiresome to record
here). It makes for provocative tippling and an
excellent case for polygamy.
Also at Booths.

16

RED £5.99

Palacio de la Vega Cabernet Sauvignon/ SPAIN
Tempranillo Crianza Navarra 2000
The tannins have a racily thrilling edge.

16

WHITE £8.03

Villa Maria Private Bin Sauvignon NEW ZEALAND
Blanc 2004
Screwcap. 17.5 points in 2007. Bitingly purposeful,
elegant, dry, fish-friendly.
Also at Asda, Sainsbury, Somerfield, Tesco.

16

WHITE £7.03

Villa Maria Private Bin Riesling 2004 NEW ZEALAND
Screwcap. 18 in 2010–12. Impressive now. Stonking
in 5 years.
Also at Majestic.

16

WHITE £5.99

Brown Brothers Dry Muscat 2004 AUSTRALIA
Screwcap. 16.5 in 2009. One of Oz's best-shrouded

secrets: a floral-edged, grapefruit– toned, subtle spicy
tipple of great charm.
Also at Asda, Somerfield.

16

WHITE £6.49

Montana Marlborough Sauvignon   NEW ZEALAND
Blanc 2004
Screwcap. Bargain gooseberry fruit. Real finesse here.
Also at Majestic, Tesco, Threshers.

16

RED £4.53

Concha y Toro Sunrise Merlot 2004   CHILE
Superbly polished plum and cherry immediacy, and
then leathery tannins strike home.
Also at Waitrose.

16

WHITE £5.99

Montana East Coast Unoaked   NEW ZEALAND
Chardonnay 2004
Screwcap. Very cosy melon/pear fruit. Terrific price
for such class.
Also at Majestic.

OTHER WINES 15.5 AND UNDER

15.5

WHITE £6.99

Wolf Blass Yellow Label Chardonnay 2004   AUSTRALIA
Screwcap. Also at Tesco.

WHITE £4.99

Cono Sur Chardonnay 2004   CHILE

RED £5.53

Torres Sangre de Toro 2003   SPAIN

RED £6.99

Wolf Blass Yellow Label Cabernet Sauvignon/   AUSTRALIA
Shiraz 2003

15

RED £6.99

Ravenswood Vintners Blend Zinfandel 2002   USA
Also at Booths, Tesco, Waitrose.

RED £9.99

Château Caronne St Gemme Haut Médoc Cru   FRANCE
Bourgeois 1999

RED £7.49

Hardy's Tintara Cabernet Sauvignon 1999   AUSTRALIA

ROSÉ £6.03

Lindemans Bin 35 Rosé 2004   AUSTRALIA

RED £3.53

Louis Eschenauer Merlot,   FRANCE
Vin de Pays d'Oc 2003
Screwcap.

ROSÉ SPARKLING £5.99

Marqués de Monistrol Rosé Cava NV   SPAIN

WHITE £5.49

Oxford Landing Chardonnay 2004   AUSTRALIA
Screwcap. Also at Sainsbury, Tesco.

	WHITE £10.03	
Pouilly-Fumé Fouassier Père et Fils 2004		FRANCE

	RED £5.03	
Peter Lehmann Wildcard Shiraz 2003		AUSTRALIA
Also at Co-op.		

	WHITE £5.49	
Torres Viña Sol 2004		SPAIN
Screwcap. Also at Tesco.		

	WHITE £5.49	
Oxford Landing Sauvignon Blanc 2004		AUSTRALIA
Screwcap. Also at Sainsbury, Tesco.		

	RED £5.99	
Fetzer Zinfandel/Shiraz 2003		USA
Also at Co-op.		

14.5

	RED £6.99	
Brown Brothers Merlot 2002		AUSTRALIA

	WHITE £4.53	
Concha y Toro Sauvignon Blanc 2004		CHILE

	WHITE £5.99	
Fetzer Chardonnay/Viognier 2003		USA

	WHITE £4.53	
Château Mouchetière Muscadet Sur Lie,		FRANCE
Gérard Sourice 2003		

	RED £4.83	
Mezzomondo Montepulciano d'Abruzzo 2003		ITALY

RED £5.49

Oxford Landing Cabernet Sauvignon/ AUSTRALIA
Shiraz 2003
Also at Co-op.

WHITE £5.03

Timara Sauvignon Blanc/ NEW ZEALAND
Sémillon 2003

ROSÉ £3.99

Van Loveren Blanc de Noirs 2003 SOUTH AFRICA

WHITE SPARKLING £26.49
Veuve Clicquot Ponsardin Brut NV FRANCE

RED £4.83

Viña Albali Reserva Valdepeñas 2000 SPAIN
Also at Asda.

WHITE £5.99

Wolf Blass Red Label Chardonnay/ AUSTRALIA
Sémillon 2004
Screwcap. Also at Tesco.

RED £6.49

McWilliams Hanwood Estate Shiraz 2003 AUSTRALIA
Also at Tesco.

14

WHITE £5.99

Brown Brothers Chenin Blanc 2004 AUSTRALIA
16.5 in 2010.

WHITE £6.99

Bonterra Chardonnay/Sauvignon/Muscat 2002 USA

	WHITE £5.99	
Blason de Bourgogne Côtes Chalonnaise		FRANCE
Chardonnay 2004		

	RED £6.03	
Château Bel Air Bordeaux 2003		FRANCE

	RED £5.03	
Da Luca Primitivo Merlot 2004		ITALY

	RED £9.49	
Fleurie Domaine Fonfotin 2002		FRANCE

	RED £6.99	
Fetzer Eagle Peak Merlot 2003		USA

	ROSÉ £5.99	
Fetzer Syrah Rosé 2004		USA
Screwcap.		

	WHITE SPARKLING £7.99	
Lindauer Brut NV		NEW ZEALAND

	WHITE £3.43	
Langenbach Spätlese 2003		GERMANY

	WHITE SPARKLING £7.99	
Marqués de Monistrol Vintage Cava 2000		SPAIN

	RED £5.99	
Marqués de Griñon Rioja 2003		SPAIN

	RED £5.49	
Oxford Landing Merlot 2003		AUSTRALIA

WHITE £12.03

Pouilly-Fuissé Bouchard 2003 FRANCE

WHITE £9.03

Sancerre Les Chasseignes Fouassier Père et Fils 2004 FRANCE

RED £7.99

Wolf Blass Red Label Cabernet Sauvignon/ Shiraz 2003 AUSTRALIA

WHITE SPARKLING £6.99

Lindemans Bin 25 Brut Cuvée NV AUSTRALIA
Also at Co-op, Morrison's, Waitrose.

CO-OP

Co-operative Wholesale Society Limited,
PO Box 53,
New Century House,
Manchester M60 4ES

Tel: (0161) 834 1212
Fax: (0161) 827 5117

Website: www.co-opdrinks2u.com

For tasting notes of Co-op wines scoring less than
16 points, and ratings of wines less than 14 points,
visit www.superplonk.com

17

RED £4.99

Da Luca Primitivo Merlot 2003   ITALY

Terrific! Like lava it flows over the taste-buds with
rich cherries, plum, blackcurrants and brilliant
roasted tannins.

Also at Tesco.

16.5

WHITE £5.99

Co-op Adelaide Hills Chardonnay   AUSTRALIA
Reserve 2004

Screwcap. Finely smoky, under-ripe, oily-textured
fruit of class, precision and real finesse. Has subtlety
yet weight.

16.5

RED £3.99

Graffigna Shiraz/Cabernet Sauvignon 2003   ARGENTINA

Superb levels of dark jammy, brisk fruit relieved by
warm tannins, plus a hint of spice. It does seem
absurd in this day and age that there are wines like
this offering themselves for less than four quid – so
this is something of a rarity.

16

RED £9.99

Bethany Cabernet/Merlot 2002   AUSTRALIA

Chunky chocolate-edged berries, warm and very
savoury. But this brashness, exposed to air by
decanting (5–10 hours), reveals mint, licorice and a
lovely sweet-edged grilled fruitiness of huge charm.
It shows itself infinitely polished and svelte but also
deep and characterful. One bottle I enjoyed reached

18 points after 6 hours' exposure to air, Jazz-FM and various tasty morsels.

16

WHITE SPARKLING £5.49

Co-op Australian Sparkling Brut NV   AUSTRALIA

Very elegant, dry, stylishly self-contained fruit. Less pretentious, slicker textured, much smarter value for money than umpteen champagnes.

My life is dedicated to research. Every morsel of food I consume is research. I am, as I write this very paragraph at 7.50 on a Tuesday evening, also preparing to walk up the hill to a local BYOB Indian eatery to research how well or ill certain wines will perform with spicy grub. Do you imagine I do this because I am starving and thirsty, having had but two slices of toast (from my own home-baked spelt-flour loaf) all day? Shame on your cynicism. This is a hard-nosed research exercise and so I am dragging my appetite up the hill with Italian and Chilean bottles in tow.   How did we get on? Not wholly successfully. The Italian buckled under the onslaught of the chicken tikka and prawn puri but was okay with the onion bhaji. The spiced pilau rice, sag paneer and tarka daal took the edge off the wine's very attractive cherry/plum richness. The Chilean was a weightier wine and had the tang of new leather along with a firm spiciness, far more tannins than the Italian, and a richly chewy edge of roasted cherry and raspberry. Even so, the level of spicing in the food was not wholly to its liking, perhaps because it was not sweet enough to counteract the chillies. But in all other respects it was a most engaging wine but it would, I reckon, be most at home with a moussaka or roasted vegetables with melted halloumi cheese on top.

16

Co-op Argentinian Malbec 2004　　ARGENTINA
Thoroughbred bargain. Very finely wrought plums,
blackberries (plus thorns and pips), and a touch of
sweet prune.

16

Co-op Coonawarra Cabernet Sauvignon　　AUSTRALIA
Reserve 2003
Lovely coarse edge to the tannins takes the
prissiness out of the smooth berries (hint of thyme
and mint helps here too).

16

Co-op Centolla Pinot Noir 2003　　CHILE
Most untypical Pinot Noir – the wild cherry
gaminess is choked with coal dust. But this
atypicality is irrelevant given its otherwise
tremendous charm and rough, tough, nicely burly,
easy-to-swallow fruit.

16

Co-op Moses Lake Cabernet Sauvignon 2003　　USA
Firm and rich and has a most agreeable tannic
oomph without making the alcohol (a high 13.6.%)
blush with shame. It is essential red wines high in
alcohol have tannins to balance them, otherwise they
come across like fruit soups.

16

WHITE £6.99

Château du Bluizard Beaujolais Blanc 2002 FRANCE
You should experience this rustic artefact. It has a
dry, wry style of incisive individuality which gives
the Chardonnay grape a fresh appeal.

16

WHITE SPARKLING £17.99

Drappier Carte d'Or Champagne NV FRANCE
If you wish to discover why a good champagne
is worth the money, try this subtle, dry, very
elegant liquid. It's as finely tailored as a couture silk
suit.

16

RED £3.99

La Finca Cabernet Sauvignon 2004 ARGENTINA
Bright plummy fruit saved from injudicious
jamminess by a smearing of tannins. Excellent price
for such savoury depth.

16

RED £4.99

Les Jamelles Syrah, Vin de Pays d'Oc 2003 FRANCE
A truly serious red, which develops various subtle
twists and turns – plums, earth, herbs, cherries – as it
proceeds lustily from nose to digestive tract.

16

WHITE £7.49

Oyster Bay Sauvignon Blanc 2004 NEW ZEALAND
Screwcap. Very, very classy. Very confident gooseberry
richness.
Also at Morrison's, Sainsbury.

16

**St Hallett Poacher's Blend Sémillon/
Sauvignon Blanc 2004**

Screwcap. Also has some Riesling in the recipe and
this lifts the wine into the premier league. Good
light-but-serious fruit of huge charm.

16

The Cork Grove Fernao Pires 2004

Dry, hint of wax to the texture, fragrant yet not
frivolous. Most individual and throat caressive.

16

Trio Merlot/Carmenere/Cabernet Sauvignon 2004

Huge, mouth-filling fruit – mostly well charred and
chewy.
Also at Somerfield.

Only the Alsatians, as far as the French are concerned, routinely
put grape varieties on their labels, and if a wine is blended it
must use different nomenclature. In Bordeaux, whatever its
myriad other failings, wines are given château or domaine
names and, in the absence of a back label, you may not know a
wine is a blend of Cabernets Sauvignon and Franc, Merlot and
Malbec. In Australia, on the other hand, some years back now, I
recall drinkers reacting in horror to the idea of blending
Sémillon with Chardonnay on the grounds that it was diluting
the purity of the latter grape. But in fact the blend of those two
grapes often results in a far superior, more complex wine, able
to develop better in bottle over a longer time.

16

Viña Misiónes Cabernet Franc Reserve 2003 CHILE
Plums and blackberries – roasted, ripe and very
ready for anything from a casserole to a hunk of
hard cheese.

OTHER WINES 15.5 AND UNDER

15.5
WHITE £4.99

Atlantique Sauvignon Blanc 2004 FRANCE
Screwcap.

RED £5.99

Caldora Sangiovese 2003 ITALY

RED £5.35

Château Laurençon Bordeaux 2003 FRANCE

RED £4.49

Co-op Australian Lime Tree Grenache 2004 AUSTRALIA

RED £5.49

Leopards Leap Shiraz 2002 SOUTH AFRICA

RED £6.99

La Cuvée Mythique, Vin de Pays d'Oc 2001 FRANCE

WHITE £4.99

The Boulders Viognier 2003 USA
Screwcap.

WHITE £5.99
Trio Chardonnay/Pinot Grigio/Pinot Blanc 2004 CHILE
Also at Somerfield.

15

WHITE £6.99
Alsace Gewürztraminer 2003 FRANCE

RED £8.99
Château Sissan, Premières Côtes de FRANCE
Bordeaux 2001

WHITE £3.99
Co-op Island Vines Cyprus White 2004 CYPRUS

WHITE £4.99
Co-op Moses Lake Chardonnay 2004 USA

RED £3.99
Co-op Romanian Prairie Merlot 2003 ROMANIA

WHITE £6.99
Co-op Cape Seal Bay Chardonnay SOUTH AFRICA
Reserve 2003

WHITE £5.29
Co-op French Organic Chardonnay/ FRANCE
Sauvignon Blanc 2004

RED £3.99
Co-op Jacaranda Hill Shiraz 2004 AUSTRALIA

RED £5.99
Fetzer Zinfandel/Shiraz 2003 USA
Also at Budgens.

	RED £4.79
Las Moras Bonarda 2004	ARGENTINA

	WHITE £4.29
Lily White, Côtes de Gascogne 2004	FRANCE

	RED £5.49
Masterpeace Shiraz 2004	AUSTRALIA

	RED £4.99
Peter Lehmann Wildcard Shiraz 2003	AUSTRALIA

Also at Budgens.

	RED £5.99
St Hallett Gamekeeper's Reserve Shiraz/	AUSTRALIA

Grenache 2004
Screwcap.

	RED £4.99
Thandi Cabernet/Merlot 2004	SOUTH AFRICA

	RED £6.49
Valréas Côtes du Rhône,	FRANCE

Domaine de la Grande Bellance 2003

	RED £5.49
Yellow Tail Merlot 2004	AUSTRALIA

14.5

	WHITE £4.99
French Connection Reserve	FRANCE

Chardonnay 2004

	RED £4.99
French Connection Reserve Merlot 2004	FRANCE

WHITE £7.99	
Las Brisas Estate Chardonnay Reserve 2002	CHILE

WHITE £4.99	
Les Jamelles Viognier, Vin de Pays d'Oc 2004	FRANCE

ROSÉ £4.49	
Masterpeace Rosé 2004	AUSTRALIA
Screwcap.	

RED £4.99	
Viña Albali Tinto Reserva 1999	SPAIN

ROSÉ £3.99	
Valley of the Roses Cabernet Sauvignon	BULGARIA
Rosé 2004	

ROSÉ £4.49	
Andrew Makepeace 'Masterpeace'	AUSTRALIA
Rosé 2004	
Screwcap. Also at Small Merchants (Nisa, Unwins).	

RED £5.49	
Oxford Landing Cabernet Sauvignon/	AUSTRALIA
Shiraz 2003	
Also at Budgens.	

14

RED £4.49	
Americana Merlot 2004	USA
Screwcap.	

RED £3.99	
Co-op Elephant Trail Pinotage/	SOUTH AFRICA
Shiraz 2004	

	RED £4.99
Co-op Fair Trade Cape Affinity Red 2004	SOUTH AFRICA

	WHITE £4.79
Co-op Casa del Sol Sauvignon Blanc/ Verdejo 2004	SPAIN

	WHITE £4.99
Co-op Pinot Grigio 2004	ITALY

	WHITE £6.49
Co-op Explorer's Vineyard Sauvignon Blanc 2004	NEW ZEALAND
Screwcap.	

	RED £5.49
Co-op Starlight Coast Zinfandel 2003	USA
Screwcap.	

	WHITE £4.79
Co-op Cape Limited Release Gewürztraminer 2004	SOUTH AFRICA

	WHITE £3.89
Co-op Vin de Pays du Jardin de la France Sauvignon Blanc 2004	FRANCE

	WHITE £4.99
Co-op Soave Classico 2004	ITALY

	WHITE £3.99
Jon Josh Estate Chardonnay 2003	HUNGARY

	RED £8.99
Las Brisas Estate Pinot Noir Reserve 2004	CHILE

WHITE £5.49

Leopards Leap Sauvignon Blanc 2004 SOUTH AFRICA

WHITE £4.59

**Lily White, Vin de Pays
des Côtes de Gascogne 2002** FRANCE

RED £4.29

Lily Red, Côtes de Gascogne 2004 FRANCE

RED £6.99

Morgon Les Charmes Domaine Brisson 2003 FRANCE

WHITE £4.49

**Robert's Rock Chardonnay/
Sémillon 2004** SOUTH AFRICA

RED £3.99

Robert's Rock Pinotage/Pinot Noir 2004 SOUTH AFRICA

WHITE £3.99

Viñas del Vero Chardonnay/Macabeo 2004 SPAIN

WHITE SPARKLING £6.99

Lindemans Bin 25 Brut Cuvée NV AUSTRALIA
Also at Budgens, Morrison's, Waitrose.

E-TAILERS

EVERYWINE

E-mail: admin@everywine.co.uk
Website: www. everywine.co.uk
Tel: (01772) 329700
Fax: (01772) 329709

LAITHWAITES

E-mail: orders@laithwaites.co.uk
Website: www.laithwaites.co.uk
Tel: (0870) 4448383
Fax: (0970) 4448282

VINTAGE ROOTS (ORGANIC WINES)

E-mail: info@vintageroots.co.uk
Website: www.vintageroots.co.uk
Tel: (0118) 9761999
Fax: (0118) 9761998

VIRGIN WINES

E-mail: help@virginwines.com
Website: www.virginwines.com
Tel: (0870) 164034
Fax: (01603) 619277

For tasting notes of E-tailers' wines scoring less than
16 points, and rating of wines less than 14 points,
visit www.superplonk.com

17.5

Errazuriz Estate Sangiovese 2003
CHILE

Everywine

Stunning mouthful! Spicy plums, chocolate and an overall richness of tone, with a wonderful characterful undertow dragging the fruit along, which defies slotting into any conventional slot. Is there no grape variety on earth the Chileans can't turn their deft digits to?

Also at Small Merchants (D. Byrne & Co., Luvians, Vicki's of Chobham, Wimbledon Wine Cellars).

17

WHITE £5.99

Errazuriz Estate Sauvignon Blanc 2004
CHILE

Everywine

A lovely textured rich gooseberry/melon wine. It oozes class, sophistication and effortless fluency. You know what I mean by that last extravagance? If you think of a grape variety as a language then some winemakers speak it crudely, some well, some confidently, but the slickest speak it with polished bi-linguality. This is the case here.

Also at Oddbins, Threshers.

17

RED £5.99

Errazuriz Estate Merlot 2003
CHILE

Everywine

Melted chocolate dripped over grilled plums. Did the winemaker steal the recipe from Nigella? The

comments regarding winemakers made about the
wine above apply here as well.

Also at Oddbins, Sainsbury, Tesco, Threshers.

16.5   RED £9.50

Coyam 2002   CHILE

Vintage Roots

A toothsome blend of 36% Syrah, 30% Cabernet
Sauvignon, 17% Carmenere, 15% Merlot and 2%
Mourvèdre which achieves maximum fruity velocity
with, paradoxically, a slow moving lava-like tannic
finish.

The mail-order wine merchant, Laithwaites, describes the
vineyards of Moldova as being on the same latitude as
Burgundy in the hope that this will encourage the
ignoramus to believe the ex-Soviet slave-state has potential
greatness. It is a fatuous comparison, which wine merchants
short on wit are wont to favour. Burgundy's brilliance as a
wine region, a few exceptional producers apart, has been
hopelessly sullied by additions of pesticides to the grapes,
artificial fertilisers to the soil, and sugar to the fermenting
must. These small matters apart, the idea that a
geographical relationship means much viticulturally is as
misguided as the author of this book claiming to be
a putative soccer genius because he shares the same
postal address as the Arsenal star Robert Pires
(which he happens to do).

16.5

Errazuriz Estate Cabernet Sauvignon 2003   CHILE

Everywine

Very gripping, vivid fruit, a combination of chocolate
and burned berries, and the tannins cut a wave of
flavour to finish up kicking their well-shod heels in
the throat before quitting.

Also at Asda, Oddbins, Somerfield, Waitrose.

16.5

Errazuriz Estate Chardonnay 2004   CHILE

Everywine

Delicious! Superb edge of tropicality (pineapple and
mango). Delicate to finish.

Also at Budgens, Oddbins, Sainsbury, Somerfield,
Tesco.

16.5

Errazuriz Estate Carmenere 2003   CHILE

Everywine

A superb cheese wine of great berried depth, soft
plums and blackberries and ripe tannins with a
black olive edge.

Also at Asda, Small Merchants (D. Byrne & Co.,
Luvians, Vicki's of Chobham, Wimbledon Wine
Cellars).

16.5

RED £8.49

Mont Gras Quatro Reserva 2002   CHILE
Everywine
A generous blend of Cabernet Sauvignon,
Malbec, Carmenere and Merlot which creates a
wine of broad shoulders (once fully decanted 4–5
hours), lovely ruffled satin texture, and deep
berries.
Also at Small Merchants (Unwins).

16.5

RED £6.70

Novas Carmenere/Cabernet Sauvignon 2002   CHILE
Vintage Roots
A deft blend of Carmenere, Cabernet Sauvignon and
Syrah which combines cocoa, plums and roasted
berries with adult tannins.
Also at Asda.

16.5

RED £6.70

Novas Cabernet Sauvignon/Merlot 2003   CHILE
Vintage Roots
Very chewy Green & Black's edge to the nutty fruit.
Delicious.

16

RED £7.50

Novas Syrah/Mourvèdre 2003   CHILE
Vintage Roots
Bouncy, rich, very sassy.

16

WHITE £7.99
CHILE

Concha y Toro Winemakers Lot Chardonnay 2002
Virgin
Very elegant stylish melon/pineapple/creamy peach.

16

WHITE £9.39
FRANCE

Vieux Château Gaubert 2001
Laithwaites
A real star. Classy, hints of vegetal peach. Lovely texture.

OTHER WINES 15.5 AND UNDER

15.5

RED £14.99
NEW ZEALAND

Villa Maria Reserve Merlot 2002
Everywine
Screwcap. Also at Waitrose.

15

RED £5.75
CHILE

Adobe Carmenere 2003
Vintage Roots

RED £5.75
CHILE

Adobe Cabernet Sauvignon 2003
Vintage Roots

RED £15.99

Esk Valley Reserve Merlot/Malbec/ NEW ZEALAND
Cabernet Sauvignon 2002
Everywine
Screwcap. Also at Small Merchants (Vicki's of
Chobham, Wimbledon Wine Cellars).

WHITE £5.50

Touchstone Sauvignon Blanc 2004 CHILE
Vintage Roots

RED £5.50

Touchstone Merlot 2002 CHILE
Vintage Roots

WHITE £4.99

Sutter Home Unoaked Chardonnay 2003 USA
Everywine

14.5 **RED £7.99**

De Martino Legado Carmenere Reserva 2003 CHILE
Virgin

WHITE £7.50

Novas Sauvignon Blanc 2004 CHILE
Vintage Roots

WHITE £7.50

Novas Chardonnay/Marsanne/Viognier 2004 CHILE
Vintage Roots

RED £5.50

Touchstone Cabernet Sauvignon 2003 CHILE
Vintage Roots

RED £19.99

Villa Maria Single Vineyard Taylors Pass NEW ZEALAND
Pinot Noir 2003
Everywine
16.5 points in 2007-8. Also at Small Merchants
(Luvians, Wimbledon Wine Cellars).

14

WHITE £7.99

De Martino Legado Sauvignon Blanc CHILE
Reserva 2004
Virgin

RED £9.99

De Martino Single Vineyard Pinot Noir 2002 CHILE
Virgin

RED £7.99

Errazuriz Estate Dos Valles Reserve Syrah 2002 CHILE
Virgin

WHITE £5.49

Monos Locos Chardonnay 2004 CHILE
Virgin

WHITE £5.49

Monos Locos Sauvignon Blanc 2004 CHILE
Virgin

RED £6.99

Monos Locos Cabernet Sauvignon 2001 CHILE

Virgin

RED £9.99

De Martino Single Vineyard Syrah 2003 CHILE

Virgin

WHITE £8.99

Mud House Riesling 2004 NEW ZEALAND

Everywine

Screwcap.

RED £14.99

Villa Maria Reserve Cabernet Sauvignon/ NEW ZEALAND
Merlot 2002

Everywine

Screwcap. Also at Small Merchants (Vicki's of
Chobham, Wimbledon Wine Cellars).

MAJESTIC

Head Office:
Majestic House,
Otterspool Way,
Watford,
Hertfordshire WD25 8WW

Tel: (01913) 298200
Fax: (01923) 819105

E-mail: info@majestic.co.uk
Website: www.majestic.co.uk

For tasting notes of Majestic wines scoring less than
16 points, and ratings of wines less than 14 points,
visit www.superplonk.com

17

WHITE £10.99

Catena Chardonnay 2003 ARGENTINA

Attractive creamy woodiness which lingers lushly yet
not gawkily. A seriously yummy white of character,
svelteness and deep class.
Also at Waitrose.

17

RED £10.99

Clos de Los Siete 2003 ARGENTINA

Beautifully composed fruit playing on several
instruments including sax and drums.
Also at Waitrose.

17

RED £4.99

Casillero del Diablo Concha y Toro CHILE
Carmenere 2004

Simply stunningly deft berries and softly savoury
tannins.
Also at Sainsbury, Tesco, Threshers.

16.5

WHITE £4.99

Argento Chardonnay 2004 ARGENTINA

Always a classy, confident wine whatever the vintage,
the '04 shows lingering smokiness, genteel yet
deliciously insistent. Considerable finesse for an
under-a-fiver white wine.
Also at Sainsbury.

16.5 RED £11.99

Beringer Appellation Collection Napa Valley USA
Cabernet Sauvignon 1999
Superior texture, nicely chunky without deformities
or weirdnesses, lovely smooth-yet-characterful sweet
fruit. Simply delicious. Nay, scrumptious!

16.5 WHITE £4.99

Casillero del Diablo Concha y Toro CHILE
Sauvignon Blanc 2004
A crisp classic Sauvignon Blanc of length and
crunchy concentration. Has a very subtle resin edge
– most attractive.
Also at Asda, Oddbins, Somerfield, Tesco, Threshers.

16.5 RED £9.99

Errazuriz Estate Max Reserva Syrah 2002 CHILE
Sheer velvet berries. Utterly seductive richness.
There's a young bloke in China who, bizarrely,
amazingly, drags a car along by ropes attached to
his ears whilst he walks on eggs without crushing
them. This wine has that kind of stealth yet
muscle.

16.5 WHITE £4.99

Finca Las Moras Viognier 2004 ARGENTINA
Delicious herby apricot and citrus. Dry, elegant, very
firm and at ease with itself. I hate a wine which
rushes you, bullies the palate, insists you must like
it.

16.5

WHITE £9.99
FRANCE

Gewürztraminer Grand Cru Eichberg Zinck 2002

Lovely dry lychee, demure spice, floral undertone. Open and decant for 5–7 hours beforehand for maximum sensuality.

16.5

RED £6.49
FRANCE

Mas de Guiot Cabernet/Syrah, Vin de Pays du Gard 2003

Baked cocoa edging to ripe plums and blackberries. A real solid mouthful of firm fruit.

16.5

RED £9.49
AUSTRALIA

Pirramimma McLaren Vale Petit Verdot 2001

Very ripe and rich but the tannins have a lovely creamy calmness. No paranoia here.

16.5

WHITE £9.99
FRANCE

Riesling Burgreben de Zelenberg Domaine Bott-Geyl 2001

18 points in 2009–11. Superbly fit and firmly developed Riesling, hint of spice, touch of apricot to the citrus and pear.

16.5

WHITE £6.99
ITALY

Riff Pinot Grigio delle Venezie, Alois Lageder 2004

A brilliant insight into fine north Italian winemaking. Has great charm this wine. If you

thought 'Who needs another Italian Pinot Grigio?'
try this and discover a revelation of subtlety and
finesse.

16.5

WHITE £11.99
FRANCE

Rully 1er Cru Vieilles Vignes,
Vincent Giradin 2003
Delicious gentility, hint of forest floor, dry
pear/melon fruit. Very classy.

Additives in Wine (2)

Additives in wine, in some climes, start with the fresh picked
grapes. Ascorbic acid is introduced to preserve the fruit
prior to reaching the winery. Enzymes may also be used to
clarify the must before the ferment. Then there is the
inoculation of the must itself with, in most wines, a special
yeast; the yeasts naturally occurring on the skins of the
grapes are employed but rarely. Wood, either in the form of
barrel aging or by chucking oak chips into vats to mimic the
effects of that maturation process, is another additive. Then
there is, in colder climates like parts of France, the
introduction of sugar (from beet) to raise the alcohol level.
In warmer climates, like Australia's, acid is often necessary
to balance the richness of the liquid. Tannin addition, in the
form of powder, is also part of some red wine recipes. Now
with all of these things, the word 'additive' is moot.
However, not with sulphur. This is essential to keep wine
from spoiling on shelf (and even organic wines must
contain some).

16.5

Sticks Yarra Valley Chardonnay 2003   AUSTRALIA

Delicious dry peach/apricot with citrus. Very finely
tailored – using satin as its material (with the odd
interesting ruffle). Interesting fascist symbol on the
label (and the name translates as such). But it's
unintentional. The fruit, though, is designed to
lushly interpret leaves, peach and citrus. Very
charming.

16.5   WHITE £9.99

Yering Station Yarra Valley Marsanne/   AUSTRALIA
Roussanne/Viognier 2004

Screwcap. A blend of 3 grapes which manages to
achieve a dry, denim-textured purposefulness of
palate-hugging richness without being cloying.

16.5   WHITE £4.99

Casillero del Diablo Concha y Toro   CHILE
Chardonnay 2004

Delicious delicate and elegant, subdued richness.
The 2003 was a lovely dry 17 pointer. The 2004 is not
quite there yet. But give it time.
Also at Asda, Oddbins, Threshers.

16.5   RED £5.49

Casillero del Diablo Concha y Toro Shiraz 2004   CHILE

How is it different from the Aussie style for the same
money? Bigger roasted coffee edge and more tannins.
Also at Sainsbury, Somerfield.

16

RED £4.99

Argento Malbec 2004 ARGENTINA

A very cool, classy customer. Supremely confident yet
not arrogant. Offers lightly burned blackberries and
smooth tannins.

Also at Budgens, Sainsbury, Tesco.

16

WHITE £4.99

Argento Pinot Grigio 2004 ARGENTINA

Dry, pert apricot. Lovely. Works stealthily, daintily,
unambiguously.

Also at Morrison's.

16

RED £5.49

Casillero del Diablo Concha y Toro Malbec 2004 CHILE

Dry, soft yet crusty to finish.

16

RED £6.99

Concha y Toro Winemakers Lot 406 Syrah 2004 CHILE

Lovely soft ripe fruit, most classily polished.

16

RED £25.00

Château Corbin St-Emilion Grand Cru FRANCE
Classé 2000

And grand and classy it is. Tannins to die for (and to
live with).

16

WHITE £3.79

Coldridge Estate Chardonnay 2004 AUSTRALIA

Fantastic smoky melon fruit.

16

RED £3.69

Coldridge Estate Merlot 2003   AUSTRALIA

What a thundering bargain! 'Dive in and enjoy me!'
it announces. Terrific balance, ripeness, serious
tannicity and effortless couthness.

16

WHITE £5.49

Cono Sur Gewürztraminer 2004   CHILE

Delicious Thai food combatant.
Also at Sainsbury.

16

RED £5.29

Château Guiot, Costières de Nîmes 2004   FRANCE

Very smooth, rich, slow-to-evolve fruit of charm and
persistence.

16

WHITE £4.99

Chardonnay Bianco di Sicilia,   ITALY
Cantine Settesoli 2003

Brilliant opulent apricot with citrus and hard pear. A
lovely white of textured finesse.

16

RED £10.99

Catena Cabernet Sauvignon 2002   ARGENTINA

Just so rich and generous. More than the perfect
fruity companion I'd say.

16

RED £3.99

Esperanza Merlot 2004 ARGENTINA

A most accommodatingly charming red which
manages to proceed at first flashily then, as it dries
in the throat, to reveal delicate touches of burned
plum and grilled nut.

16

RED £7.99

Fairview 'Peg Leg' Carignan 2003 SOUTH AFRICA

Beautifully tailored, ripe yet sane, complex, dark,
rivettingly unpretentious and of-this-earth.

16

WHITE £6.99

Fairleigh Estate Single Vineyard NEW ZEALAND
Marlborough Chardonnay 2003

Screwcap. Touch of baked cream to the melon/
peach/citrus fruit is beautifully judged. It softens
well and yet doesn't fade.

16

WHITE £4.99

Gavi Terredavino 2004 ITALY

Has a lovely oily undertone to the fruit.

16

WHITE £7.99

Gavi di Gavi La Tolcadana Raccolto ITALY
Tardivo 2004

Lovely peach fruit. If you thought Italian white wine
was bony and austere, try this and swallow your
prejudices.

16

WHITE £4.99

Griffin Vineyards Verdelho 2003 AUSTRALIA
Terrific calmness to it yet slightly exotic apricot and
Alphonse mango richness.

16

WHITE £6.99

Knappstein Hand Picked Clare Valley AUSTRALIA
Riesling 2003
Screwcap. 18.5 points in 2010–15. One of the Clare's
sassiest Rieslings.

It is sometimes difficult in wine writing to tell whether one is
saying something objective or whether one is merely erecting a
barrier against one's own personal fears. It is always a
significant question to ask about any wine writer: what is (s)he
afraid of? Of course one is afraid that the attempt to be
truthful may turn out to be meaningless or vague. Metaphor is
the only way to solve the problem because the development of
consciousness in human beings is inseparably connected with
the use of metaphor. Metaphors are not adornments, they are
fundamental forms of our awareness of our condition:
metaphors of space, metaphors of movement, metaphors of
vision (which includes smell and taste). Unlike the philosopher
Iris Murdoch whose thinking is reflected in the above, the wine
writer can nail down more precisely his objectivity with
something which transcends language: by providing a value-
for-money rating for each wine assessed. This is the only wine
guide which is organised on such a basis. In rating a wine there
is no ambiguity; the taster's rating expresses an unequivocal
view of the wine's place in the hierarchy.

16

RED £9.99

Kangarilla Road McLaren Vale   AUSTRALIA
Cabernet Sauvignon 2002
About as approachable as a Cabernet Sauvignon can
get and not be over-friendly.

16

RED £9.99

Kangarilla Road McLaren Vale Shiraz 2003   AUSTRALIA
Jam, but not frivolously so for it has an insouciant
richness. Displays sweet (yet dry to finish) open-
hearted fruit (yet not soppy or gushing), rich yet not
throat-gagging to finish.

16

WHITE £7.99

Kangarilla Road McLaren Vale   AUSTRALIA
Chardonnay 2004
Screwcap. The fruit deepens on the palate to reveal
citrussy apricot. Unfussy, elegant.

16

WHITE £5.99

Macon-Prissé Cave Co-op de Prissé 2004   FRANCE
Screwcap. A very subtle white Burgundy which proceeds
across the palate with chalky stealth. Fail to pay attention
– blink even – and its myriad virtues will be lost.

16

WHITE £5.99

Montana East Coast Unoaked   NEW ZEALAND
Chardonnay 2004
Screwcap. Very cosy melon/pear fruit. Terrific price
for such class.
Also at Budgens.

16   RED £6.49

Mas Las Cabes, Jean Gardies,   FRANCE
Côtes du Roussillon 2003
Rusticity refined by good tannins. Herbiness relieved
by fine berries. Roasted jam fruit, with pips, very
energetic. The finish has a touch of chocolate.

16   RED £6.99

Montes 'Limited Selection' Cabernet/   CHILE
Carmenere 2004
Rich and full yet goes delicately roasted on the finish
to reveal fine tannins and chewy biscuit-edged
berries.

16   WHITE £5.99

Montes Reserve Sauvignon Blanc 2004   CHILE
Finely aloof fruit of restraint yet character.

16   RED £6.99

Montes 'Limited Selection' Pinot Noir 2004   CHILE
Superbly textured, smooth, forthright richness. Very
complete, controlled gamy cherries (hint of dried
raspberry).

16   RED £4.99

Monastier Cabernet Franc,   FRANCE
Vin de Pays d'Oc 2004
Screwcap. Delicious coal-black fruit, chewy and
impactful.

16

RED £14.99

Nautilus Estate Pinot Noir 2002   NEW ZEALAND

Very attractive black cherry, gamy raspberry, firm
tannins.

Also at Small Merchants (Christopher Piper Wines,
Thomas Panton Wine Merchants).

16

WHITE £3.99

Neblina Sauvignon Blanc 2004   CHILE

Bargain tippling here. Offers demure ripeness and
melon/citrus fruit.

Where Chardonnay is a much-travelled cliché, Pinot Noir is
a closeted contradiction. Even the Canadians turn out
Chardonnay; the Chinese are at it; even Madagascar, in the
hills, boasts Chardonnay vines. Its eponym, that village in
Burgundy, had it had a mayor with the entrepreneurial
instincts of Richard Branson, would have trademarked the
word a century ago and by now the Chardonnayers would be
rolling in royalties. Their neighbours, those first growers of
the variety we now call Pinot Noir, would be the poor
relations, for though Pinot does crop up in odd places (I've
even tasted an English one by-golly-gosh and it was like
sucking on a lolly stick without the lolly), it is within the
confines of Burgundy that it is said to reach the acme of its
gamy expressiveness. The important words in that last
sentence are 'it is said'.

16

Neblina Merlot 2004　　　　　　　　　　CHILE
The jamminess doesn't weaken, but keeps up the
flavoursome effect for a full 60 seconds.

16

Roero Arneis Terre da Vino 2004　　　　ITALY
Tangy citrus – delightful, demure, dainty (yet daring).

16

Rex Goliath Giant 47-Pound Rooster　　USA
Cabernet Sauvignon NV
Like tasting grapes off the vine, lightly toasted in the
sun, sprinkled with grilled nuts and some spice. The
name is a lot crazier than the fruit.

16

Sauvignon de Touraine,　　　　　　　　FRANCE
Domaine de la Prévote 2004
Delicious! What an individual Sauvignon Blanc (yet
not eccentric, so no grass or asparagus). Very classy
and complete.

16

Saumur Champigny 'Les Tuffeaux',　　　FRANCE
Château de Targe 2003
Black truffle-edged and darkly cherried red of
intense cheeriness. Very, very dry.

16

WHITE £6.99

Santa Rita Reserva Sauvignon Blanc 2004 CHILE
More peach to the gooseberry than is typical, but it's
delicious.

16

RED £13.99

Vergelegen Cabernet Sauvignon 2003 SOUTH AFRICA
Sheer sensual ripeness.

16

WHITE £7.99

Vergelegen Chardonnay 2003 SOUTH AFRICA
Screwcap. Complexity with a woodiness held by
creamy fruit and a finely tailored texture.

16

RED £9.99

Valpolicella Classico Superiore Ripasso ITALY
La Casetta di Ettore Righetti 2001
The tight patchwork of flavours and textures is pure
Italian – rococo, confident, very pretty.

16

RED £6.99

Concha y Toro Winemakers Lot Merlot/ CHILE
Syrah 2003
Character with polish – difficult trick to pull off.

16

WHITE £6.99

Yering Frog Yarra Valley Chardonnay 2003 AUSTRALIA
Wood with dignity and in proper obeisance to the
fruit.

16

**Yering Station Yarra Valley
Chardonnay 2003**
Screwcap. One of the Yarra Valley's most deftly
judged fruit/wood Chardonnays.

16

**Yering Station Yarra Valley Pinot Noir
Rosé 2004**
Screwcap. One of the most attractive rosés I've tasted
with its dry cherry/raspberry fruit. Delicate,
determined.

16

Cono Sur Viognier 2004
How Viognier should be at this price. Gorgeous
apricot/citrus fruit which fattens on the tongue but
does not go florid.
Also at Somerfield, Threshers, Waitrose.

Almost all young wines will benefit from being opened and
fully decanted into a jug and allowed to breathe for several
hours. Air is wine's greatest friend and its greatest enemy;
for all wine's destiny is to become acetic acid eventually. Yet,
long before that, the same liquid will reach an apogee of
mellow fruitiness and/or concentrated minerality
(depending on its grape variety and wine-making style) and
exposing it fully to air is an attempt to capture that moment.

16

WHITE £6.99

Villa Maria Private Bin Riesling 2004   NEW ZEALAND
Screwcap. 18 in 2010–12. Impressive now. Stonking
in 5 years.
Also at Budgens.

16

RED £11.99

Wolf Blass President's Selection   AUSTRALIA
Cabernet Sauvignon 2002
Big, rich, yet only lightly grilled berries with firm
tannins of velvet with denim patches. Very well
modulated Cabernet of some class.
Also at Somerfield, Waitrose.

16

WHITE £6.49

Montana Marlborough Sauvignon   NEW ZEALAND
Blanc 2004
Screwcap. Bargain gooseberry fruit. Real finesse
here.
Also at Budgens, Tesco, Threshers.

16

RED £4.99

Cono Sur Pinot Noir 2004   CHILE
Stunningly complete – the tobacco-edged, gamy
cherries linger for ages in the throat.
Also at Somerfield, Threshers, Waitrose.

OTHER WINES 15.5 AND UNDER

15.5

RED £7.99

Concha y Toro Winemakers Lot 1006
Merlot 2004
CHILE

WHITE £5.99

Château Saint-Jean-des-Graves 2004
FRANCE
Screwcap. Also at Waitrose.

RED £5.99

Domaine La Galine 2003
FRANCE

RED £6.49

Domaine de Piaugier Côtes de Rhône-Villages
FRANCE
Sablet 2002

WHITE £7.99

Gavi Brico Battistina 2004
ITALY

WHITE (half bottle) £4.69

Concha y Toro Late Harvest Sauvignon
CHILE
Blanc 2001
17.5 points in 2010–15.

WHITE £4.49

Marc Ducourneau, Vin de Pays des Côtes
FRANCE
de Gascogne 2002

RED £6.99

Santa Rita Reserva Merlot 2003
CHILE

RED £2.99
SPAIN

Tempranillo La Serrana Vino de la Tierra 2003

RED £9.99
AUSTRALIA

Vasse Felix 'Adams Road' Cabernet/ Merlot 2003

WHITE £8.99
NEW ZEALAND

Waimea Estate Sauvignon Blanc 2004
Screwcap.

15

RED £4.99
ITALY

Aglianico Rosso di Sicilia, Cantine Settesoli 2003

RED £6.99
FRANCE

Beaujolais-Villages, Domaine de Nuges 2004

WHITE £7.49
FRANCE

Coulée d'Argent Bourillon d'Orléans Vouvray Sec 2004

RED £6.99
SPAIN

Durius Arribes del Duero Tempranillo 2003

WHITE £6.99
NEW ZEALAND

Fairleigh Estate Single Vineyard Marlborough Sauvignon Blanc 2004
Screwcap.

WHITE £4.99
FRANCE

Les Argelières Chardonnay, Vin de Pays d'Oc 2004

RED £9.99

Montana Reserve Pinot Noir 2003   NEW ZEALAND

Also at Oddbins, Threshers.

WHITE £12.99

Mercurey 1er Cru 'Clos des Barrault'   FRANCE

Domaine Juillot 2000

WHITE £7.99

Pinot d'Alsace Domaine Bott-Geyl 2002   FRANCE

17 points in 2007.

WHITE £7.49

Quincy Jean-Charles Borgnat 2004   FRANCE

WHITE £8.99

St-Véran Orchys 2003   FRANCE

WHITE £8.99

Sancerre Domaine Gerard Fiou 2004   FRANCE

ROSÉ £5.85

Santa Rita Cabernet Sauvignon Rosé 2004   CHILE

RED £16.99

Waimea Estate Pinot Noir 2003   NEW ZEALAND

WHITE £6.99

Zondernaam Sauvignon Blanc 2004   SOUTH AFRICA

Screwcap.

14.5

RED £5.99

Beaujolais Cuvée Vieilles Vignes   FRANCE

Cave de Bully 2004

RED £15.99

Cloudy Bay Pinot Noir 2003   NEW ZEALAND

Also at Small Merchants (Harrods), Waitrose
(selected stores).

ROSÉ £5.29

Château Guiot Rosé, Costières de Nîmes 2004   FRANCE

WHITE £3.49

Cuvée des Amandiers Blanc,   FRANCE
Vin de Pays d'Oc 2004

RED £7.99

El Malbec de Ricardo Santos,   ARGENTINA
La Madras Vineyard 2003

ROSÉ £4.99

Finca Les Moras Shiraz Rosé 2004   ARGENTINA
Screwcap.

RED £4.99

La Rectorie Côtes du Rhône-Villages 2004   FRANCE

RED £3.49

Les Marquières Vin de Pays des Coteaux   FRANCE
de Fontcaude 2004
Screwcap.

RED £9.99

Moulin-à-Vent Les Michelons,   FRANCE
Louis Latour 2003

RED £8.49
Premier Vin du Château de Pitray, FRANCE
Côtes de Castillon 2001

RED £7.99
Perrin Cairanne 'Peyre Blanche', FRANCE
Côtes du Rhône-Villages 2003

RED £15.99
Quartz Reef Pinot Noir 2003 NEW ZEALAND
Screwcap.

ROSÉ £5.85
Stormhoek Select Rosé 2004 SOUTH AFRICA

WHITE £4.99
Saumur Blanc Reserve des Vignerons 2004 FRANCE

WHITE £4.69
Verdicchio dei Castelli di Jesi ITALY
Croce del Moro 2004

WHITE £9.99
Vasse Felix 'Adams Road' Chardonnay 2004 AUSTRALIA

RED £9.99
Yering Station Yarra Valley Pinot Noir 2002 AUSTRALIA

RED £7.99
Oyster Bay Merlot 2004 NEW ZEALAND
Screwcap. Also at Sainsbury, Waitrose.

14

WHITE £8.49

Amberley Estate Margaret River Sauvignon   AUSTRALIA
Blanc 2004
Screwcap.

WHITE £7.99

Bellingham 'The Maverick'   SOUTH AFRICA
Viognier 2004
Screwcap.

WHITE £11.99

Beringer Appellation Collection Napa Valley   USA
Chardonnay 2004

RED £5.49

Bardolino Classico Tedeschi 2003   ITALY

ROSÉ £4.09

Cuvée des Amandiers Rosé,   FRANCE
Vin de Pays d'Oc 2004

WHITE £3.05

Cuvée de Richard Blanc, Vin de Pays   FRANCE
du Comte Tolosan 2004

RED £3.49

Cuvée des Amandiers, Vin de Pays d'Oc 2004   FRANCE

ROSÉ £8.99

Château de Sours Rosé 2004   FRANCE
Screwcap.

RED £6.49

FRANCE

Château de l'Abbaye de St-Ferme Bordeaux Supérieur 2002

RED £30.00

AUSTRALIA

Cullen Estate Diana Madelaine Cabernet/ Merlot 2001
St Johns Wood branch only.

RED £7.49

FRANCE

Domaine de la Janasse Terre de Bussière, Vin de Pays de la Principauté d'Orange 2003

RED £7.99

ITALY

Dogajolo Carpineto Toscana 2003

WHITE £3.99

ARGENTINA

Esperanza Sauvignon Blanc 2004

WHITE £7.99

NEW ZEALAND

Fairleigh Estate Riesling 2004
Screwcap.16.5 points in 2010.

WHITE SPARKLING £31.99

FRANCE

Laurent Perrier Ultra Brut NV

ROSÉ SPARKLING £26.65

FRANCE

Lanson Rosé NV

WHITE £3.49

FRANCE

Les Marquières, Vin de Pays du Comte Tolosan 2004
Screwcap.

RED £19.99

La Réserve de Léoville-Barton, St-Julien 2000   FRANCE

WHITE £6.49

Mas Las Cabes, Jean Gardies, Vin de Pays   FRANCE
des Côtes Catalanes Muscat Sec 2004

RED £28.00

Nuits-St-Georges 1er Cru Les Chaignots,   FRANCE
Robert Chévillon 2002
St Johns Wood branch only.

RED £8.99

Perrin & Fils Rasteau 'L'Andeol',   FRANCE
Côtes du Rhône 2003

RED £7.49

Pinot Noir Valmoissine Louis Latour,   FRANCE
Vin de Pays des Coteaux du Verdon 2002

WHITE £8.49

Reuilly 'Les Bouchauds' Gerard   FRANCE
Bigonneau 2004

WHITE £4.49

Robertson Winery Sauvignon Blanc 2004   FRANCE

WHITE £6.99

Southbank Estate Sauvignon Blanc 2004   NEW ZEALAND
Screwcap.

WHITE £7.99

Sonoma Creek Chardonnay 2001   USA

RED £7.99	
Sonoma Creek Merlot 2000	USA
RED £16.99	
Savigny 1er Cru La Bataillière aux Vergelesses Albert Morot 2001	FRANCE
RED £7.99	
Sticks Yarra Valley Pinot Noir 2003	AUSTRALIA
RED £4.99	
Viña Alta Mar Jumilla Monastrell/ Cabernet Sauvignon 2001	SPAIN

MARKS & SPENCER

Waterside House,
35 North Wharf Road,
London W2 1NW

Tel: (020) 7268 1234
Fax: (020) 7268 2380

Customer Services: (0845) 302 1234

E-mail: customer.services@marks-and-spencer.com
Website: www.marksandspencer.com

For tasting notes of Marks & Spencer wines scoring
less than 16 points, and ratings of wines less than of
14 points, visit www.superplonk.com

18

WHITE £7.99

AUSTRALIA

Lenbridge Forge Yarra Valley Chardonnay 2003

Quite pungently attractive and mildly raffish euphoriant. Has creamy fruit offering layers of melon, pear and citrus, but it's the texture which is so scrumptiously sensual.

18

RED £14.49

Villalta Amarone della Valpolicella Classico 2000   ITALY

Ravishing, complete, baroque Italian with brickwork of roasted berries, ornaments of prune and almond, and gargoyles of licorice and black cherry. The result is a wine you don't so much drink as inhabit.

17.5

RED £5.50

FRANCE

Château des Lanes Corbières 2001

This engaging red wine moves slowly but very surely across the palate, revealing charcoal, raspberry and very gripping tannins. A most elegant claret-style bargain.

17.5

RED £7.99

Dorrien Estate Bin 442 Barossa Shiraz 2003   AUSTRALIA

Impossible to dislike (unless you've spent the last 20 years at the bottom of the sea). Quintessential Barossa Shiraz: muscled, rich, deep, soft, spicy – hugely gluggable and uncomplicated (yet complex to contemplate if you've a mind to be distracted). Great energy and ripeness with a lengthy, well-textured finish of great class. Very vivid, exciting, rich.

17.5   RED £9.99

Leon de Oro Merlot/Cabernet Sauvignon 2003   CHILE
A toweringly plummy, sensually ripe and heady red
wine of character yet great polish. A vibrant
mouthful of great class and clout.

17.5   WHITE £5.99

Tupagato Chardonnay 2003   ARGENTINA
Beautifully plump and vivid but still possesses
delicacy as the mango/citrus/pear fruit dries out in
the throat.

17   WHITE £7.99

Banwell Farm Eden Valley Riesling 2004   AUSTRALIA
18.5 points in 2008–10. Already an immediately
sensuous liquid with its subtle kerosene undertone
laced with citrus and grapefruit. Will mature
dazzlingly.

17   WHITE £7.99

Banwell Farm Barossa Valley Sémillon 2002   AUSTRALIA
Magically Aussie in its Sémillonosity. That is to say it
wears a variety of colours and textures whilst the
fruit has that teasing waxy citrus/grapefruit
undertone. Hugely elegant.

17   RED £6.50

Casa Leona Reserve Cabernet Sauvignon 2003   CHILE
Chunky, cocoa-edged plums and berries with superb
tannins.

17 RED £7.99

Harrowgate Shiraz 2003 AUSTRALIA
A super-duper blend of only 86% Shiraz in fact, with
10% Mourvèdre and 4% Grenache to provide variety.
This massive red shuffles along with an air of
dishevelment yet it reveals itself to be a dandy
underneath. A most unusually couth yet raffish
Aussie.

17 WHITE £6.99

La Prendina Estate Pinot Grigio 2004 ITALY
Gorgeous oily richness! What a superb vintage of
this Superplonkers' fave M & S white. The opulence
of the apricot is more pronounced and there are deft
balancing acids.

17 RED £13.99

Shady Grove Cabernet Sauvignon 2001 AUSTRALIA
A stunningly complete Cab fully fitted out with
leather seats, a leather fascia, and a beautifully soft
purrer of an engine. Takes you from nose to throat
in great style and comfort.

16.5 WHITE £7.99

Bush View Margaret River Chardonnay 2003 AUSTRALIA
Most individual: a triumph of M & S peculiar–to-
itself blending preferences. Nice smoky intro leads
to citrus, papaya and, would you credit, a hint of
lime.

16.5   RED £4.99
Casa Leona Merlot 2004   CHILE
Deliciously nut chocolate finish to cherry and
blackcurrant. The tannins are soft but determined.

If the retailers this book covers are animals then M & S is
surely the oddest. It is a rhinoceros with Cerberus' heads atop
a leopard's legs – yet in spite of these peculiarities it wishes it
was a chameleon. In other words it is bulky and thick-
skinned, always in several minds at once, saved from being
lumbering by that elegant undercarriage which it can
sometimes employ to speedy effect, but dominating all its
moods is the burning desire to blend into any landscape in
which it finds itself. Is it a fast-food retailer? A grocer? An
underwear emporium? A fashion house? A sandwich bar? A
wine merchant? It is all of these things; and in some
branches it also sells kitchen utensils and home furnishings. I
am only surprised it has not caused to be designed and
manufactured, in Korea, its own make of motor vehicle. It is
certainly the only retailer known to me - I suspect the whole
world - which can blithely shift a multi-lingual master of wine,
who has had the rare professional experience of studying
oenology and making wine herself, from fronting its wine
department to its flower department where her hard-won
qualifications and skills are, amongst all those flawless bug-
free blooms, utterly irrelevant. At such times, Marks &
Spencer manifests all the idiosyncratic solipsism of a
mediaeval princedom and one discovers this remarkable
company is a law unto itself.

16.5

RED £4.99

Casa Leona Cabernet Sauvignon 2004 CHILE

Unusual Cab in that it moves between playful, strikingly dry berries and soft, raspberry-edged tannins. Utterly delicious. Wonderfully satisfying quaffing here.

16.5

RED £7.50

Château Plo du Roy Minervois 2000 FRANCE

Superb blend of 80% Syrah and 20% Grenache which is beautifully berried up to its neck in rich fruit.

16.5

RED £6.99

Chianti Burchino Superiore 2003 ITALY

What an exciting modern yet echoic old-fashioned Chianti. Has earthy cherries with frisky tannins. Demanding, strict, yet sensually charged from nose to throat.

16.5

RED £11.00

Domaine Bunan Bandol 2001 FRANCE

A mouth-rippling, palate-punching, throat-tickling blend of 65% Mourvèdre, 15% Cinsault, 15% Grenache and 5% Syrah. It moves along briskly and very aromatically.

16.5

**Gold Label Cabernet Sauvignon/
Merlot, Vin de Pays d'Oc 2002**

Chocolate appears once the roasted plums quit the
stage. But then it too must make way for Falstaffian
tannins.

16.5

Mandorla Syrah Sicilia 2003

Very chewy, slightly coffee-edged blackberries with
spicy tannins. Undercurrent of raspberry is
suggested as another theme.

16.5

Oudinot Brut 2000

The hint of feral melon and suggestion of leafiness
are very tantalising.

16.5

**Shepherds Ridge Marlborough
Sauvignon Blanc 2004**

Proceeds on various botanical levels:

> Grass
> Earth
> Flowers
> Fruits

In sum, a provocative tipple of class and great
interest. (True, it's made by a man whose Mercedes
has a glass roof, but even world-class winemakers
must have their little indulgences.)

16.5
RED £3.29
FRANCE

Vin de Pays de l'Ardèche Gamay 2004
Superb! Like Beaujolais used to be. Has perfect
12% alcohol weight, good cherries and plums,
and velvet-edged tannins embroidered within. A
truly terrific glug which, lightly chilled, recalls a
bygone era.

16
WHITE £4.99
ITALY

Aramonte Catarratto 2004
How to be vague yet committed, rich yet slim, very
dry yet hugely entertaining.

16
WHITE £5.99
FRANCE

Burgundy Bourgogne Chardonnay 2004
Very finely wrought melon/lemon co-ordination.
Delicious.

16
RED £7.99
ITALY

Chianti Colli Fiorentini Terre de'Nocenti 2003
In complete contrast to many Chiantis, this has a
ripe plum, taffeta-textured ripeness which is truly a
revelation.

16
WHITE £9.99
NEW ZEALAND

Clocktower Sauvignon Blanc 2004
A Kiwi thickly disguised as an old-fashioned
Sancerre. Bravo, boys!

16

RED £6.99
FRANCE

Clos Roque d'Aspes Faugères 2001

A lovely marriage of 60% Mourvèdre, 20% Grenache and 20% Syrah which contrives to be couth yet rustic, polished yet rugged.

16

WHITE £5.99

Darting Estate Michelsberg Riesling 2004   GERMANY

Try it! Be not afeared, citizens! This Riesling will not bite. It is deliciously touched by grapefruit and citrus.

16

WHITE £4.49

Domaine Galatis Chardonnay/Viognier 2004   FRANCE

Offers ripe peach/melon with citrus and under-ripe passionfruit. Unusually toothsome tippling for the money.

16

WHITE SPARKLING £18.99

Desroches Champagne NV   FRANCE

Has that classic touch of melon/raspberry to its dry elegance.

16

WHITE £4.99
ARGENTINA

El Dueño Chardonnay 2004

Dry yet waxy, this wine is a sum of many parts – delicious melon/citrus/peach/pear and something indefinably...savoury... could it be nuts? (Or maybe it's just me.)

16

Friuli Sauvignon Blanc 2004 ITALY
The very subtle peach is deliciously undercut by
lemon.

16

Fitou 2002 FRANCE
Warm but not overcoated, rustic yet smooth,
tantalising yet not frustrating, hearty yet not bulky.

16

Gold Label Chardonnay, Vin de Pays d'Oc 2004 FRANCE
Very firm and elegant.

Many supermarkets now employ wine advisers to patrol
the booze aisles and offer advice. However, I must
question why M & S, as a prime example of this trend,
took some of these advisers to France last year and
introduced them to what it, fatuously, called 'the art of
blending'. Blending wine is not, for a start, an art; it can
hardly claim to be more than a creative skill and it is as
much use to a wine adviser as knowledge of blast furnace
alloys is to a car salesman. M & S, like all supermarkets,
should encourage their wine advisers to spend their time
in restaurants, eating and drinking and discovering how to
match wine and food. That is the most relevant skill of
any wine adviser.

16

WHITE £7.99
AUSTRIA

Grüner Veltliner Atrium 2004
Very dry, classily elegant and beautifully textured.

16

WHITE £7.99
AUSTRALIA

Honey Tree Reserve Chardonnay 2004
Delicious fruity at first (melon, citrus, the usual suspects) then it goes coy and dry. Most charming manners displayed here.

16

WHITE £5.99
NEW ZEALAND

Kaituna Hills East Coast Riesling 2004
17.5 points in 2010. Combines the richness of ripe melon with the cheekiness of dry citrus.

16

RED £5.49
SPAIN

Las Almenas Bobal Crianza 2002
Vivid plums and lovely soft tannins. A gorgeous, supple red of lushness yet lithe, shapely fruit.

16

RED £4.99
SPAIN

La Basca Uvas Tintas 2004
Tannins like velvet, fruit like taffeta, acids like silk. This is the normal Spanish mode of dress at this price? Fantastic! Cheap chic. (Like many of the same retailer's clothes.)

16

WHITE £4.99
SPAIN

La Basca Uvas Blancas 2004
Fat pear and gentle peach/citrus. Individual, nicely textured, very relaxed.

16

WHITE £8.99
FRANCE

Chablis La Chablisienne 2002
Mature, beautifully paced fruit which offers a complete performance from nose to throat.

16

RED £5.49
FRANCE

Minervois 2003
A controlled, rustic assembly line of 40% Carignan, 30% Grenache, 20% Syrah and 10% Mourvèdre. The resultant liquid is put together very prettily.

16

WHITE £20.00
FRANCE

Meursault 2003
Lovely old-fashioned woody richness which defines a style of Chardonnay one can only characterise as haughty and very finely tailored. More *Daily Telegraph* than *Guardian* perhaps, but what's life without variety?

16

WHITE £9.99
GERMANY

Martin Estate Riesling 2004
By stealth it works magic as a steady pear and gooseberry slither over the taste-buds.

WHITE £5.99

Mineralstein Riesling 2004 GERMANY

Classy, nervous, very demure and daintily peach/
pineapple.

WHITE SPARKLING £16.99

Oudinot Cuvée Brut NV FRANCE

One of the most elegant of supermarket 100%
Chardonnay bubblies.

WHITE SPARKLING £6.99

Pinot Grigio NV ITALY

Delicious. A real find. Has very elegant, crisp
fruit with a hint – just a hint – of dry peach and
nut.

It is a common misconception that wine from an individual
vineyard is superior to a blend of several. All this, to my
mind, is an ingenious scheme to protect real-estate values.
If you can attach greatness to a small area of wine
production, the vineyard, rather than the people who make
the wine, the product's value is permanently enhanced. Even
when the wine is mediocre, or less than thrilling, it remains
revered. By the same token a premiership football team
bottom of the league could point to its hallowed turf
as conferring world-class status to whatever home team
played on it. How long would even the most besotted
fan buy that idea?

16

RED £8.99

FRANCE

**Rasteau Cuvée Chambert,
Côtes du Rhône-Villages 2003**
Marvellously polished yet has jagged edges to the
tannins to give it real character and bite.

16

RED £6.99

CHILE

Secano Estate Pinot Noir 2004
18 points in 2007–8. Ripe and gamy, good
cherry/raspberry richness. Needs time to concentrate
its aroma and fruit to even higher sensuous levels.

16

RED £10.99

FRANCE

Terre du Lion Saint Julien Bordeaux 1999
Perfectly mature Cabernet Sauvignon and Merlot
marriage of ripeness, most accommodating berried
richness, and with a very relaxed, take-it-or-leave-it
demeanour. It oozes class yet is unpretentiously,
immediately drinkable.

16

WHITE £6.99

SPAIN

Torresoto Rioja 2003
A white Rioja I can enthuse over! The hint of grilled
wood and nuts is decisive. The gentle smoky
undertone which results is nicely weighted.

16

RED £4.99

SOUTH AFRICA

Trackers Trail Shiraz 2004
Intense cigar-smoke fruit of great entertainment
value.

16 WHITE £4.99

Verdicchio dei Castelli di Jesi 2004 ITALY

Elegance, finesse, chic understated citrus, melon, and some kind of nut unknown precisely to this drinker.

16 WHITE £4.99

Vin de Pays d'Oc Sauvignon Blanc 2004 FRANCE

Superb under-ripe fruit of great style and elegance.

16 RED £4.99

Woodhaven Shiraz 2004 USA

Bargain Film Star glitz here. The fruit is a combination of Tom Cruise and Jennifer Lopez – handsome, slightly relaxed, and even-featured with a hint of exotic paranoia beneath.

16 WHITE £5.50

Vouvray Domaine de la Pouvraie 2003 FRANCE

18 points in 2010–12. Off dry richness slowly raises its game as the liquid reaches the back of the throat to reveal grapefruit and a hint of chive.

OTHER WINES 15.5 AND UNDER

15.5 RED £3.99

Dolphin Bay Shiraz 2004 SOUTH AFRICA

WHITE £4.99

Organic Villa Masera 2004 ITALY

RED £11.00

Pago Real Rioja 2002   SPAIN

WHITE SPARKLING £21.99

St Gall Grand Cru 2000   FRANCE

15

WHITE SPARKLING £5.99

Asti NV   ITALY

RED £4.99

El Dueño Shiraz 2004   ARGENTINA

RED £12.99

Initial de Desmirail Margaux 2002   FRANCE

RED £6.99

Kaituna Hills Merlot/   NEW ZEALAND
Cabernet Sauvignon 2003

RED £9.99

Kaituna Hills Reserve Pinot Noir 2003   NEW ZEALAND

WHITE £4.99

Kaituna Blue Sauvignon Blanc/   NEW ZEALAND
Sémillon 2004

RED £9.99

Marin Ridge Lodi Malbec 2002   USA

WHITE £4.99

Pinot Grigio 2004   GERMANY

RED £7.99

Quinta de Fafide 2003   PORTUGAL

14.5

	RED £7.99
Bush View Margaret River Shiraz 2002	AUSTRALIA

	WHITE £7.99
Kaituna Hills Reserve Sauvignon Blanc 2004	NEW ZEALAND

	WHITE £4.99
Pheasant Gully Sémillon/ Sauvignon Blanc 2004	AUSTRALIA

	WHITE SPARKLING £6.99
Prosecco NV	ITALY

	ROSÉ SPARKLING £5.99
Rosado Cava NV	SPAIN

	WHITE SPARKLING £18.99
St Gall Brut Premier Cru NV	FRANCE

	WHITE £4.99
Via Ulivi Pinot Grigio 2004	ITALY

	RED £6.99
Zamora Zinfandel 2003	USA

	WHITE £6.99
Alsace Gewürztraminer (M & S) 2004	FRANCE

14

	WHITE £5.99
Alsace Riesling (M & S) 2004	FRANCE

	RED £8.99
Clos de Reynard 2004	USA

Yep, it really is a Californian wine.

	RED £7.50
Château Planèzes,	FRANCE
Côtes du Roussillon-Villages 2001	

	RED £5.49
Corbières (M & S) 2003	FRANCE

	WHITE £4.29
Domaine Mandeville Viognier 2004	FRANCE

	WHITE £9.99
Ernst Loosen Erdener Treppchen Riesling	GERMANY
Kabinett 2004	
16.5 points in 2010.	

	RED £4.99
Gold Label Cabernet Sauvignon,	FRANCE
Vin de Pays d'Oc 2004	

	ROSÉ £4.99
Gold Label Rosé, Vin de Pays d'Oc 2004	FRANCE

	RED £7.99
Houdamond Pinotage 2004	SOUTH AFRICA

	RED £6.99
Honey Tree Shiraz/Cabernet Sauvignon 2004	AUSTRALIA

	WHITE £5.99
Kaituna Hills Chardonnay 2004	NEW ZEALAND

	WHITE £7.99
Langhorne Creek Estate Pinot Grigio 2004	AUSTRALIA

	WHITE £5.99
Macon-Villages 2004	FRANCE

RED £4.99

Old Vines Grenache Noir,
Vin de Pays des Côtes Catalanes 2004

FRANCE

ROSÉ SPARKLING £17.99

Oudinot Rosé Champagne NV

FRANCE

WHITE £6.99

Secano Estate Sauvignon Blanc 2004

CHILE

WHITE £3.99

Sauvignon Blanc, Vin de Pays du Jardin
de la France 2004

FRANCE

MORRISON'S

**Hillmore House,
Thornton Road,
Bradford,
West Yorkshire BD8 9AX**

Tel: (01274) 494166
Fax: (01274) 494831

Website: www.morereasons.co.uk

For tasting notes of Morrison's wines scoring less
than 16 points, and ratings of wines less than
14 points, visit www.superplonk.com

16

RED £4.99
ARGENTINA

Argento Bonarda 2004
Bruising soft, rich and ripe yet it is not OTT or
ungainly.

16

RED £5.99
CHILE

Castillo de Molina Reserva Shiraz 2003
One of the classiest reds on Morrison's shelves: real
salivatory chocolate-edged fruit and high-class
tannins.

16

WHITE £5.99
CHILE

Castillo de Molina Reserva Chardonnay 2004
Lovely balance between softly spicy (though subtle)
melon and fine, textured lemon.

16

WHITE £5.49
CHILE

**Casillero del Diablo Concha y Toro
Viognier 2004**
Very elegant, stylish under-ripe apricot.

16

RED £2.99
CHILE

Cielo de Luz Cabernet Sauvignon 2004
Screwcap. Lightly grilled berries and a touch of nutty
chocolate on the finish.

16

RED £2.99
CHILE

Cielo de Luz Carmenere 2004
Screwcap. Plump, pleasing plummy, unpretentious
tippling – and utterly terrific with cheese dishes.

Is so-called (i.e. self-proclaimed) great champagne really worth the dosh? Very rarely, as far as I can tell. The house of G.H. Mumm, for example, sent me its Mumm de Cramant, a non-vintage 100% Chardonnay blend, and I had some hopes that, for £39.99, there might be in such a bottle a gaseous liquid the emphatic sublimities of which could be shouted from the rooftops. But it was not to be. My neighbours were undisturbed as I sipped and cogitated. Mumm de Cramant is certainly a curiousity but its price tag is prohibitive. It has claims to exclusivity, perhaps, but who in his right mind wants to indulge in exclusivity only to be mugged by a price tag? The wine has been maintained as a tradition, an in-house wine (strictly for Mumm's executives and favourite customers) for years, and departs from the style of this champagne house in that it does not have any Pinot Noir grapes in its make-up as do other Mumm wines. It has an agreeable grapefruit undertone to a restrained, dry, Charentais melon edginess and it exhibits a certain po-facedness which gives it an amusingily starchy, almost sacerdotal serenity. Being as charitable as I can, I've rated it 14 points out of 20. If it were a third of the price, it would be more charming; but if it was so easy to acquire what mystery would it have for the status seeker? Would the sparkling wine snob give it a second glance? Probably not. A high price is an essential part of a champagne's image.

16

WHITE £2.99
CHILE

Cielo de Luz Sauvignon Blanc 2004
Screwcap. Stunningly well tailored for £2.99! The patches on the sleeves are designer labels, not repaired wear and tear.

16

ROSÉ £4.99
ITALY

Inycon Cabernet Sauvignon Rosé 2003
One of the most elegant rosés around.

16

WHITE £4.99
ITALY

Inycon Chardonnay 2004
Classy, dry, very firm melon/citrus fruit.
Also at Tesco.

16

RED £4.49
ARGENTINA

Santa Julia Bonarda/Sangiovese 2004
Nicely controlled, only slightly exuberant berries, nicely charred, with firm tannins.
Also at Waitrose.

16

WHITE £5.99
CHILE

Villa Montes Reserve Sauvignon Blanc 2003
Very classy amalgam of under-ripe melon, pineapple and citrus.
Also at Sainsbury, Waitrose.

16

RED SPARKLING £7.99
AUSTRALIA

Wyndham Estate Bin 555 Sparkling Shiraz NV
Dry, vivacious, brilliantly able to handle sweetly sauced game dishes.

16

WHITE £5.99

Peter Lehmann Barossa Sémillon 2003   AUSTRALIA
Screwcap. 18 points in 2010. Drink it with abandon
now. With extra special care in 5 years.
Also at Asda, Booths, Sainsbury.

16

WHITE £6.99

Oyster Bay Sauvignon Blanc 2004   NEW ZEALAND
Screwcap. Very, very classy. Very confident gooseberry
richness.
Also at Co-op, Sainsbury.

16

WHITE £4.99

Argento Pinot Grigio 2004   ARGENTINA
Dry, pert apricot. Lovely. Works stealthily, daintily,
unambiguously.
Also at Majestic.

OTHER WINES 15.5 AND UNDER

15.5

WHITE £9.99

Domaine Carrette Pouilly-Fuissé 2003   FRANCE

WHITE £5.99

Inspire Sauvignon Blanc 2004   SOUTH AFRICA

WHITE £5.99

Kingston Empiric Selection Viognier 2002   AUSTRALIA
Screwcap.

	RED £4.99
Les Marionettes Ancient Vines Carignan 2002	FRANCE

	RED £6.99
Marqués de Casa Concha Cabernet Sauvignon 2003	CHILE

	RED £4.99
Misiónes de Rengo Carmenere 2003	CHILE

	WHITE £6.99
Oyster Bay Chardonnay 2003 Screwcap.	NEW ZEALAND

15

	RED £4.49
Cano Cosecha Toro 2003	SPAIN

	WHITE £4.49
Distinto Catarratto/Chardonnay 2004	ITALY

	WHITE £4.99
Jindalee Chardonnay 2003	AUSTRALIA

	WHITE £4.69
Woolpunda Chardonnay 2002	AUSTRALIA

	RED £5.29
Woolpunda Cabernet Sauvignon	AUSTRALIA

14.5

	RED £4.99
Myrtle Grove Shiraz 2001	AUSTRALIA

Macon-Villages Teissèdre 2003
WHITE £4.99
FRANCE

Navasques Tempranillo Navarra 2003
RED £4.49
SPAIN

Pink Pink Fizz Cava
ROSÉ SPARKLING £4.99
SPAIN

Peter Lehmann Grenache 2002
RED £4.99
AUSTRALIA
Screwcap. Also at Tesco.

14

Brindisi Rosso 2001
RED £4.99
ITALY

Cape Cinsault Ruby Cabernet 2004
RED £3.99
SOUTH AFRICA

Cava Cristalino Brut
WHITE SPARKLING £3.99
SPAIN

Gewürztraminer d'Alsace Preiss Zimmer 2003
WHITE £6.49
FRANCE

Hardy's Stamp of Australia Grenache/ Shiraz Rosé 2004
ROSÉ £5.49
AUSTRALIA

Jindalee Shiraz 2003
RED £4.99
AUSTRALIA

Kendall-Jackson Vintners Reserve Cabernet Sauvignon 2001
RED £9.99
USA

RED £5.99

Kingston Empiric Selection Durif 2001　AUSTRALIA

WHITE £8.99

Kendall-Jackson Vintners Reserve Chardonnay 2003　USA

WHITE SPARKLING £6.99

Lindemans Bin 25 Brut Cuvée NV　AUSTRALIA
Also at Budgens, Co-op, Waitrose.

RED £4.99

La Marca Madrid Tempranillo 2003　SPAIN

WHITE SPARKLING £10.99

Nicole d'Aurigny Brut Champagne　FRANCE

WHITE £4.99

The Gables Chardonnay 2004　SOUTH AFRICA

RED £4.99

Terramar Cabernet Sauvignon/Merlot 2002　SPAIN

ODDBINS

31–33 Weir Road,
Wimbledon,
London SW19 8UG

Tel: (020) 8944 4400
Fax: (020) 8944 4411

E-mail: customer.service@oddbinsmail.com
Website: www.oddbins.com

For tasting notes of Oddbins' wines scoring less than
16 points, and ratings of wines less than 14 points,
visit www.superplonk.com

17.5

RED **(magnum)** £22.99

Casa Lapostolle Cuvée Alexandre Library   CHILE
Cabernet Sauvignon 2000
So controlled, svelte, charming, civilised – and its
14.5% alcohol is expertly (and pertly) balanced by the
tannins, so it is not overwhelming. The magnum has
such a wonderful presence on a dinner table that it's
almost a shame to decant the contents. My
suggestion is to decant anyway, for 2 hours, and then
pour the contents back before your guests turn up to
demolish it.

17.5

RED £14.99

Vergelegen Cabernet Sauvignon 2001   SOUTH AFRICA
Remarkably textured like ruffled taffeta. Gorgeous
smoky berries with a rich, herby undertone.
Remarkably lovely red wine.

17

RED £8.39

Château de Valcombe 'Prestige',   FRANCE
Costières de Nîmes 2003
Recipe: chunks of melted chocolate are slowly heated
and into the rich mass oven-roasted plums are
stirred with lots of coal dust and crushed coffee
beans.

17

RED **(magnum)** £29.99

Casa Lapostolle Cuvée Alexandre Library   CHILE
Merlot 2000
Stunning quality, still young (critically) and evolving
even though the tannins are softening. This

magnum is more immediate than its Cabernet
cousin above so it needs little decanting if it seems
like a lot of trouble.

WHITE £7.99
AUSTRALIA

**D'Arenberg 'The Olive Grove'
Chardonnay 2003**
Screwcap. Superb waxy melon, citrus, and a genteel
smokiness. That screwcap gives it developmental
potential over many years (if you keep the wine).

WHITE £8.99
AUSTRALIA

**D'Arenberg 'The Money Spider'
Roussanne 2003**
Screwcap. Delicious smoky pear and peach fruit,
undertoned by citrus and pineapple. A really
impactful yet genteel white wine.

WHITE £5.59
AUSTRALIA

Thomas Mitchell Marsanne 2003
Screwcap. Superbly waxy touches to rich peach and
melon given balance by citrus. Superbly refreshing.
Fantastic value for the money and could reach 19
points in 2010 (when it will turn more eccentrically
delicious).

RED £13.99
SOUTH AFRICA

Vergelegen Merlot 2001
Classic herbaceous, slightly floral Merlot. A real
brute of a Merlot in fact: craggy yet succulent.

17

Errazuriz Estate Sauvignon Blanc 2004   CHILE

A lovely textured rich gooseberry/melon wine. It
oozes class, sophistication and effortless fluency. You
know what I mean by that last extravagance? If you
think of a grape variety as a language then some
winemakers speak it crudely, some well, some
confidently, but the slickest speak it with polished
bi-linguality. This is the case here.

Also at E-tailers (Everywine), Threshers.

Imagine a scene of bucolic bliss. By one of those lily- and
weed-bedecked rivulets, which at any moment will surely
bear Ophelia downstream singing to herself, a hungry,
thirsty couple prepares to feast. Lassoed at the neck with
string, a bottle of white wine is coolingly submerged
amongst the lilies. Can any scene be more English? Could
there be any alfresco pleasure more delightful? And then the
wine is hauled in, the man – it's always the fella –
manipulates the corkscrew, and...the wine is corked. It is not
horribly corked. It does not smell of festering lilies (which
the sonneteer tells us smell worse than weeds). It has been
only marginally tainted by its cork, but the pleasure of the
moment is marred. The man sulks. The woman puts on a
brave face (which somehow makes her prettier but the man
fails to notice). What was surely destined to be a picnic to
remember has become besmirched. Moral? Always go on
picnics with wines sealed with screwcaps.

17

Errazuriz Estate Merlot 2003
Everywine
Melted chocolate dripped over grilled plums. Did
the winemaker steal the recipe from Nigella? The
comments regarding winemakers made about the
Errazuriz wine on page 143 apply here as well.
Also at E-tailers (Everywine), Oddbins, Sainsbury,
Tesco, Threshers.

16.5

Avila Cabernet Sauvignon 2002
The most clearly scrumptious of the Avila wines
with its stunning tannins, rich raspberry and plum
fruit, and lovely textured jammy finish. Very
powerful punch to it.

16.5

**Casillero del Diablo Concha y Toro
Sauvignon Blanc 2004**
A crisp classic of length and crunchy concentration.
Also at Asda, Majestic, Somerfield, Tesco,
Threshers.

16.5

Casa Rivas Merlot Reserva 2002
Great craggy tannins and ripe plum, blackberries
and herbs. Very persistent.
Also at Small Merchants (Adnams).

16.5
RED £11.99

AUSTRALIA

**D'Arenberg 'The Bonsai Vine' Grenache/
Shiraz/Mourvèdre 2001**

Sticks to the teeth like nougat. Astonishing tannic
berries of great depth.

16.5
RED £6.99

FRANCE

**Domaine Borie de Maurel Esprit
d'Automne 2003**

Lovely rich berries, roasted and warm, with firm
tannins and a herbal undertone.

16.5
WHITE SPARKLING £14.99

ITALY

Ferrari Brut NV

Explodes with smoky rich fruit. Really fine and rich.
Much better company than Krug, more
concentrated, sexier.

16.5
WHITE £6.09

GERMANY

Lingenfelder Owl Label Pinot Grigio 2003

Screwcap. Wonderful roasted pear edge to
pineapple and dry peach. Lingers lovingly on the
palate.

16.5
WHITE £6.49

GERMANY

**Lingenfelder Hare Label
Gerwürtztraminer 2003**

Screwcap. Lively spicy aromatic fruit, apricot and
lychee.

16.5   WHITE £13.99

Monferrato Bianco 'Alteserre' Bava 2000   ITALY
Utterly delicious smoky fruit with complex acids and
hard/soft fruit. Really high-class tippling here.

16.5   WHITE £6.99

Snake Creek Marsanne 2002   AUSTRALIA
Screwcap. Dry, really vibrant dryness and tangy,
purposeful precision. It's steely, yet full of twists and
turns (and that is not a pun on its seal).

16.5   RED £8.39

Wakefield Estate Shiraz 2003   AUSTRALIA
Screwcap. Brilliant savoury, soft stuff.
Also at Small Merchants (Unwins).

Oddbins has a great deal in common with Arsenal Football
Club. Both are managed by the French. In the latter
instance, as we all know, the success which has accrued
from this *entente cordiale* is massive, *sans pareil*. But the jury
is out on the wine retailer, some wine critics perceiving a
shift in its once whacky stance (and perceived flair) to one of
greater conformity. However, Oddbins is, in one respect, the
greatest force for change on the high street, and with
supermarkets only Tesco is superior. I refer to screwcapped
wines. Oddbins now offers well over a 100, more on the way,
and who would have thought it?

16.5   WHITE £4.99

Casillero del Diablo Concha y Toro   CHILE
Chardonnay 2004

Delicious delicate and elegant, subdued richness.
Also at Asda, Majestic, Threshers.

16.5   RED £5.99

Errazuriz Estate Cabernet Sauvignon 2003   CHILE

Very gripping, vivid fruit, a combination of chocolate
and burned berries, and the tannins cut a wave of
flavour to finish up kicking their well-shod heels in
the throat before quitting.
Also at Asda, E-tailers (Everywine), Somerfield,
Waitrose.

16.5   WHITE £5.99

Errazuriz Estate Chardonnay 2004   CHILE

Delicious! Superb edge of tropicality (pineapple and
mango). Delicate to finish.
Also at Budgens, E-tailers (Everywine), Sainsbury,
Somerfield, Tesco.

16   WHITE £9.99

Avila Chardonnay 2004   USA

Good oily texture, touch of whisky (it seems) on the
spirited finish.

16   RED £8.49

D'Arenberg 'Footbolt' Old Vine Shiraz 2002   AUSTRALIA
Jam with great style and savoury-to-finish richness.

16

RED £8.49

Bleasdale Shiraz/Cabernet Sauvignon 2001   AUSTRALIA

Seems quite sturdy and rich on first slurp then turns
delicate and sly.

16

RED £7.99

Bertie Collection Saint-Chinian Grenache 2002   FRANCE

Big jammy, vigorous wine of great woven berries,
and cocoa-edged tannins.

16

RED £6.79

Château Maris Tradition Minervois 2003   FRANCE

Meaty, soft, vivid herby and very attractively textured.

16

WHITE £7.99

Carmen Nativa Chardonnay 2004   CHILE

Lean, stylish, thrusting.

16

WHITE £5.99

Concha y Toro Winemakers Lot   CHILE
Gewürztraminer 2004

Chile goes in for these dry Gewürztraminers. They
are terrific with shellfish (and for sipping listening
to complex, demanding music like Abba).

16

RED £10.49

Clos Petite Bellane 'Les Echalas' Valréas,   FRANCE
Côtes du Rhône-Villages 2003

Lovely crunchy tannins coating smooth, chocolate-
burned berries.

16

WHITE £9.49

FRANCE

**Domaine Bégude Sauvignon Blanc,
Vin de Pays d'Oc 2004**
Deliciously crisp pineapple and citrus.

16

RED £5.99

Dancing Monkey 'Alpha Series' Merlot 2003   ARGENTINA
Huge vibrancy of plums/cherries with startling
X-certificate tannins.

16

RED £4.99

ARGENTINA

**Dancing Monkey Cabernet Sauvignon/
Merlot/Malbec 2003**
Great-value healthy slurping. Real tannic
excitement.

16

WHITE £4.99

ARGENTINA

**Dancing Monkey Chardonnay/
Sémillon 2004**
Delightfully impish citrus, peach and pear fruit. The
monkey doesn't so much dance as caper nimbly (to
the lascivious pleasings of any wind instrument you
care to name).

16

WHITE £6.49

FRANCE

**Deux Soleils 'Les Romains' Chardonnay/
Viognier, Vin de Pays d'Oc 2003**
Crisp apricot, classily dry and dainty, with lemon.
Stylish act here.

16

RED £6.69

Domaine de Saint-Antoine 'Selection Coin du Murier', Costières de Nîmes 2003

FRANCE

Offers coal-chewy tannins to raspberry-edged fruit.

16

WHITE £9.79

Falanghina Feudi di San Gregorio 2003

ITALY

Wonderfully invigorating liquid of stealthy class and complex, cohesive layers of dryness and gently over-ripe pear/citrus.

It is generally supposed that the only people who keep wine are the very rich. As a corollary of this notion it is further presumed that only expensive wines repay keeping. It is possible to open a chain of shoe shops on the strength of the load of old cobblers talked about wine and maturation perceptions. Do you need a cellar or cellar-like conditions? Yes, if the wines have traditional corks and you want to put the wines down for over five years. However, I mature wines, many of them cheapies, in a cupboard with no central heating or hot water pipes near; so far the wines have grown old gracefully therein for four years. Screwcapped wines do not need laying down (no cork to keep moist) and will age better without cork. This applies not only to whites but also to reds as the tannins stay friskier. Many wines can profitably be laid down. But the word 'profitably' does not imply monetary gain from future re-sale, it means that greater pleasure should result when the wines are opened in years to come.

16

RED £9.29

Feudi di Santa Teresa 'Nivuro' Nero d'Avola/ ITALY
Cabernet Sauvignon 2001

Works on three levels.
1. Juiciness.
2. Sensuality.
3. Tannic tenacity.

16

WHITE SPARKLING £11.99

Green Point Chardonnay/ AUSTRALIA
Pinot Noir Brut 1999

If you love that rich yeasty style, you'll fall for this.

16

WHITE SPARKLING £16.49

Henri Harlin Champagne NV FRANCE

Beautifully tailored and crisp.

16

WHITE SPARKLING £9.99

Jansz Premium Cuvée NV AUSTRALIA

Came top in a blind tasting, conducted (hic) by me,
alongside champagnes twice the price.
Also at Small Merchants (Selfridges, Noel Young
Wines).

16

RED £8.09

Knappstein Shiraz 2001 AUSTRALIA

Gosh! What a mouthful of vibrant, rich, roasted
berries and supple tannins is presented here.

16

WHITE £7.09

Lingenfelder Bee Label Morio Muskat 2003   GERMANY
Screwcap. 18 points possibly in 2010. Great smoky
muscatty richness – pear and passionfruit – that will
deepen over the years.

16

DESSERT WHITE (50cl bottle) £8.99

Muscat de Saint Jean de Minervois 2002   FRANCE
18 points in 2012-18. Has honied peach with a touch
of spicy pear. Lovely summer-pudding wine.

16

WHITE £7.59

Nepenthe 'Tryst' 2003   AUSTRALIA
Screwcap. A crisp, clean, delightfully dry shellfish
wine.

16

RED £7.59

Nepenthe 'Tryst' Cabernet/Zinfandel/   AUSTRALIA
Tempranillo 2003
Screwcap. Firmly, plummily approachable thanks to
its most appealing, slow-moving dry fruit.
Also at Somerfield.

16

RED £8.99

Peter Lehmann Barossa Cabernet   AUSTRALIA
Sauvignon 2001
It has the insouciant class and hefty demeanour of a
liquid which has nothing to prove.

16 WHITE £9.99

Riesling Paul Blanck Alsace 2003 FRANCE
Screwcap. Delicious melon and rich citric apricot.
Will improve to 17.5 points by 2010-12.

16 WHITE £9.99

Scotchmans Hill Geelong AUSTRALIA
Chardonnay 2003
Screwcap. A fine, elegant Chardonnay of restrained
opulence.

16 RED £13.29

Septombre Minervois 2002 FRANCE
Ripe, soft, very individual, persuasively more-ish and
tannicly svelte.

16 WHITE £8.49

Vergelegen Chardonnay 2003 SOUTH AFRICA
Woody, rich, creamy finishing, touch exotic, very
forthright yet has some delicacy. Cheaper than
Puligny-Montrachet.

16 WHITE £8.39

Wakefield Estate Riesling 2003 AUSTRALIA
Screwcap. 18.5 points in 2010–15. Real crisp, dry,
tangy understatement. Petroleum undertone already
subtly insistent.

16   RED £13.99

Wither Hills Pinot Noir 2003   NEW ZEALAND
Screwcap. 16.5 points in 2007. Beautiful gamy
cherries and raspberries.
Also at Booths, Waitrose.

OTHER WINES 15.5 AND UNDER

15.5   RED £9.99

Avila Pinot Noir 2003   USA

                                                RED £9.99

Avila Syrah 2003   USA

                                                RED £6.99

Bertie Collection Minervois/Syrah 2002   FRANCE

                                              WHITE £9.99

Blind River Sauvignon Blanc 2004   NEW ZEALAND
Screwcap. 17 points in 2007.

                                   WHITE SPARKLING £18.99

H. Blin & Co. Brut Tradition NV   FRANCE

                                              WHITE £4.99

Deakin Estate Colombard/Chardonnay 2004 AUSTRALIA
Screwcap.

                                                RED £5.99

Dancing Monkey 'Alpha Series' Malbec 2003 ARGENTINA

RED £5.99
ARGENTINA

Dancing Monkey 'Alpha Series'
Cabernet Sauvignon 2003

WHITE £4.99
SOUTH AFRICA

Flagstone Noon Gun 2004

WHITE £9.99
SOUTH AFRICA

Flagstone Two Roads 2004
Screwcap.

WHITE £6.09
GERMANY

Lingenfelder Bird Label Riesling 2003
Screwcap.

WHITE £9.49
FRANCE

Le Big Macon, Jean-Luc Terrier 2001

RED £8.49
ITALY

Monferrato Rosso 'Le Monache'
Michele Chiarlo 2003

RED £5.99
CHILE

Santa Rita 120 Merlot 2003

RED £17.99
NEW ZEALAND

Peregrine Pinot Noir 2003
Screwcap.

RED £9.99
CHILE

Stella Aurea Cabernet Sauvignon 2001

RED £9.99
Stella Aurea Cabernet Sauvignon 2002 CHILE

WHITE £8.49
Vergelegen Sauvignon Blanc 2004 SOUTH AFRICA

WHITE £9.99
Voyager Estate Sauvignon Blanc/ AUSTRALIA
Sémillon 2004
Screwcap.

15

ROSÉ £6.99
Antipodean Sangiovese Rosé 2004 AUSTRALIA
Also at Small Merchants (Hoults).

WHITE SPARKLING £6.99
Angas Brut Premium Cuvée Pinot Noir/ AUSTRALIA
Chardonnay NV
Also at Small Merchants (Unwins).

RED £9.99
Avila Côte d'Avila 2002 USA

WHITE £7.99
Concha y Toro Winemakers Lot 20 Riesling 2004 CHILE
Screwcap. 16.5 points in 2008.

WHITE £11.39
Crozes-Hermitage Blanc, FRANCE
Domaine Belle Père et Fils 2002

RED £14.99
Château Marsau Bordeaux, Côte de Francs 2001 FRANCE

WHITE SPARKLING £7.99

Deakin Estate Chardonnay/ AUSTRALIA
Pinot Noir Brut NV
Also at Small Merchants (Bibendum).

RED £16.99

Domus Aurea Cabernet Sauvignon 1999 CHILE

RED £9.99

Flagstone The Berrio SOUTH AFRICA
Cabernet Sauvignon 2004

ROSÉ £5.99

Flagstone Fish Hoek Rosé 2004 SOUTH AFRICA
Screwcap.

RED £8.99

Katnook Founders Block AUSTRALIA
Cabernet Sauvignon 2002

WHITE £5.99

Lingenfelder Fish Label Riesling 2003 GERMANY
Screwcap. 17.5 points in 2010–12.

RED £14.99

Lost Valley Hazy Mountain Merlot 2003 AUSTRALIA

RED £9.99

Montana Reserve Pinot Noir 2003 NEW ZEALAND
Also at Majestic, Threshers.

RED £6.99

Peñalolen Cabernet Sauvignon 2002 CHILE

	RED £7.49
Scaranto Rosso 1999	ITALY

14.5

	ROSÉ £5.99
Flagstone Semaphore Rosé 2004	SOUTH AFRICA
Screwcap.	

	ROSÉ £7.99
Scotchmans Hill Swan Bay	AUSTRALIA
Pinot Noir Rosé 2004	
Screwcap.	

	WHITE £13.99
Voyager Estate Chardonnay 2003	AUSTRALIA
Screwcap.	

	RED £6.99
Viña Porta Reserva Pinot Noir 2003	CHILE

14

	RED £23.99
Amarone della Valpolicella Musella 1999	ITALY

	RED £9.19
Brookland Valley 'Verse 1'	AUSTRALIA
Cabernet Sauvignon/Merlot 2002	

	WHITE £9.19
Brookland Valley 'Verse 1' Sémillon/	AUSTRALIA
Sauvignon Blanc 2004	
Screwcap.	

	WHITE £11.99
Bourgogne Blanc, Domaine de Montmeix	FRANCE
Mestre-Michelot 2003	

RED £19.99

Barnett Vineyards Sleepy Hollow Vineyard   USA
Pinot Noir

WHITE SPARKLING £22.99

Champagne Pommery Blanc de Blancs NV   FRANCE
Also at Small Merchants (Unwins).

WHITE £5.99

Casillero del Diablo Concha y Toro Riesling 2004   CHILE

RED £8.49

Cusumano Benuara Nero d'Avola/Syrah 2003   ITALY

RED £5.49

Cusumano Nero d'Avola 2003   ITALY

RED £23.99

Château Yon-Figéac, St-Emilion Grand Cru 2001   FRANCE

RED £5.99

Comte Cathare Le Parfait Syrah 2002   FRANCE
Screwcap.

WHITE £5.99

Comte Cathare Le Parfait Chardonnay 2003   FRANCE
Screwcap.

ROSÉ £6.49

Deakin Estate Rosé 2004   AUSTRALIA
Screwcap. Also at Small Merchants (Bibendum).

WHITE £5.99

Dancing Monkey 'Alpha Series'   ARGENTINA
Chardonnay 2004

WHITE £7.59
Dashwood Sauvignon Blanc 2004 NEW ZEALAND
Screwcap.

WHITE (50cl bottle) £10.49
Domaine Cady Harmonie, FRANCE
Coteaux du Layon 2001
16.5 points in 2009–10.

RED £16.99
Domus Aurea Cabernet Sauvignon 2001 CHILE

WHITE £9.99
Flagstone The Berrio Sauvignon SOUTH AFRICA
Blanc 2004
Screwcap.

WHITE SPARKLING £19.99
Ferrari Brut Perle NV ITALY

WHITE £5.99
Fleur du Cap Sauvignon Blanc 2004 SOUTH AFRICA

WHITE £7.99
Katnook Founders Block Sauvignon AUSTRALIA
Blanc 2004

RED £6.99
La Palmeria Huachitos Estate Carmenere/ CHILE
Cabernet Sauvignon 2001

WHITE £13.99
Lost Valley Cortese 2004 AUSTRALIA
Fine Wine Shops only. Screwcap.

RED £6.99

Montana Merlot/Cabernet Sauvignon 2003 NEW ZEALAND
Screwcap. Also at Somerfield, Waitrose.

RED £8.99

Matahiwi Estate Pinot Noir 2004 NEW ZEALAND
Screwcap.

WHITE £12.19

Montana Brancott Estate Sauvignon NEW ZEALAND
Blanc 2002

WHITE £4.99

Oracle Sauvignon Blanc 2004 SOUTH AFRICA

RED £7.19

Orobio Rioja Artadi 2003 SPAIN

WHITE SPARKLING £19.99

Pierre Gimonnet & Fils Premier Cru Cuvée FRANCE
Gastronome NV

WHITE £7.99

Scarbolo Sauvignon Blanc 2003 ITALY

RED £7.99

Scotchmans Hill Swan Bay Shiraz 2003 AUSTRALIA
Screwcap.

RED £7.99

Tukulu Pinotage 2002 SOUTH AFRICA

WHITE £11.49

Voyager Estate Sémillon 2002 AUSTRALIA
Screwcap. 16.5 points in 2008–9.

	RED £12.49
Voyager Estate Shiraz 2003	AUSTRALIA
Screwcap.	

	RED £14.99
Voyager Estate Cabernet/Merlot 2000	AUSTRALIA

SAINSBURY

Head Office:
33 High Holborn,
London EC1N 2HT

Tel: (020) 7695 6000
Fax: (020) 7695 7610

Customer Careline: (0800) 636262

Website: www.sainsburys.co.uk.

For tasting notes of Sainsbury wines scoring less
than 16 points, and ratings of wines less than
14 points, visit www.superplonk.com

18

RED £12.99

Casa Lapostolle Cuvée Alexandre   CHILE
Apalta Vineyard Merlot 2002

Sheer hedonistic luxury. Romantic, confident,
beautifully textured (satin with hints of denim) and
with richly fruity berries which offer at least three
subtle twists in the tale (and tail as the wine
finishes). £13 is not a lot to pay for such a delicately
provocative liquid.

17.5

WHITE £9.99

Casa Lapostolle Cuvée Alexandre   CHILE
Casablanca Valley Chardonnay 2003

Stunning class here showing demure wood,
fine minerally acids and subtle (yet curiously
decisive) soft and hard fruit which play footsie
with one another thus making it difficult to assign
a precise fruit metaphor to either. This is no bad
thing. With a wine of this class, like its relative
above, the factor which makes it so superior is
texture.

17

RED £6.99

Château Jouanin, Côtes du Castillon 2003   FRANCE
Stunning chocolate-edged claret. Has oodles of class
and stylishly grilled berries. Engaging perfume is a
lovely overture; the chocolate and roasted
blackberries a smooth finale.

RED £12.99

Casa Lapostolle Cuvée Alexandre Merlot 2001　　CHILE
The usual high-class fruit from one of my favourite,
whatever the vintage, Merlots. Has crunchy fruit with
elegant tannins and the character of the wine is
emphatic without being, as some New World Merlots
can be, overly brash (with that dreadful *you-must-
give-me-your-attention* boisterousness).

RED £5.49

Conde de Siruela Ribera del Duero,　　SPAIN
Tinto Roble 2003
Superb chocolate-rich fruit here of uncommon
civility yet potency. Tobacco, prunes, herbs, berries –
and wonderfully roasted tannins. This is a totally
smashing Spanish red; it yields to the drinker
without kow-towing and surrendering its integrity.

The pressure to find more and more outlandish metaphors
has been one of the defining factors in modern wine writing.
It becomes part of the individual wine writer's style and as
long as no-one is left in any doubt of the writer's true opinion
of the wine, then we can surely smile on any indulgence as
long as it does not mislead or bewilder. For all these
reasons, to provide that unequivocal opinion, I insist on a
rating system with every wine I taste. This provides
something which transcends the paucities and extravagances
of language. It offers an absolute, which language by itself
cannot. To me, the rating is the most important symbol
attached to any wine I describe.

17

RED £5.49

Domaine du Colombier Chinon 2003 FRANCE

Best vintage of this wine for a dozen years.
Marvellously acute tannins coagulating with dry
raspberry and blackberries with a touch of tar, a hint
of thyme, a suggestion of black olive.

17

RED £5.99

Errazuriz Estate Merlot 2003 CHILE

Melted chocolate dripped over grilled plums. An
irresistible recipe.
Also at E-tailers (Everywine), Oddbins, Tesco,
Threshers.

17

RED £3.99

Frontera Cabernet Sauvignon/Merlot 2004 CHILE

A beautifully savoury, bitter-cherry, rich red of tannic
elegance and no little depth.
Also at Small Merchants (Spar).

17

RED £4.99

Casillero del Diablo Concha y Toro CHILE
Carmenere 2004

Simply stunningly deft berries and softly savoury
tannins. Carmenere is not a grape much trumpeted
any more in Europe, since it was chased out of
France on the grounds of being a sympathiser with
separatist movements, but in Chile its stand-alone
qualities are recognised and justifiably so.
Also at Majestic, Tesco, Threshers.

16.5

WHITE £6.99

Argento Chardonnay Reserva 2003   ARGENTINA

Classily smoky, confident and hugely entertaining
on several levels. Has an aloof sense of its status.

16.5

RED £10.99

Brolio Chianti Classico 2002   ITALY

And Classic Chianti it is (and the modern touches of
ripeness to the earthiness do not obscure this effect).

16.5

WHITE SPARKLING £14.79

Sainsbury's Premier Cru Extra Dry   FRANCE
Champagne NV

Really a classic champagne: dry, hugely elegant, with
crisp citrus and a reassuring wild strawberry edge.

16.5

WHITE £5.99

Errazuriz Estate Chardonnay 2004   CHILE

Delicious! Superb edge of tropicality (pineapple and
mango). Delicate to finish.
Also at Budgens, E-tailers (Everywine), Oddbins,
Somerfield, Tesco.

16.5

RED £5.49

Casillero del Diablo Concha y Toro Shiraz 2004   CHILE

Ripe yet has several layers of richly cunning fruit
which suggest one thing whilst delivering another.
For a wine to be so knowing yet so young is a feature
of Chileans.
Also at Majestic, Somerfield.

16.5
RED £6.99

Doña Dominga Carmenere Reserva 2002   CHILE

Pulsates with savoury cherries and chocolate berries.
Also at Waitrose.

16.5
WHITE £4.99

Sainsbury's Classic Selection Muscadet   FRANCE
Sèvre et Maine Sur Lie 2004

Brilliant crisp fruit. Wonderfully elegant and
stylishly crisp and it completely justifies the Classic
Selection label. Is this evidence that British
supermarkets can be the saviours of Muscadet?

16.5
FORTIFIED £4.29

Sainsbury's Medium Dry Amontillado   SPAIN
Sherry NV

Quite superb. Lovely oily richness with toasted
nutty fruit and a very dry subtly-treacle texture
(which sounds thicker than in fact it is, but no
other metaphor comes to mind). Try it, well chilled,
as an early evening tipple with almonds or
charcuterie.

16.5
RED £4.99

Sainsbury's Bin 60 Australian   AUSTRALIA
Cabernet Sauvignon/Shiraz 2004

Has baked damsons, hint of clove, lovely ripe plums
and blackberries, and soft-as-wool tannins which
caress the palate.

16.5

RED £4.99
CHILE

Sainsbury's Reserve Selection Chilean Cabernet Sauvignon 2004

Quite brilliant berries here, convincingly classly and ripe, with chocolate-coated nuts. Very warm-hearted red.

16.5

WHITE £5.99
NEW ZEALAND

Sanctuary Marlborough Pinot Gris 2004

Screwcap. Lovely ripe apricot and crisp acids in classy collusion. The Pinot Gris grape seems to me to offer a superb alternative to Sauvignon Blancs and Chardonnays, as it has an individuality, in its various Kiwi manifestations, which sets it deliciously apart.

16.5

WHITE £4.99
ARGENTINA

Argento Chardonnay 2004

Wax, lemon, pineapple, apples, touch of dry peach – this is a superb Chardonnay for anyone's money, and at £4.99 it is a minor miracle.
Also at Majestic.

At one tasting of organic wines in 2004 I was never so glad to have a spittoon handy as one dull wine followed another. Why do we expect organic wines to be superior when so many are utterly mediocre? Another example of our gullibility when it comes to making judgements about wine.

16

ROSÉ SPARKLING £15.99

Sainsbury's Rosé Brut Champagne NV   FRANCE

Justifies being a rosé courtesy of its strawberry
undertone.

16

RED £13.99

Alain Graillot Crozes-Hermitage 2003   FRANCE

Available Sainsbury's Wine eShop only. How to be
ripe yet firmly dry and brackeny. Very high-class
ambitions here. Has that coal-edged richness this
Rhône region flaunts with its fruit – which can come
from the stems and pips of the grapes – and this
greenness may strike some as uncongenially
youthful, and therefore prefer to wait a couple of
years for the wine to soften. Personally, I like it
younger, fully decanted 5–10 hours before being
offered to sensitive guests.

16

RED £4.99

Argento Malbec 2004   ARGENTINA

The plumminess is inherent, not baked on, and so
the sincerity of the fruit gives it no sharp edges, no
untoward creases in its well-cut cloth.
Also at Budgens, Majestic, Tesco.

16

RED £5.99

Altos de Tamaron Ribera del Duero 2003   SPAIN

It slides down beautifully. Quite why the label claims
'Fuego y Hielo' is a mystery to me (fire and ice – sort
of thing you'd get in a cocktail isn't it?).

16

RED £5.99

ITALY

Brindisi Rosso Cantine Due Palme 2003
Ripe plums tempered by tobacco-ey cherries. Great
tannins, too. What a little beaut.

16

RED SPARKLING £7.99

Banrock Station Sparkling Shiraz NV　　AUSTRALIA
Brilliant roasted plum fruit, sweet but very far from
juvenile. The prunes, dry and savoury, help bolster
the wine, making it a great companion to game
dishes with rich sauces.
Also at Asda.

16

WHITE £5.99

FRANCE

**Bernard Germain Anjou, Barrel Fermented
Chenin Blanc 2002**
One of the most individual, vibrantly interesting
white wines on sale under six quid. The mineral
edging is tight, the melon/peach/gooseberry fruit is
elegantly under-ripe, and the texture is teasingly
plump yet not over-eager. It will age interestingly,
if cellared, for several years.

16

RED £4.49

CHILE

Chileño Shiraz/Cabernet Sauvignon 2004
Excellent curry red. The savoury/sweet edge to the
fruit hugs chillies like old friends.
Also at Somerfield, Waitrose (15 in 3 litre box).

16 RED £14.99

Château La Vieille Cure Fronsac 2000 FRANCE
Really confident claret, smooth yet characterful,
tobacco-rich yet not fumacious, elegant yet very deep
and satisfying. Very classily assembled.

16 WHITE £4.99

Cono Sur Gewürztraminer 2004 CHILE
A superb aperitif, welcome-home white wine. Has
lovely subtle touches of spicy peach and lychee. But
it is very dry, not sweet.
Also at Majestic.

16 WHITE £4.99

Calvet Limited Release Sauvignon Blanc FRANCE
Bordeaux 2004
Has a deliciously chalky chewy edge.

16 RED £6.99

Carmesi Oak Aged Calatayud Garnacha/ SPAIN
Tempranillo 2003
Ripe, alcoholic (14.5%) but well balanced. A red for
roast meats and spicy casseroles.

16 RED £6.99

Durius Tempranillo Alto Duero 2003 SPAIN
Ripe yet vegetal, smooth yet characterful, herby, rich,
and food friendly.

16

RED £7.99
NEW ZEALAND

Delegat's Oyster Bay Central Otago Merlot 2004

This is one of those New World reds where the fruit is so persuasive that it doesn't seem like alcohol at all.

16

WHITE £4.49
GERMANY

Devil's Rock Riesling 2003

Screwcap. Complex attempts at demotic richness frustrated by youthful aristocratic Riesling acidity. Delightful tension here.

The emphasis on a grape variety on the label has led to certain grapes becoming almost brands in their own right. 'I'd like a glass of Chardonnay please,' said a woman next to me at a pub bar one night, and the barman responded, 'Coming up.' I doubt she would have dreamed of saying 'What I really fancy is a Sémillon, Chardonnay and Viognier blend,' and for the barman to nod and reach for the appropriate bottle. Did she get a 100% Chardonnay? I have no idea. Even if the bottle claimed the wine to be so, it may contain other grape varieties because it is legal for wines from New World countries to claim to be a Chardonnay, or Shiraz, or any other variety like Cabernet Sauvignon or Sauvignon Blanc for that matter, yet only lay claim on the label to the major component of the blend (which may comprise only 85% of the wine). In my view, no wine should be permitted to say it is a grape variety on the label unless it is 100% of that variety.

16

RED £6.03

Errazuriz Estate Syrah 2003   CHILE

It has the most uncommonly polite way of
proceeding – it even wipes its feet and doffs its cap –
but as it dries in the throat it makes its insidiously
delicious character felt and one is seduced.

16

RED £5.99

Excelsior Paddock Shiraz 2004   SOUTH AFRICA

Sweet, jammy and seemingly heading for a 14-point
rating but the finish pulls off a surprise – class and
cohesion, richness without brashness – and so the
money is well spent.
Screwcap. Also at Somerfield.

16

WHITE £3.99

Frontera Sauvignon/Chardonnay 2004   CHILE

Not a crisp/lean classic blend but superbly rotund
and not without elegance as it settles in the throat.
Also at Small Merchants (Spar).

16

RED £4.99

La Chasse du Pape Syrah, Vin de Pays d'Oc 2004   FRANCE
Good rustic richness and dryness. A terrific casserole
red.

16

RED £8.99

Las Brisas Estate Pinot Noir Reserve 2003   CHILE

16 points is a provisional rating for a wine which
should be exquisite. Sulphur levels in the last two
bottles I tried at Sainsbury, however, gave it an off-

putting pong. I am reluctant to condemn it (in any event decanting and aerating the wine for a few hours would get rid of the aberrant aroma) for Pinot from this valley and this producer can be fantastic.

16

RED £4.99
SPAIN

Los Monteros Valencia 2003
Jammy but huge fun. Why? The bottle's whacky – its glass has contracted a rare dose of DIY shingles – and the label's a riot.

16

WHITE £5.99
AUSTRALIA

Lindemans Bin 65 Chardonnay 2004
Always one of Oz's finest non-sporting achievements (for the money), the '04 vintage offers some new chalky touches.
Also at Tesco.

16

RED £8.99
FRANCE

Les Crouzels Fitou 2003
Smooth ruggedness. Quite a charmer here with its slow-to-develop tarry ripeness. Very glamorous tannins.

16

WHITE £2.99
FRANCE

Muscadet La Régate 2004
Screwcap. Astonishing level of tangy melon/lemon for the money. Will develop well if laid down for 18 months (and even longer) or wholly decant 2–3 hours.

16

RED £5.99
SPAIN

Muruve Roble Toro 2003
Terrific casserole red. Rustic, very enthusiastic
(heartily tannic and dry to finish).

16

RED £8.99
ITALY

Polizano Rosso di Montepulciano 2004
Very jammy but the insistent tannins refuse to allow
the wine to go soppy and wilt on the palate.

16

WHITE £4.49
FRANCE

**Prestige du Roc Sauvignon Blanc
Bordeaux 2004**
Wow! Bordeaux blanc back on course. This is a
superbly crisp, clean specimen (under-ripe
gooseberry with citrus).

16

RED £4.99
FRANCE

**Réserve des Tuileries, Côtes du
Roussillon 2004**
Chunky tannins turning plummily climactic to
provide a firmly berried richness. Very controlled,
calm, svelte.

16

RED £7.99
USA

Ravenswood Lodi Old Vine Zinfandel 2002
Sheer vivacious fun juice. Heady, exuberant,
unabashed, very far from shy.

16   DESSERT WHITE (50cl) £14.99
Ruppertsberger Riesling Eiswein 2001   GERMANY
19 in 2015. Getting better (first tasted last year)
because the acids are settling down but the chunky
fruit, white peach with honey, is only just emerging
and can only get better over time.

16   WHITE £4.49

Réserve St Marc Sauvignon Blanc,   FRANCE
Vin de Pays d'Oc 2004
Interestingly complex layers of citrus and very
under-ripe gooseberry.

16   RED £10.99

Sainsbury's Classic Selection Amarone   ITALY
della Valpolicella Valpentena 2002
Delicious licorice-undertoned baked plums with
black cherries and a nice sprinkling of tannins.

16   RED £6.99

Sainsbury's Classic Selection Barossa   AUSTRALIA
Shiraz 2003
Most unusually elegant and well-tailored.

16   RED £4.99

Sainsbury's Reserve Selection Chilean   CHILE
Carmenere 2003
Utterly delicious, smooth, proud, uncluttered, and so
warm you could bathe in it.

16

RED £3.99

Sainsbury's Argentinian Malbec NV   ARGENTINA
Juicy but firm, ripe and relaxed. The plum and
cherries cruise home in style.

16

FORTIFIED £4.69

Sainsbury's Pale Dry Manzanilla Sherry NV   SPAIN
Beautifully textured, saline-undertoned fruit which
goes gloriously nutty and gently rich.

16

FORTIFIED £4.69

**Sainsbury's Medium Sweet Oloroso
Sherry NV**   SPAIN
Try it with fresh grapes and blue cheese after a meal
or before a meal with TV (though viewers of such
things as *Celebrity Love Island* are warned not to drink
more than a glass as it may turn yukky).

16

RED £6.99

Sainsbury's Classic Selection Western   AUSTRALIA
Australia Cabernet Sauvignon/Merlot 2003
Good sour edge to the plums (with tannins) once the
cherries ceasing buzzing in the mouth.

16

WHITE £4.99

Santa Julia Viognier 2004   ARGENTINA
Screwcap. The texture provides a vehicle for the
peach/apricot fruit to motor in chic style across the
palate.

16

RED £5.99
SOUTH AFRICA

Sainsbury's Classic Selection South African Cabernet Sauvignon/Merlot 2002
Has a very classy sheen to it. Impressively well berried and firm.

16

WHITE £6.99
NEW ZEALAND

Stoneleigh Vineyards Marlborough Sauvignon Blanc 2004
Screwcap. Touches of grapefruit, pear and gooseberries. Yum!
Also at Waitrose.

16

WHITE £6.99
SOUTH AFRICA

Sincerely Sauvignon Blanc 2004
Screwcap. And surely sincerely more crisp than many a Sancerre it apes.

16

RED £6.99
CHILE

Santa Rita Cabernet Sauvignon Reserva 2003
Blackberry jam with attitude (courtesy of rich, dark tannins with a hint of cherry liqueur).

16

RED £3.49
ARGENTINA

Sainsbury's Argentinian Bonarda NV
Bargain baked plum tippling. Finishes with a hint of chewy chocolate.

What price individuality in a wine? Well, amongst the credulous fools who believe there is such a thing as fine wine (when there is only wine: very good, good, passable and mediocre) there is unanimous adherence to the concept of *terroir*. These poor souls are little different from the members of the Elvis-Presley-Is-Alive-and-Living-on-Mars congregation. The fine wine yahoos would have you believe their beverages are always unique expressions of a particular piece of dirt and its peculiar climatic conditions. A good deal of the time, such expressions are expensive; some are established luxury brands (Château Lafite, Krug, Pétrus, Vega Sicilia, and certain of the so-called super-Tuscans); some are parvenus (like the surreal Screaming Eagle Merlot from California which the last time I saw a bottle, in Selfridges, had a £2,300 price tag attached). What in truth makes these products seductive commercial entities is one factor: their high prices and limited availability. This makes acquisition difficult, restricted to a few people. Tasting them, extremely infrequently, one is struck by their struggle, much of the time, to be any better than wines costing a lot less. But we all understand this. Rich people are addicted to rare playthings, badges of success perceived to indicate superior taste, and so they are gullible targets for anyone who cares to create the products to satisfy this passion. What makes wine in this context different, however, is agriculture and its annual vagaries; every year a vintage-dated wine cannot help but be to some extent a reflection of the weather during its growing and picking season. From this obvious fact it is easy to extrapolate a marvellous fiction: that such a wine is the unique product of an individual vineyard *and it is this which justifies the vast cost of sampling its uniqueness.* Do not buy this bullshit. Bullshit is the fertiliser the so-called fine wine market delights in pouring on vineyards.

16

RED £4.99

Sainsbury's Reserve Selection   CHILE
Chilean Merlot 2004
It's difficult to decide whether the spicy cherries or
the nutty tannins steal the show.

16

WHITE £6.99

Sainsbury's Classic Selection   FRANCE
Alsace Gewürztraminer 2003
Opens with lovely aromatic richness and then hints
of waxy lemon appear to fat, vaguely peachy fruit.
A dynamic aperitif.

16

WHITE £6.99

Sainsbury's Classic Selection   AUSTRALIA
Padthaway Chardonnay 2004
Plump fruit relieved by resolute acids. Balanced,
sane, very civilised tippling here.

16

WHITE £5.79

Sainsbury's Chilean Reserve Chardonnay 2002   CHILE
Very dainty dryness (in spite of the apricot and
citrus) with a nutty undertone.

16

RED £4.49

35 South Cabernet Sauvignon 2003   CHILE
Grand quaffing here – ripe damsons with a nutty
undertone. Very immediate but not flashy or
superficial.

16

WHITE £4.99

Vouvray La Couronne des Plantagenets 2003 FRANCE

18 points in 2009–12. This is a demi-sec white of delicious apricot/lychee richness with young acids, good with mild Thai food now or cellar for future excitement. I am currently drinking the 1996 vintage bought in 1999 at a Sainsbury's sale for a quid off. If I waited 3 more years I would be rewarded by even greater funkiness and entertainment.

16

RED £6.99

Valdivieso Reserve Cabernet Sauvignon 2002 CHILE

Serious yet playful, rich yet not superficial, slow-moving yet not backward – this is a delicious Cabernet of great class.

16

WHITE £5.99

Villa Montes Reserve Sauvignon Blanc 2003 CHILE

Very classy amalgam of under-ripe melon, pineapple and citrus.

Also at Morrison's, Waitrose.

16

RED £7.49

Weinert Malbec 1999 ARGENTINA

Terrific energy and softly incisive devotion to duty.

16

RED £5.99

The Wolftrap Boekenhoutskloof 2004 SOUTH AFRICA

Screwcap. 17.5 in 2007 (spring). One of the Cape's great chutzpah bargains. Lovely dark chocolate fruit which time will deepen.

16   ROSÉ £6.99

Zonte's Footsteps Langhorne Creek   AUSTRALIA
Cabernet/Petit Verdot Rosé 2004
Screwcap. A most convincingly firm, stylish, subtly
rich, dry, plum-edged rosé.
Also at Small Merchants (Unwins).

16   WHITE £5.99

Peter Lehmann Barossa Sémillon 2003   AUSTRALIA
Screwcap. 18 points in 2010. Drink it with abandon
now. With extra special care in 5 years.
Also at Asda, Booths, Morrison's.

16   WHITE £7.99

Villa Maria Private Bin   NEW ZEALAND
Sauvignon Blanc 2004
Screwcap. 17.5 points in 2007. Bitingly purposeful,
elegant, dry, fish-friendly.
Also at Asda, Budgens, Somerfield, Tesco.

16   RED £5.49

Casillero del Diablo Concha y Toro   CHILE
Cabernet Sauvignon 2003
So quaffable it's a sin. And what can be more
satisfying than that kind of indulgence?
Also at Asda, Tesco.

16

WHITE £8.99

Jackson Estate Marlborough   NEW ZEALAND
Sauvignon Blanc 2004
Screwcap. 16.5 points in 2007. Beautiful gamy
cherries and raspberries.
Also at Booths, Somerfield.

16

WHITE £6.99

Oyster Bay Sauvignon Blanc 2004   NEW ZEALAND
Screwcap. Very, very classy. Very confident gooseberry
richness.
Also at Co-op, Morrison's.

16

WHITE £4.99

Wolf Blass Eagle Hawk Chardonnay 2004   AUSTRALIA
Rich yet far from over-cooked, delicate yet not close
to being a shrinking violet, cosy but not sycophantic.
Also at Asda, Somerfield.

OTHER WINES 15.5 AND UNDER

15.5

RED £4.99

Cono Sur Merlot 2004   CHILE

ROSÉ £4.49

Cape Grace Pinotage Rosé 2005   SOUTH AFRICA
Screwcap.

ROSÉ £3.89

Cabernet Rosé, Vin de Pays du Jardin   FRANCE
de la France 2004
Screwcap.

WHITE £5.99

Château Vonnet Entre-Deux-Mers 2004   FRANCE
Screwcap.

DESSERT WHITE (50cl) £6.99

Domaine Leonce Cuisset, Saussignac 2003   FRANCE
17.5 in 5 years.

RED £4.99

Doña Dominga Cabernet Sauvignon/   CHILE
Carmenere 2003

RED £12.99

Don Reca Limited Release Merlot 2002   CHILE
Also at Waitrose.

RED £6.03

Errazuriz Estate Merlot 2004   CHILE
Screwcap.

WHITE SPARKLING £7.49

Hardy's Nottage Hill Sparkling   AUSTRALIA
Chardonnay 2004
Also at Somerfield.

ROSÉ £6.99

Skuttlebutt Shiraz/Merlot Rosé 2004   AUSTRALIA

WHITE £7.49

Sainsbury's Classic Selection Pinot Grigio 2004 ITALY

WHITE £6.99

Sanctuary Marlborough Sauvignon NEW ZEALAND
Blanc 2004

RED £7.99

Zonte's Footsteps Langhorne Creek Shiraz/ AUSTRALIA
Viognier 2004
Screwcap. Also at Somerfield.

15

WHITE £6.99

Graham Beck Viognier 2004 SOUTH AFRICA

WHITE £5.79

Jacob's Creek Dry Riesling 2003 AUSTRALIA
Screwcap. 18 in 2010–12. Also at Tesco, Waitrose.

WHITE SPARKLING £7.99

Jacob's Creek Sparkling Chardonnay/ AUSTRALIA
Pinot Noir Brut Cuvée NV
Also at Asda, Tesco, Waitrose.

WHITE £6.99

Ken Forrester Chenin Blanc 2004 SOUTH AFRICA
Screwcap.

WHITE £4.49

Kendermanns Pinot Grigio 2004 GERMANY

WHITE £4.99

La Baume Sauvignon Blanc, FRANCE
Vin de Pays d'Oc 2004
Screwcap.

	RED £7.99
Marqués de Casa Concha Merlot 2003	CHILE

	WHITE £4.99
Sainsbury's New Zealand Sauvignon Blanc 2004	NEW ZEALAND
Screwcap.	

	RED £2.80
Sainsbury's Australian Ruby Cabernet Sauvignon/Shiraz 2004	AUSTRALIA

	WHITE £3.49
Sainsbury's Argentinian Torrontes NV	ARGENTINA

	WHITE £7.49
Springfield Estate Special Cuvée Sauvignon Blanc 2004	SOUTH AFRICA

	RED £4.99
Sainsbury's Reserve Selection Minervois 2002	FRANCE

	WHITE £6.99
Sainsbury's Classic Selection Western Australia Sauvignon Blanc/Sémillon 2004	AUSTRALIA
Screwcap.	

	RED £6.99
Shingle Peak Pinot Noir 2004	NEW ZEALAND
Screwcap.	

	RED £6.99
Santa Rita Cabernet Sauvignon Reserva 2002	CHILE

WHITE £5.49

Oxford Landing Sauvignon Blanc 2004 AUSTRALIA
Screwcap. Also at Budgens, Tesco.

WHITE £5.49

Oxford Landing Chardonnay 2004 AUSTRALIA
Screwcap. Also at Budgens, Tesco.

14.5

WHITE £5.49

Araldica Gavi, Piemonte 2004 ITALY

WHITE SPARKLING £11.99

Chapel Down Century, Bottle Fermented UK
Extra Dry NV

WHITE £4.99

Doña Dominga Chardonnay/Sémillon 2004 CHILE

RED £5.99

Delicato Shiraz 2002 USA

RED £4.99

Kumala Cabernet Sauvignon/Shiraz 2004 SOUTH AFRICA
Also at Tesco.

RED £4.99

Los Robles 'Fairtrade' Carmenere 2004 CHILE

RED £9.99

Marbore Bodega Pirineos Somontano 2000 SPAIN

RED £4.49

Sainsbury's Reserve Selection ARGENTINA
Argentinian Malbec 2003

WHITE £6.99
Santa Rita Chardonnay 2004 CHILE

ROSÉ £4.99
Wolf Blass Eagle Hawk Rosé 2004 AUSTRALIA
Screwcap. Also at Asda.

RED £7.99
Oyster Bay Merlot 2004 NEW ZEALAND
Screwcap. Also at Majestic, Waitrose.

14

ROSÉ £3.99
Agramont Navarra Garnacha Rosado 2004 SPAIN

WHITE £7.59
Cono Sur Vision Gewürztraminer 2002 CHILE

RED £7.99
Broquel Malbec 2002 ARGENTINA

WHITE DESSERT (half bottle) £5.99
Brown Brothers Late Harvested Orange AUSTRALIA
and Muscat Flora 2003
16.5 points in 2008-12.

WHITE £4.99
Cape Soleil Sauvignon Blanc 2004 SOUTH AFRICA
Organic.

RED £8.99
Château de la Garde Ilias Bordeaux FRANCE
Supérieur 2001

RED £4.99
Château Marquis de la Grange Bordeaux 2004 FRANCE

ROSÉ £5.49

Domaine de Sours Bordeaux Rosé 2004   FRANCE
Screwcap.

RED £6.99

Durius Marqués de Griñon Tempranillo 2003   SPAIN

WHITE £5.99

Dr L Riesling Mosel-Saar-Ruwer 2004   GERMANY
Screwcap. 17 points in 2012.

WHITE £6.99

El Dorado Sauvignon Blanc Reserva 2004   CHILE

RED £8.99

Excelsior Estate Special Reserve Cabernet   SOUTH AFRICA
Sauvignon 2002

RED £4.99

Excelsior Estate Merlot 2003   SOUTH AFRICA

WHITE SPARKLING £5.99

Hardy's Stamp of Australia Sparkling   AUSTRALIA
Pinot Noir/Chardonnay Brut NV
Also at Asda, Somerfield, Tesco.

WHITE £4.99

Kumala Sauvignon Blanc/Sémillon 2004   SOUTH AFRICA

RED £5.99

Lindemans Bin 50 Shiraz 2004   ARGENTINA

RED £17.99

Mount Difficulty Central Otago   NEW ZEALAND
Pinot Noir 2002

RED £5.99

Quinta des Setencostas Alenquer 2003 SPAIN

WHITE £5.99

Rosemount Estate Sémillon/Chardonnay 2004 AUSTRALIA

WHITE £4.49

Sauvignon Blanc, Vin de Pays du Jardin FRANCE
de la France 2004
Screwcap.

WHITE £8.99

Sainsbury's Classic Selection Pouilly-Fumé 2004 FRANCE

WHITE £5.99

Sainsbury's Classic Selection Vouvray 2004 FRANCE
16.5 points in 2009-10.

WHITE £5.99

Sainsbury's Classic Selection SOUTH AFRICA
South African Chardonnay 2003

RED £8.49

Sainsbury's Classic Selection St-Emilion 2002 FRANCE

RED £4.99

Sainsbury's Reserve Selection Corbières 2002 FRANCE

WHITE £4.99

Sainsbury's Bin 20 Australian AUSTRALIA
Chardonnay 2004

RED £5.99

Sainsbury's Classic Selection Vintage Claret 2004 FRANCE

RED £3.49

Sainsbury's Australian Shiraz 2004   AUSTRALIA

WHITE £8.49

Steenberg Sémillon 2004   SOUTH AFRICA

RED £6.99

Tabali Reserva Cabernet Sauvignon 2002   CHILE

RED £14.99

Two Hands Brave Faces Barossa Valley   AUSTRALIA
Shiraz/Grenache 2002

RED £6.49

Viña Albali Gran Reserva Valdepeñas 1998   SPAIN

WHITE SPARKLING £7.99

Wolf Blass Red Label Sparkling   AUSTRALIA
Chardonnay/Pinot Noir NV
Also at Asda.

SMALL MERCHANTS

ADNAMS WINE MERCHANTS
Sole Bay Brewery,
East Green, Southwold,
Suffolk IP18 6JW

Tel: (01502) 727222
Fax: (01502) 727223

E-mail: wines@adnams.co.uk
Website: www.adnamswines.co.uk

ALDI STORES LTD
Holly Lane, Atherstone,
Warwickshire CV9 2SQ

Tel: (01827) 711800
Fax: (01827) 710899

Customer help-line: (08705) 134262

Website: www.aldi.com

AMEY'S WINES
83 Melford Road, Sudbury,
Suffolk CO10 1JT

Tel: (01787) 377144

AMPS FINE WINES
6 Market Place, Oundle,
Peterborough PE8 4BQ

Tel: (01832) 273502
Fax: (01832) 273611

E-mail: info@ampsfinewines.co.uk
Website: www.ampsfinewines.co.uk

AVERY'S OF BRISTOL
Head Office:
Orchard House, Southfield Road,
Nailsea, Bristol BS48 1JN

Tel: (01275) 811100
Fax: (01275) 811101

E-mail: sales@averys.com
Website: www.averys.com

BACCHUS FINE WINES
Warrington House Farm Barn,
Warrington, Olney,
Buckinghamshire MK46 4HN

Tel: (01234) 711140
Fax: (01234) 711362

E-mail: wine@bacchus.co.uk
Website: www.bacchus.co.uk

BEACONSFIELD WINE CELLARS
38 London End, Beaconsfield,
Buckinghamshire HP9 2JH

Tel: (01494) 675545
Fax: (01494) 681066

E-mail: info@beaconsfieldwinecellars.com
Website: www.beaconsfieldwinecellars.com

BENTALLS PLC
Wood Street, Kingston upon Thames,
Surrey KT1 1TN

Tel: (020) 8546 1001
Fax: (020) 8549 6163

Website: www.bentalls.co.uk

BIBENDUM

113 Regents Park Road,
London NW1 8UR

Tel: (020) 7449 4100
Fax: (020) 7449 4121

E-mail: sales@bibendum-wine.co.uk
Website: www.bibendum-wine.co.uk

D. BYRNE & CO.

Victoria Buildings,
12 King Street, Clitheroe,
Yorkshire BB7 2EP

Tel: (01200) 423152
Fax: (01200) 429386

COCKBURN AND CAMPBELL

Cockpen House,
20–30 Buckhold Road, Wandsworth,
London SW18 4AP

Tel: (020) 8875 7007
Fax: (020) 8875 7009

E-mail: cockburnandcampbell@youngs.co.uk

COE VINTNERS

53 Redbridge Lane, East Ilford,
Essex IG4 5E4

Tel: (020) 8551 4966
Fax: (020) 8550 6312

E-mail: enquiries@coevintners.co.uk
Website: www.coevintners.co.uk

D & D WINES INTERNATIONAL LTD

Adams Court,
Adams Hill, Knutsford,
Cheshire WA16 6BA

Tel: (01565) 650952
Fax: (01565) 755295

E-mail: ddwi@ddwinesint.com

F. L. DICKINS LTD

89-91 High Street, Rickmansworth,
Hertfordshire WD3 1EF

Tel: (01923) 773636
Fax: (01923) 772981

E-mail: karendickens@hotmail.com

FLAGSHIP WINES LTD

36 Rowan Close, St Albans,
Hertfordshire AL4 0ST

Tel: (01727) 841968
Fax: (01727) 841968

E-mail: info@flagshipwines.co.uk
Website: www.flagshipwines.co.uk

GREAT WESTERN WINES

The Wine Warehouse,
Wells Road, Bath,
Somerset BA2 3AP

Tel: (01225) 322800
Fax: (01225) 442139

E-mail: orders@greatwesternwine.co.uk
Website: www.greatwesternwine.co.uk

HALIFAX WINES

18 Prescott Street, Halifax,
West Yorkshire HX1 2LG

Tel: (01422) 256333

E-mail: andy@halifaxwinecompany.com
Website: www.halifaxwinecompany.com

HALLGARTEN WINES

Dallow Road, Luton,
Bedfordshire LU1 1UR

Tel: (01582) 722538
Fax: (01582) 723240

E-mail: hdawines@aol.com
Website: www.hallgarten.co.uk

HANDFORD WINES

12 Portland Road,
London W11 4LE

Tel: (020) 7221 9614
Fax: (020) 7221 9613

E-mail: wine@handford.net
Website: www.handford.net

HARRODS

Brompton Road, Knightsbridge,
London SW1X 7XL

Tel: (020) 7730 1234
Fax: (020) 7225 5823

E-mail: food.halls@harrods.com
Website: www.harrods.com

HARVEY NICHOLS
125 Knightsbridge,
London SW1X 7RJ

Tel: (020) 7201 8537
Fax: (020) 7245 6561

E-mail: wineshop@harveynichols.com
Website: www.harveynichols.com

CHARLES HENNINGS LTD
London House,
Lower Street, Pulborough,
West Sussex RH20 2BW

Tel: (01798) 343021
Fax: (01798) 343021

E-mail: sales@chu-wine.co.uk
Website: www.chu/wine.co.uk

HOULTS WINE MERCHANTS
10 Viaduct Street, Huddersfield,
West Yorkshire HD1 5DL

Tel: (01484) 510700
Fax: (01484) 510712

E-mail: info@hoults-winemerchants.co.uk
Website: hostmaster@hoults-winemerchants.co.uk

I VINI
Unit 2, The Old Kennels,
Cirencester Park, Cirencester,
Gloucestershire GL7 1UR

Tel: (01285) 655595
Fax: (01285) 650684

E-mail: enquiries@ivini.co.uk
Website: www.i-vini.co.uk

JEROBOAMS

Head Office:
43 Portland Road,
London W11 4LJ

Tel: (020) 7259 6716

E-mail: sales@jeroboams.co.uk
Website: www.jeroboams.co.uk

LIBERTY WINES UK LTD

Unit A53, The Food Market,
New Covent Garden,
London SW8 5EE

Tel: (020) 7720 5350
Fax: (020) 7720 6158

E-mail: info@libertywine.co.uk

LUVIANS

66 Market Street, St Andrews,
Fife KY16 9NT

Tel: (01334) 477 752
Fax: (01334) 477 128

E-mail: andy@luvians.com
Website: luvians.com

JAMES NICOLSON WINE MERCHANTS

27a Killyleagh Street,
Crossgar, Downpatrick,
Co. Down BT30 9DQ

Tel: (028) 4483 0091
Fax: (028) 4483 0028

E-mail: info@inwine.com
Website: www.inwine.com

NISA-TODAY'S
Ambient Warehouse,
Park Farm Road,
Foxhills Industrial Estate, Scunthorpe,
North Lincolnshire DN15 8QP

Tel: (0845) 6044999
Fax: (10724) 278727

E-mail: info@nisa-todays.com
Website: www.nisa-todays.com

THOMAS PANTON WINE MERCHANTS
Hampton Street, Tetbury,
Gloucestershire GL8 8JN

Tel: (01666) 503088
Fax: (01666) 503113

E-mail: sales@wineimporter.co.uk
Website: www.wineimporter.co.uk

PHILGLAS & SWIGGOT
21 Northcote Road, Battersea,
London SW11 1NG

Tel: (020) 7924 4494
Fax: (020) 7924 4736

E-mail: philandswigg@aol.com

CHRISTOPHER PIPER WINES
1 Silver Street, Ottery St. Mary's,
Devon EX11 1DV

Tel: (01404) 814139
Fax: (01404) 812100

E-mail: sales@christopherpiperwines.co.uk
Website: www.christopherpiperwines.co.uk

RICHARD & RICHARD FINE WINES

6 Hebburn Drive,
Brandlesholme, Bury,
Lancashire BL8 1ED

Tel: (0161) 762 0022
Fax: (0161) 763 4477

E-mail: fine.wines@btconnect.com

SELFRIDGES

400 Oxford Street,
London W1A 1AB

Tel: (020) 7318 3730
Fax: (020) 7318 3730

E-mail: wine.club@selfridges.co.uk
Website: www.selfridges.co.uk

SPAR

Head Office:
Hygeia Building,
66–68 College Road, Harrow,
Middlesex HA1 1BE

Tel: (020) 8426 3700
Fax: (020) 8426 3701/2

E-mail: angela.buckle@spar.co.uk
Website: www.spar.co.uk

STRATFORD'S WINE AGENCIES

High Street, Cookham,
Berkshire SL6 9SQ

Tel: (01628) 810606
Fax: (01628) 810605

E-mail: alistair@stratfordwine.co.uk
Website: www.stratfordwine.co.uk

TANNERS WINES LTD

26 Wyte Cop, Shrewsbury,
Shropshire SY1 1YD

Tel: (01743) 234500
Fax: (01743) 234501

E-mail: sales@tanners-wines.co.uk
Website: tanners-wines.co.uk

UNWINS

Birchwood House,
Victoria Road, Dartford,
Kent DA1 5AJ

Tel: (01322) 272711
Fax: (01322) 294469

E-mail: admin@unwinswines.co.uk
Website: www.unwins.co.uk

VICKI'S OF CHOBHAM

79–81 Windsor Road, Chobham,
Surrey GU24 8LD

Tel: (01276) 858374

PETER WATTS WINES

Wisdoms Barn,
Colne Road, Coggeshall
Essex CO6 1TV

Tel: (01376) 561130
Fax: (01376) 562925

E-mail: sales@peterwattswines.co.uk
Website: www.peterwattswine.co.uk

WAVERLEY WINES & SPIRITS

PO Box 22,
Crieff Road, Perth,
Perthshire PH1 2SL

Tel: (01738) 472000
Fax: (01738) 630338

Website: www.waverley-group.co.uk

WIMBLEDON WINE CELLERS

1 Gladstone Road, Wimbledon,
London SW19 1QU

Tel: (020) 8540 0079
Fax: (020) 8540 9399

Website: www.wimbledonwinecellar.com

WINE CELLARS

Head Office:
The Cellar 5 Group, PO Box 476,
Loushers Lane, Warrington,
Cheshire WA4 6RQ

Tel: (01925) 454545
Fax: (01925) 454546

E-mail: david.vaughan@cellar5.com
Website: www.winecellar.co.uk

THE WINE SOCIETY

Gunnels Wood Road, Stevenage,
Herts SG1 2BG

Tel: (01438) 741177
Fax: (01438) 761167

E-mail: memberservices@thewinesociety.com
Website: www.thewinesociety.com

NOEL YOUNG WINES

56 High Street, Trumpington,
Cambridge CB2 2LS

Tel: (01223) 844744

E-mail: admin@nywines.co.uk
Website: www.nywines.co.uk

For tasting notes of all Small Merchants' wines less
than 16 points, and ratings of wines less than
14 points, visit www.superplonk.com

17.5

Château Paul Mas, Coteaux de Languedoc Grenache/Syrah/Mourvèdre 2003
Stratford's Wine Agencies
Fantastically brazen, throaty cocoa and licorice-grilled berries. It oozes class and conviction and the price is absurdly low for such robust richness. It is one of those newly emerging wines from this area of France, the Midi, totally justifying the claims made for its elevation to major league status.

17.5

Errazuriz Estate Sangiovese 2003
D. Byrne & Co., Luvians, Vicki's of Chobham, Wimbledon Wine Cellars
Stunning mouthful! Spicy plums, chocolate, and a texture which is svelte yet not without character and bite. The Sangiovese is the Chianti grape and if the Chileans decide to plant it more widely than it is at present, then what the Aussies have done to France, the Chileans could do to Italy.
Also at E-tailers (Everywine).

17

Frontera Cabernet Sauvignon/Merlot 2004
Spar
A beautifully savoury, bitter-cherry-rich red of tannic elegance and no little depth.
Also at Sainsbury.

17

RED £7.99
FRANCE

Les Faisses Grenache/Syrah 2003

Stratford's Wine Agencies

Hit of chocolate on the finish. Fine gripping
tannins. This is a most exciting specimen of
Syrah (though it's more in the Shiraz mould
I guess).

16.5

RED £5.99
FRANCE

Arrogant Frog Ribet Red (Cabernet/ Merlot) 2003

Unwins

Screwcap. Terrific tannins and plums, hint of black
cherry. Great style, great name, great fun.

16.5

RED £7.99
CHILE

Casa Rivas Cabernet Sauvignon Reserva 2002

Adnams

Vigorous berried richness, slightly roasted plums,
deeply roasted tannins.

16.5

RED £5.99
CHILE

Errazuriz Estate Carmenere 2003

*D. Byrne & Co., Luvians, Vicki's of Chobham, Wimbledon
Wine Cellars*

A superb cheese-dish wine of great berried depth,
soft plums and blackberries and ripe tannins with a
black olive edge.

Also at Asda, E-tailers (Everywine).

16.5

La Forge Viognier 2004
Stratford's Wine Agencies
Superb complex apricot/pineapple/citrus.
Another thoroughbred tipple from the Paul Mas
stable.

16.5

Mont Gras Quatro Reserva 2002
Unwins
This hearty blend of Cabernet Sauvignon, Malbec,
Carmenere and Merlot creates a wine of broad
shoulders (once fully decanted 4–5 hours), ruffled
satin texture, and deep rich berries.
Also at E-tailers (Everywine).

The Carmenere is a funny old grape. Once hugely popular in
the Médoc, perhaps because of its ability to beef up a blend
and provide vibrant colour, it fell out of favour at least a century
and a half ago; it proved fragile in the face of certain vine
diseases. It emigrated to Chile around 1850 and seems to have
been confused with, and taken for, Merlot. Only as recently as
1998 was it recognised as a distinct variety. (According to Monty
Waldin, in his splendid *Wines of South America*, Mitchell Beazley,
£25, it is, apparently, still confused with Merlot in northern Italy
where it can also be found.) Chile is the only country where
the grape is cultivated to any great extent commercially and
vinified as such. Examples generally exhibit a vivacious
fruitiness and a very poised meaty undertone, sometimes a
little eccentric in its finish.

16.5

RED £4.99

Paul Mas Cabernet Sauvignon, FRANCE
Vin de Pays d'Oc 2004
Unwins
Screwcap. Elegant, rich, complex. A remarkable price
for such finesse and class.
Also at Waitrose.

16.5

RED £7.99

Wakefield Estate Cabernet AUSTRALIA
Sauvignon 2002
Unwins
This is a 30th anniversary release of a well-sodden
war-horse of an Aussie Cabernet, but never has it
delivered such a deliciously savoury fruit as this
because…it is now screwcapped. This maintains the
wine's virility and its combativeness with food
(cheese, meat, chicken, casserole dishes it loves).
Winemaker Mitchell Taylor, the third generation of
Taylors at the estate (called Taylor's in Australia but
because of Taylor Portugal and the USA, the
producer was forced to select another name for
export), remarked 'I'm sick of having my wine at the
mercy of a bit of cork.' Right on, Mitch.

16.5

RED £8.39

Wakefield Estate Shiraz 2003 AUSTRALIA
Unwins
Screwcap. Brilliant savoury, softly spoken berries

which evolve deftly on the palate to reveal depth and
style without any over-engineering.
Also at Oddbins.

 16.5   RED £7.99

Casa Rivas Merlot Reserva 2002   CHILE
Adnams
Great craggy tannins and ripe plum, blackberries
and herbs. Very persistent.
Also at Oddbins.

 16   RED (25cl miniature bottle) £1.19

Aldi Cabernet Sauvignon 2003   CHILE
Aldi
A totally quaffable luncheon or picnic red of savoury
plums and burned berries. Has a touch of chocolate
to the tannins. Terrific with ham or cheese
sandwiches.

 16   RED £5.29

Casa Rivas Merlot 2003   CHILE
Adnams
Very dark biscuity fruit. Deliciously pugnacious.

16   RED £5.29

Casa Rivas Cabernet Sauvignon 2003   CHILE
Adnams
Characterfully roasted, spicy plums propped up by
decent tannins and a positive texture.

16
WHITE £3.99

Frontera Sauvignon/Chardonnay 2004 CHILE
Spar
Not a crisp/lean classic but superbly rotund (yet not
inelegant).
Also at Sainsbury.

16
RED £23.00

Goldwater 'Goldie' Cabernet Sauvignon/ NEW ZEALAND
Merlot/Cabernet Franc 2002
Avery's of Bristol
Very interesting mature fruit. Good tannins. Lot of
money, true, but its individuality is proudly borne.
Very interesting mature fruit. The grapes are grown
on Waiheke Island, a place where wine wankers can
run riot (with Goldwater the most notable

Not only at auctions does silly money change hands over a
bottle of wine. I was at a merchant's office last summer,
Bibendum in Regent's Park, and I was told that an American
had recently coughed up £6,000 for a single bottle of 1869
Chateau d'Yquem. It would be a miracle if the wine was
stunning, but it was one of the greatest ever vintages for this
estate (and David Peppercorn, the wine guru who drinks old
sweet Bordeaux for breakfast, has written that a bottle of the
1869 drunk in 1988 was 'marvellous'). Drinkability, however, with
a wine so ancient is not wholly the point. It is having the wine
in one's possession that counts (like a lock of Marie
Antoinette's hair).

exception). If you want to read the whole hilarious story of this fashionable island off Auckland then subscribe to superplonk.com and access the articles I have written on travelling in New Zealand and what happened when I rented a house on Waiheke for a while.

16

WHITE £4.99

Hidden Hill Sauvignon Blanc 2004 FRANCE

Stratford's Wine Agencies
Screwcap. Full-on Thai-food wine.

16

RED £14.00

Huia Pinot Noir 2003 NEW ZEALAND

Bibendum
Very charming, classy, aromatic, solid, gamy cherries which flirt with rather than wholly embrace the palate. Still, affection has to start somewhere.

16

WHITE SPARKLING £9.99

Jansz Premium Cuvée NV AUSTRALIA

Selfridges, Noel Young Wines
Came top in a blind tasting, conducted (hic) by me, alongside champagnes twice the price.
Also at Oddbins.

16

RED £4.99

Ile La Forge Cabernet Sauvignon 2003 FRANCE

Aldi
Lovely fresh plum edge to the ripe tannins.

16

RED £14.99

Nautilus Estate Pinot Noir 2002   NEW ZEALAND
Thomas Panton Wine Merchants, Christopher Piper Wines
Very attractive black cherry with gamy raspberry and
firm tannins.
Also at Majestic.

16

WHITE £5.99

Paul Mas Viognier, Vin de Pays d'Oc 2004   FRANCE
Stratford's Wine Agencies
Delicate acids with lip-smackin' apricot.

16

RED £8.99

Trinity Hill Pinot Noir 2004   NEW ZEALAND
Selfridges
Lovely tight Pinot: gamy cherry/raspberry fruit, firm
and not over-sweet on the finish.

16

WHITE SPARKLING £15.00

Yering Station Yarrabank Cuvée Pinot   AUSTRALIA
Noir/Chardonnay 2000
Philglas & Swiggot, Wine Cellars
Great finesse and class here.

16

ROSÉ £6.99

Zonte's Footsteps Langhorne Creek   AUSTRALIA
Cabernet/Petit Verdot Rosé 2004
Unwins
Screwcap. A most convincingly firm, stylish, subtly
rich, dry-plum rosé.
Also at Sainsbury.

OTHER WINES 15.5 AND UNDER

15.5
                                  WHITE £5.29

Casa Rivas Sauvignon Blanc 2004   CHILE
Adnams

ROSÉ £4.99

Paul Mas Rosé de Syrah, Vin de Pays   FRANCE
d'Oc 2004
Stratford's Wine Agencies
Screwcap.

RED £7.99

Stoneleigh Vineyards Marlborough   NEW ZEALAND
Pinot Noir 2003
Richard & Richard Fine Wines, Halifax Wines
Screwcap.

RED £7.99

Sherwood Estate Pinot Noir 2004   NEW ZEALAND
I Vini

15
                                RED £25.95

Ata Rangi Pinot Noir 2002   NEW ZEALAND
Harrods, Jeroboams
Screwcap.

ROSÉ £6.99

Antipodean Sangiovese Rosé 2004   AUSTRALIA
Hoults
Also at Oddbins.

WHITE SPARKLING £6.99

Angas Brut Premium Cuvée Pinot Noir/ AUSTRALIA
Chardonnay NV
Unwins
Also at Oddbins.

WHITE £5.29

Casa Rivas Chardonnay 2004 CHILE
Adnams

WHITE SPARKLING £7.99

Deakin Estate Chardonnay/ AUSTRALIA
Pinot Noir Brut NV
Bibendum
Also at Oddbins.

RED £15.99

Esk Valley Reserve Merlot/Malbec/ NEW ZEALAND
Cabernet Sauvignon 2002
Vicki's of Chobham, Wimbledon Wine Cellars
Screwcap. Also at E-tailers (Everywine).

RED £9.99

Forrest Estate Pinot Noir 2003 NEW ZEALAND
Adnams
Screwcap.

RED £8.99

Kim Crawford Pinot Noir 2004 NEW ZEALAND
Amps Fine Wines, Bacchus Fine Wines, Beaconsfield Wine
Cellars
Screwcap.

RED £8.99
CHILE

Kuyen 2002
Adnams

WHITE £8.99
NEW ZEALAND

Mud House Sauvignon Blanc 2004
Bentalls, Harrods, Harvey Nichols, Selfridges
Screwcap. Also at Booths.

RED £8.99
NEW ZEALAND

Oyster Bay Pinot Noir 2004
Wimbledon Wine Cellars
Screwcap.

RED £19.00
NEW ZEALAND

Seresin Pinot Noir 2003
Selfridges, Handford Wines

RED £10.99
NEW ZEALAND

Seifried Pinot Noir 2003
Peter Watts Wines, F.L. Dickins, Flagship Wines
Screwcap.

14.5

RED £19.99
CHILE

Antiyal 2002
Adnams

RED £15.99
NEW ZEALAND

Cloudy Bay Pinot Noir 2003
Harrods
Also at Majestic, Waitrose (selected stores).

Craggy Range Te Muna Pinot Noir 2003
RED £15.99
NEW ZEALAND
Amey's Wines, The Wine Society

Casa Rivas Chardonnay Reserva 2003
WHITE £7.99
CHILE
Adnams

Geoff Merrill Grenache Rosé 2004
ROSÉ £6.50
AUSTRALIA
Amey's Wines, Charles Hennings, Christopher Piper Wines
Screwcap.

Montana Pinot Noir 2004
RED £6.99
NEW ZEALAND
Waverly Wines & Spirits
Screwcap. Also at Waitrose.

Tuatara Bay Pinot Noir 2004
RED £8.99
NEW ZEALAND
Hallgarten Wines, Selfridges
Screwcap.

Spy Valley Pinot Noir 2003
RED £9.99
NEW ZEALAND
Bibendum

Villa Maria Single Vineyard Taylors Pass Pinot Noir 2003
RED £19.99
NEW ZEALAND
Luvians, Wimbledon Wine Cellars
16.5 in 2007–8. Screwcap. Also at E-tailers (Everywine).

RED £18.50
CHILE

Via Leyda Pinot Noir 'Lot 21' 2002
Adnams

RED £9.95
NEW ZEALAND

West Brook Pinot Noir 2004
Great Western Wines
Screwcap.

ROSÉ £10.95
AUSTRALIA

Yering Station 'ED' Pinot Noir Rosé 2003
Philglas & Swiggot

ROSÉ £4.49
AUSTRALIA

Andrew Makepeace 'Masterpeace' Rosé 2004
Nisa, Unwins
Screwcap. Also at Co-op.

14

ROSÉ £5.29
CHILE

Casa Rivas Rosé 2003
Adnams

RED £12.50
NEW ZEALAND

Churton Pinot Noir 2003
Tanners Wines

WHITE SPARKLING £22.99
FRANCE

Champagne Pommery Blanc de Blancs NV
Unwins
Also at Oddbins.

ROSÉ £6.49
AUSTRALIA

**Chain of Ponds Novello Rosso Sangiovese/
Grenache Rosé 2003**
D. & D. Wines

Delta Vineyards Pinot Noir 2004
Liberty Wines

RED £9.95
NEW ZEALAND

Deakin Estate Rosé 2004
Bibendum
Screwcap. Also at Oddbins.

ROSÉ £6.49
AUSTRALIA

Gladstone Vineyards Pinot Noir 2004
James Nicolson Wine Merchants
Screwcap.

RED £11.49
NEW ZEALAND

Mondiale Sauvignon Blanc NV
Aldi

WHITE £3.49
SOUTH AFRICA

Matua Valley Pinot Noir 2004
Cockburn & Campbell
Screwcap.

RED £7.99
NEW ZEALAND

Old Coach Road Pinot Noir 2003
Peter Watts Wines, F. L. Dickins, Flagship Wines
Screwcap.

RED £9.99
NEW ZEALAND

Aldi Pinot Blanc 2003
Aldi

WHITE (25cl miniature bottle) £1.19
GERMANY

RED £10.99
NEW ZEALAND

Stoneleigh Vineyards Rapaura Series Pinot Noir 2003
Coe Vintners

RED £18.00
NEW ZEALAND

Te Kairanga Reserve Pinot Noir 2003
Bibendum

RED £14.99
NEW ZEALAND

Villa Maria Reserve Cabernet Sauvignon/ Merlot 2002
Vicki's of Chobham, Wimbledon Wine Cellars
Screwcap. Also at E-tailers (Everywine).

WHITE £10.83
CHILE

Viña Leyda Chardonnay 2001
Adnams

RED £10.59
CHILE

Viña Leyda Pinot Noir 2004
Adnams

ROSÉ £6.99
AUSTRALIA

Windy Peak Cabernet Rosé 2004
Amps Fine Wines
Screwcap.

SOMERFIELD

Somerfield House,
Whitchurch Lane,
Bristol BS14 0TJ

Tel: (0117) 935 9359
Fax: (0117) 978 0629

E-mail: customer.service@somerfield.co.uk
Website: www.somerfield.co.uk

For tasting notes of Somerfield wines of less than
16 points, and ratings of wines less than 14 points,
visit www.superplonk.com

17.5   WHITE SPARKLING £6.99

Somerfield Vintage Cava Brut 2000   SPAIN

Slicker (shyer, more compact) than many a much-
vaunted champagne at three to four times the price.
A hugely elegant, demurely rich bubbly.

17   RED £5.49

Vacqueyras 2003   FRANCE

What a wonderfully meaty wine! Has huge character,
commitment and charm which give the wine length,
breadth and depth from the roasted berries to the
chunky tannins.

16.5   RED £5.49

Casillero del Diablo Concha y Toro Shiraz 2004   CHILE

Delicious. Multi-layered berries and soft tannins.
Also at Majestic, Sainsbury.

16.5   WHITE £5.99

Errazuriz Estate Chardonnay 2004   CHILE

Superb edge of tropicality (pineapple and mango).
Delicate to finish so no spicy food with this wine
(smoked fish is perfect).
Also at Budgens, E-tailers (Everywine), Oddbins,
Sainsbury, Tesco.

16.5   RED £5.99

Errazuriz Estate Cabernet Sauvignon 2003   CHILE

Very gripping, vivid fruit. A combination of
chocolate and burned berries, with the tannins, cuts

a swathe of flavour which lingers lustily.
Also at Asda, E-tailers (Everywine), Oddbins,
Waitrose.

16.5   RED £4.99

Ken Forrester Petit Pinotage 2004   SOUTH AFRICA
Sweet spicy plum fruit slowly coagulates to reveal
chocolate and licorice and black olive.
Also at Asda (but rated at 14).

There is still the odd wine drinker bemoaning the rise in non-
natural cork seals on the grounds it threatens Portuguese
wildlife. On the 29th of July 2004 in the *Guardian*'s G2
supplement Hannah Berry, who writes for *Ethical Consumer*
magazine, wrote that plastic corks are 'causing profound
problems for Europe's cork *dehesas*, which are sustainably
managed habitats rich in wildlife'. The truth is that the only
problem non-cork seals are causing cork manufacturers, and
their ability to exploit the cork forests, is how to widen the
use of cork now it no longer has so large a captive wine-
bottle market. Cork has myriad uses outside wine, but due to
the ingenuity of one PR woman the cork industry concocted a
story that wildlife would be threatened if non-cork seals
became popular. It is a wonderful piece of PR poppycock.
Inside a decade the majority of our everyday drinking wines
will be screwcapped and the Iberian eagle will still be flying
over and rare pigs will still be rootling around the base of all
those majestic cork oaks because, just like any other business
facing competition, the cork industry expanded its product's
multiple other uses (as it is now doing).

16.5   RED £6.99

La Forge Syrah 2003   FRANCE

Oh what a beauty! Lovely polished sheen to the
rugged berries which display damsons, roasted nuts
and a hint of herbiness to the tannins.
Also at Threshers.

16.5   RED £6.99

L'Hospitalet 2002   FRANCE

Chokes the throat thrillingly with raw chocolate,
blackberries, tar, licorice and very even-tempered
tannins of great character.

16.5   RED £4.99

Santa Julia Tempranillo 2004   ARGENTINA

Very smooth plums and blackberries with licorice.
Also at Tesco.

16.5   WHITE £3.99

Somerfield Argentine Chardonnay NV   ARGENTINA

What a lovely waxy-textured bargain here. Lushness
tempered by acids from the lemon/peach and
pineapple fruit.

16.5   WHITE £4.99

Casillero del Diablo Concha y Toro   CHILE
Sauvignon Blanc 2004

A crisp classic of length and crunchy concentration.
Also at Asda, Majestic, Oddbins, Tesco, Threshers.

16

RED £11.99

Wolf Blass President's Selection Cabernet Sauvignon 2002

AUSTRALIA

Big, rich, yet only lightly grilled berries with firm tannins of velvet with denim patches. Very well modulated Cabernet of some class.
Also at Majestic, Waitrose.

16

RED £3.99

Amanti Rosso

ITALY

Amazing value! – and its delicious screwcap will keep its pert, savoury tannins in the fettle they need to be to support the nicely charred berried fruit.

16

WHITE £6.99

Botham/Merrill/Willis Chardonnay 2002

AUSTRALIA

The most convincing reason to follow the world's most impossible-to-understand sport (cricket, though I believe sumo snow wrestling also has its complex side). Has a forthright elegance this wine, which its first vintage release lacked.

16

RED £4.99

Blueridge XR Merlot

BULGARIA

Screwcap. Terrific! Ignore the baroque bottle and wallow in the soft plums on offer here. In fact, the bottle's not so bad once you ignore it.

16   WHITE £4.99

Brown Brothers Dry Muscat 2004   AUSTRALIA
Screwcap. 16.5 in 2009. One of Oz's best-shrouded
secrets: a floral-edged, grapefruit-toned, subtle spicy
tipple of great charm.
Also at Asda, Budgens, Tesco.

16   RED £4.49

Chileño Shiraz/Cabernet Sauvignon 2004   CHILE
Excellent curry red. The savoury/sweet edge to the
fruit hugs chillies like old friends.
Also at Sainsbury, Waitrose (15 in 3 litre box).

16   WHITE £5.99

Cono Sur Viognier 2004   CHILE
How Viognier should be at this price. Gorgeous
apricot/citrus fruit which fattens on the tongue but
does not go florid.
Also at Majestic, Threshers, Waitrose.

It is always assumed that it is red wine which is enhanced with
laying down and great aging. The oldest red wine I have
consumed a bottle of was a 1933 Château Lafite in 1983 and it
was reasonably characterful for half-an-hour, but hardly
stupendous. Sweet wines, Trockenbeerenauslesen, Sauternes,
Tokajis, are much more likely to react congenially from
longevity because of the degree of sugar in their make-up (and
30 or 40 years would not be an outrageous age at which to
experience them and find them exciting).

16

RED £4.99

Cape Grace Cabernet Sauvignon/ SOUTH AFRICA
Merlot 2003
Screwcap. The burned rubber after-tang is nicely
judged. The fruit is soft, coated with velour-textured
tannins. A terrific glugging red.

16

RED £9.99

Châteauneuf-du-Pape La Volonté des FRANCE
Papes 2001
Fine mature fruit of class and cohesion. Catch it
while its fruit is still so vigorous and sprightly.

16

RED £8.49

Château Fongaban FRANCE
Puisséguin- St-Emilion 2002
A no-nonsense claret of class and great character.
Has serious tannins allied to fine berries.

16

RED £4.99

Canaletto Primitivo 2002 ITALY
Lovely biting, brisk fruit with tannins which stride
with aplomb and confidence across the palate.

16

WHITE £5.99

Chileño Gold Sauvignon Blanc 2004 CHILE
Very elegant with under-ripe fruit and friendly
balanced acids.

16

WHITE £6.99

Cono Sur Reserve Chardonnay 2004 CHILE
Lean, elegant, tangy, very refreshing – even members
of the ABC club (Anything But Chardonnay) will find
reasons to defect.

16

RED £4.99

Emiliana Syrah 2004 CHILE
Rich and very ripe. Full of personality and
interesting touches – not least the cherries and spicy
tannins.

16

WHITE £6.99

Goundrey Unwooded Chardonnay 2004 AUSTRALIA
Screwcap. Firm ripe gooseberry, melon and half dry
peach.

16

RED £6.99

Ironstone Cabernet Franc 2002 USA
Hugely plummy polish and chutzpah. Brilliant with
spicy vegetarian food.

16

WHITE £6.99

Jackson Estate Marlborough NEW ZEALAND
Sauvignon Blanc 2004
Screwcap. 16.5 points in 2007. Finely modulated
gooseberry/citrus fruit. A fine tipple by any
standards.
Also at Booths, Sainsbury.

16   RED £6.99

La Capitana Merlot Barrel Reserve   CHILE
Viña La Rosa 2002
Tobacco – that's the theme. And it's aromatically and
very dryly expressed.

16   WHITE £6.99

L'Hospitalet White 2002   FRANCE
Stunning! Lovely waxy, creamily textured hard/soft
fruitiness well tempered, couth and very civilised.

16   WHITE £4.99

Masterpeace Chardonnay 2004   AUSTRALIA
One of Andrew Peace's best Chardonnays under a
fiver for it has rich melon mitigated by calm acids.
Well textured and sane.

16   RED £5.99

Mont Tauch Fitou 2003   FRANCE
Ripe yet beautifully cocoa-edged berries strike the
taste-buds with rustic abandon. Highly civilised yet
slightly feral.

16   FORTIFIED £6.99

Navigators' LBV Port 1999   PORTUGAL
A delicious well-berried port of finesse and character
helped by cherry-edged tannins.

16

RED £8.99

Alemena Real Reserva Rioja 1998 SPAIN

Selected stores only. Slightly craggy but soft-centred.
Mature tannins cloaking earthy plums.

16

RED £3.99

Riverview Cabernet Sauvignon 2000 HUNGARY

Bitter cherry which expands on the palate to reveal a
touch of green olive to the tannins. Fantastically
serious wine for the money.

16

WHITE £6.99

Rutherglen Estates Marsanne/ AUSTRALIA
Chardonnay 2004

Screwcap. Understated yet emphatic, subtle yet
impactful, weighty yet has a fleet-of-foot fruitiness. A
statuesque white wine.

16

FORTIFIED £3.99

Somerfield Pale Cream Sherry SPAIN

A lovely sippin' liquid which deserves to bring
people back to that much under-appreciated
welcome-home-from-the-coalface-darling drink
called sherry. This example has the saline nutty
undertone of fino with an off-sweet melon edge – so
the result is harmonious, cheerful, life-enhancing. A
delicious, well-chilled aperitif.

16

RED £3.99

Somerfield First Flight Shiraz/Cabernet 2003 AUSTRALIA
Screwcap. Bargain soft fruit yet has good tannins and
character. Terrific glugging.

16

RED £4.99

Somerfield First Flight Reserve Shiraz 2003 AUSTRALIA
This one has spicy undertones from plum and
cherry and the tannins have a fresher edge than is
normal with Aussie Shirazes.

16

RED £5.99

Trio Merlot/Carmenere/Cabernet CHILE
Sauvignon 2004
Lovely grilled plums in firm collusion with ripe
tannins.
Also at Co-op.

16

WHITE £4.99

Terra Organica Chenin Blanc 2004 ARGENTINA
Complex, bold, striking as it hits the palate then
goes dry and coy on the finish to then return with
gooseberry and citrus.

16

WHITE £4.99

Terra Organica Bonarda/Sangiovese 2004 ARGENTINA
Lovely ripe fruit, not soppy or OTT, just bonny,
generous and plummy. It wilts deliciously under the
tongue.

16

WHITE £7.99
NEW ZEALAND

Villa Maria Private Bin Sauvignon Blanc 2004

Selected stores only. Screwcap. 17.5 points in 2007.
Forward rich style, beautifully textured like satin.
Has an effortlessly classy feel.
Also at Asda, Budgens, Sainsbury, Tesco.

16

RED £6.99
CHILE

Veramonte Cabernet Sauvignon 2001
Coffee and cream fruit, edging towards the mature.

16

WHITE £8.99
AUSTRALIA

Wolf Blass Eagle Hawk Chardonnay 2004
Rich yet far from over-cooked, delicate yet not close
to being a shrinking violet, cosy but not sycophantic.
Also at Asda, Sainsbury.

Wine writing is being kept alive by its doyen: Hugh Johnson Esq.
In a single sentence, in the *Guardian* in 2004, he got 'crystalline',
'penetrating', 'poised', 'luxurious', 'fragrant' and 'foghorn' into a
single sentence whilst describing Aussie wine. I humble myself
at the feet of his inkhorn. Others have tried to imitate his
linguistic delicacy and freshness. One aspiring (and perspiring)
wine critic, who deserves the anonymity of namelessness, once
said of Palo Cortado that it was a 'strange hermaphroditic
sherry', a descriptor so extravagant that the reader is left utterly
confused instead of enlightened (let alone titillated to try an
often richly engaging sherry style).

16

WHITE £6.99
AUSTRALIA

Zonte's Footsteps Langhorne Creek Verdelho 2004

Nice spicy undertone to peach, pear and citrus.
Terrific with mild Thai food.

16

RED £6.99
AUSTRALIA

Nepenthe 'Tryst' Cabernet/Zinfandel/ Tempranillo 2003

Screwcap. Firmly, plummily approachable thanks to
its most appealing, slow-moving dry fruit.
Screwcap. Also at Oddbins.

16

RED £4.99
CHILE

Cono Sur Pinot Noir 2004

Stunningly complete – the tobacco-edged, gamy
cherries linger for ages in the throat.
Also at Majestic, Threshers, Waitrose.

16

RED £5.99
SOUTH AFRICA

Excelsior Paddock Shiraz 2004

Sweet, jammy and seemingly heading for a 14-point
rating but the finish pulls off a surprise – class and
cohesion, richness without brashness – and so the
money is well spent.
Screwcap. Also at Sainsbury.

OTHER WINES 15.5 AND UNDER

15.5

WHITE £5.99
Trio Chardonnay/Pinot Grigio/Pinot Blanc 2004 CHILE
Also at Co-op.

RED £7.99
Zonte's Footsteps Langhorne Creek AUSTRALIA
Shiraz/Viognier 2004
Screwcap. Also at Sainsbury.

WHITE £4.99
Domaine du Bois Viognier, FRANCE
Vin de Pays d'Oc 2003

RED £4.99
Goundrey Cabernet/Merlot 2003 AUSTRALIA

WHITE SPARKLING £7.49
Hardy's Nottage Hill Sparkling AUSTRALIA
Chardonnay 2004
Also at Sainsbury.

RED £6.99
Inti Reserve Shiraz 2004 ARGENTINA

ROSÉ £4.99
Misiónes de Rengo Cabernet Rosé 2004 CHILE

RED £3.99
Riverview Kekfrankos Merlot NV HUNGARY

RED £6.99
The Reserve Yellow Tail Shiraz 2002 AUSTRALIA

RED £7.99
Wolf Blass Yellow Label AUSTRALIA
Cabernet Sauvignon 2003
Also at Tesco.

RED £6.49
Wakefield Promised Land Cabernet/ AUSTRALIA
Merlot 2002

WHITE £6.99
Nobilo Marlborough NEW ZEALAND
Sauvignon Blanc 2004
Screwcap. Also at Tesco, Threshers.

15

WHITE £4.49
Divinum Riesling 2004 GERMANY
Screwcap.

WHITE £6.99
Inti Reserve Chardonnay 2004 ARGENTINA

WHITE £6.99
Ironstone Viognier 2003 USA

WHITE £4.99
Misiónes de Rengo Chardonnay 2004 CHILE
Also at Asda.

WHITE £6.99
Nepenthe 'Tryst' Sauvignon Blanc/ AUSTRALIA
Sémillon 2004
Screwcap.

Rutherglen Estates Grenache/Shiraz/ Mourvèdre 2004
Screwcap.

RED £6.99
AUSTRALIA

Spier Inspire Cabernet Sauvignon 2003

RED £5.99
SOUTH AFRICA

Somerfield First Flight Reserve Chardonnay 2003

WHITE £4.99
AUSTRALIA

Tariquet Famille Grassa Sauvignon Blanc 2004

WHITE £4.99
FRANCE

Tariquet Vin de Pays des Côtes Gascogne Blanc 2004

WHITE £4.99
FRANCE

Veramonte Sauvignon Blanc 2004
Screwcap.

WHITE £7.03
CHILE

Wolf Blass Yellow Label Cabernet Sauvignon 2002

RED £7.99
AUSTRALIA

Wolf Blass President's Selection Chardonnay 2003

WHITE £9.99
AUSTRALIA

14.5

Buzet Rouge Cuvée 44 2003
Selected stores only.

RED £4.99
FRANCE

Boland Cellar Sauvignon Blanc 2004

WHITE £4.99
SOUTH AFRICA

Somerfield First Flight Unoaked Chardonnay 2004
Screwcap.

WHITE £3.99
AUSTRALIA

Tariquet Famille Grassa Rosé 2004

ROSÉ £5.99
FRANCE

Wolf Blass Eagle Hawk Shiraz/Merlot/ Cabernet 2003

RED £4.99
AUSTRALIA

14

Brown Brothers Tarrango 2003

RED £4.99
AUSTRALIA

Champagne Paul Reisder NV

WHITE SPARKLING £10.99
FRANCE

Cape Grace Chardonnay/Sémillon 2004

WHITE £4.99
USA

Emiliana Chardonnay 2004

WHITE £4.99
CHILE

Hardy's Stamp of Australia Sparkling Pinot Noir/Chardonnay Brut NV
Also at Asda, Sainsbury, Tesco.

WHITE SPARKLING £5.99
AUSTRALIA

RED £11.99
NEW ZEALAND

Jackson Estate Marlborough Pinot Noir 2003
16.5 points in 2007–8.

WHITE £4.99
USA

Leaping Horse Chardonnay 2003

RED £7.29
FRANCE

Louis Jadot Beaujolais-Villages 2004

RED £6.99

Montana Merlot/Cabernet Sauvignon 2003 NEW ZEALAND
Screwcap. Also at Oddbins, Waitrose.

RED £4.99

Masterpeace Cabernet Sauvignon/Merlot 2004 AUSTRALIA

WHITE £6.99
FRANCE

Somerfield Chablis 2003

TESCO

Head Office:
Tesco House,
PO Box 18,
Delamare Road,
Cheshunt,
Hertfordshire EN8 9SL

Tel: (01992) 632222

Customer Services Helpline: (0800) 505555

Email: customer.services@tesco.co.uk
Website: www.tesco.com

For tasting notes of Tesco wines scoring less than
16 points, and ratings of wines less than 14 points,
visit www.superplonk.com

17.5

RED £9.99
ARGENTINA

Familia Zuccardi 'Q' Tempranillo 2002

Wonderful rich, ripe cherries and plums, dusty prunes on the side and a touch of tar to the very ripe tannins. This is an exciting updating of the Spanish style of the Tempranillo grape, called in its most notorious form Rioja, but the Zuccardi version is more perfumed, more sensual, altogether more decadent.

17.5

WHITE £8.99
AUSTRALIA

Tim Adams Sémillon 2003

19 points in 2010. A beautifully oily wine, smoky, ripe, complex, utterly convincing. Superbly structured and fine, it will reach near-perfection in 5 years.

17.5

RED £5.99
ITALY

Vigneti di Montegradella Valpolicella Classico 2001

Superb tannins give the spicy cherry/plum/prune fruit great grip. Wonderful with game dishes with fruit sauces. Complex, bold, concentrated, amazingly sensual.

17

WHITE £4.99
SOUTH AFRICA

Danie de Wet Chardonnay Sur Lie 2004

One of the loveliest, dry under-a-fiver whites in the store. Intense yet subtle, delicate yet firm, expressive but not flamboyant, this is a major Chardonnay statement.

17

RED £4.99

Da Luca Primitivo Merlot 2003 ITALY

Terrific! Like lava it flows over the taste-buds with
rich cherries, plum, blackcurrants and brilliant
roasted tannins. With an abundance of wines priced
and fruited like this, Italy could take on Australia,
South Africa and Chile, but to the great relief of those
three wine exporters the Italians aren't competing.
Also at Co-op.

17

RED £8.99

Errazuriz Estate Max Reserva CHILE
Cabernet Sauvignon 2001

Bung it in a jug for 3–5 hours. And then watch it
motor over the taste-buds like a Ferrari. Has a lovely
Italianate growl to its purring fruit and sleekly
fruited richness, but its oomph is all South
American.

17

WHITE £8.99

Neil Ellis Stellenbosch Chardonnay 2003 SOUTH AFRICA

Out-points many more expensive Chardonnays with
its complex, chalky melon fruit, minerally citrus
undertone and finish of light creamy wood.

17

WHITE £7.49

Tesco Finest Marlborough NEW ZEALAND
Sauvignon Blanc 2004

Screwcap. Delicious touch of peach to the
gooseberry and citrus. Very finely structured.

**Tesco Finest Denman Estate Reserve
Sémillon 2002**

Screwcap. 18.5 points in 2009-10. A wonderful smoky,
minerally citrussy, lean, gorgeous Sémillon of real
class and distinction. Wines like this, from this
grape, are much more compelling, for far less
money, than many expensive white Burgundies.

Errazuriz Estate Merlot 2003

Melted chocolate dripped over grilled plums. An
irresistible recipe.
Also at E-tailers (Everywine), Oddbins, Sainsbury,
Threshers.

It is always more difficult for a wine critic to find highly
recommendable white wines than it is red because the white
wine maker has so much less to play with. This is because skin
contact time with whites, though in some instances it does
permit colour and tannin to leach into the must which will then
ferment, is so much shorter than with reds. For wine owes its
colour to the skin of its grapes and since tannin, which the
berry produces as an antioxidant (protection of the sugars
required to make the pips, when brown and ripe, enticing to
animals to eat), is only significantly present in the skins of red
wines. So it is that white wines can be less substantial than red
and indeed less complex (though of course there are
winemakers who conjure white wines, from Riesling,
Chardonnay, Chenin, Grüner Veltliner and Viognier grapes, of
provocative depth and concentration to rival any red).

17   RED £5.03

Casillero del Diablo Concha y Toro   CHILE
Carmenere 2004
Simply wonder-juice. Joy from eye to nose, lips to
throat (via a thrilled palate).
Also at Majestic, Sainsbury, Threshers.

16.5   WHITE £4.99

Argento Chardonnay 2003   ARGENTINA
Scrumptious, classy, lovely ripe peach/pineapple,
finishing with waxy lemon. Works a treat on the
taste-buds.

16.5   RED £5.99

Errazuriz Estate Shiraz 2003   CHILE
A relaxed style subtle to open, then it goes
emphatically rich and complex, and then it lingers
with cocoa and nuts and burned berries. It is
wickedly unfair of the Chileans to manufacture
wines like this for this kind of money. The rest of
the winemaking world has a difficult job competing.
Also at Waitrose.

16.5   WHITE £12.99

Cloudy Bay Sauvignon Blanc 2004   NEW ZEALAND
Screwcap. A superbly complete Sauvignon Blanc
from a fine vintage. Indeed, for me this is the best
C.B. from this grape for some years.

16.5

Errazuriz Estate Chardonnay 2004
Screwcap. Absolutely stunningly textured and
amazingly smooth on the palate (without being
either anodyne or superficial).
Also at Budgens, E-tailers (Everywine), Oddbins,
Sainsbury, Somerfield.

16.5

**Finest New Zealand Hawkes Bay
Chardonnay 2002**
Screwcap. Lovely waxy complexity:
gooseberry/melon/lemon, hint of herb to the
peach. A stunning wine and in its screwcap it'll
age brilliantly for 2–3 years more and age
interestingly.

16.5

Inycon Merlot 2003
The second best Italian red in the store. It flaunts
plummy ripeness, an oily/waxy texture, and rich
vigorous tannins. Real class in a glass here.

16.5

**Casillero del Diablo Concha y Toro
Sauvignon Blanc 2004**
Very elegant, dry, subtly saline edge to the under-
ripe gooseberry fruit.
Also at Asda, Majestic, Oddbins, Somerfield, Threshers.

16.5

RED £4.99

Railroad Red Cabernet Sauvignon/   SOUTH AFRICA
Shiraz 2003
One of the glugging reds of the year. Has youth,
chutzpah, wit, richness and muscle.
Also at Asda.

16.5

RED £8.99

Marqués de Griñon Reserva Rioja 2000   SPAIN
Always one of the most svelte and accomplished of
Riojas, edging towards a New World level of
excitement.

16.5

WHITE £5.03

Peter Lehmann Sémillon 2002   AUSTRALIA
Screwcap. A superbly complex, thought-provoking
white wine, offering gooseberry, grapefruit, lemon
and a hint of coriander.

16.5

WHITE £6.99

Pazo Serantellos Albarino 2004   SPAIN
One of the most elongated Albarinos I've tasted. A
fine white wine of style and finesse from Galicia,
Spain's rainiest region.

16.5

WHITE £9.99

Rawnsley Estate Chardonnay 2003   AUSTRALIA
Screwcap. A treat. Very expressive, slightly waxy
lemon/melon/ pineapple/Cox's Orange Pippin fruit.
Very elegant.

16.5

FORTIFIED £4.99

Tesco Finest Oloroso Sherry NV SPAIN

Stunning oily, nutty richness with touches of black
olive and tomato. Dry but wickedly subtly fruity and
complete.

16.5

WHITE £5.99

Tesco Finest Gavi 2004 ITALY

Delightful creamy touch to apricot and citrus.
Outstanding.

Readers must trust this book in the face of mild or even
vociferous contradiction when one retailer or another, in the
shape of a counter assistant or supermarket employee,
declares that the prices are all wrong, or the wines do not exist,
or that 'being just a journalist, Martin Fluck don't know better
than me what should be on sale here.' Last year, 2004, was
better than most, I suppose, but I still got the odd letter or
e-mail from an outraged reader who, on the evidence of, say, a
£3.99 red at Somerfield turning out to boast a £4.99 price ticket
(like Mr Lowry of Sheffield), or a Tesco Californian Voignier not
costing £3.99 but the staff insisting it is £4.99 (like Mr Hoskins
of Banstead), wondered if I knew my coccyx from my ulna.
Some readers go further and tell me I am bonkers and that my
scoring system is up the creek because it is based on value for
money. Now I am not perfect, but do you imagine I write
about wine in the dark? Do you think I make the numbers up?
Is it remotely possible that I would allow to appear in print facts
I knew to be skew-whiff? No, sir/madam. No wine appears here
if it has not been checked with the retailer or retailers first, but
even I cannot prevent a wine selling out early in this book's life.

16.5

WHITE £9.99
AUSTRALIA

Tesco Finest Barossa Old Vines Sémillon 2003

Screwcap. Lean, oily, complex, stylish and a very neatly tailored wine.

16.5

RED £7.99
AUSTRALIA

Tesco Finest Howcroft Estate Reserve Cabernet/Merlot 2003

Screwcap. Delicious minty blackberries with really swinging tannins. Great style and individuality here from the Limestone Coast.

16.5

RED £4.99
ARGENTINA

Santa Julia Tempranillo 2004

Very smooth plums and blackberries with licorice. Also at Somerfield.

16.5

RED £2.86
CHILE

Tesco Chilean Red NV

Screwcap. Raunchy, crunchy, spicy, hugely mouth-filling bargain. Offers smoked plums, burned tannins and a hint of chocolate. Amazing length of flavour for a red so humbly priced.

16.5

RED £6.03
CHILE

Trio Shiraz/Cabernet Sauvignon/ Cabernet Franc NV

A superb classy, throaty red of mannered yet fruity roasted berries with even-flowing molten tannins.

16.5

RED £4.99
CHILE

Valdivieso Cabernet Sauvignon 2004
Screwcap. So soft it steals across the palate like a
velveteen slipper and than unleashes leather-soled
tannins which slap the tongue about nicely.

16.5

RED £4.99
CHILE

Valdivieso Merlot 2004
Screwcap. Slight bacon edge to the roasted berries
supported by gently incendiary tannins.

16.5

RED £4.99
CHILE

Valdivieso Cabernet Sauvignon 2003
Brilliant smoked berries and plums, hint of spiced
herb, excellent tannic oomph to the finish.

16

WHITE £4.98
ITALY

Inycon Chardonnay 2004
Hugely classy, well-textured under-ripe fruit of style,
charm and concentration. New World meets Old
stylistically, and the result is compelling.
Also at Morrison's.

16

WHITE £7.98
NEW ZEALAND

**Villa Maria Private Bin
Sauvignon Blanc 2004**
Screwcap. Simply wonderful complex pineapple/
gooseberry/lime/peach fruit. And it'll age
interestingly for 2–3 years.
Also at Asda, Budgens, Sainsbury, Somerfield.

16

RED £12.99
ITALY

Ascheri Barolo Sorano 1998
A real mean lean Barolo, barely alive when compared
with, say, a Pinotage or a Shiraz, but hugely
provocative if you enjoy a necrophiliac experience in
a wine glass.

16

WHITE £7.69
SOUTH AFRICA

**Boschendal Grande Cuvée
Sauvignon Blanc 2004**
Touch of grapefruit earthiness to the gooseberry is
entertaining without being brash.

16

RED £5.03
CHILE

Cono Sur Merlot 2003
Melts in the mouth like nutty chocolate. Oh my!
What a sinful experience!

16

RED £5.03
CHILE

Cono Sur Cabernet Sauvignon 2004
Very lively, dark cherry/plum/blackcurrant richness
with unguent tannins.

16

RED £5.49
CHILE

**Casillero del Diablo Concha y Toro
Cabernet Sauvignon 2003**
Chewy, rich, firm (yet yielding to the tannins on the
finish), this is a hugely well-tailored Cabernet.
Also at Asda, Sainsbury.

16 WHITE £5.03

Cono Sur Chardonnay 2003 CHILE
Plump, polished, very pretty melon fruit.

16 RED £5.03

Cono Sur Pinot Noir Reserve 2002 CHILE
A real Pinot: gamy, black cherryish, hint of tannins
to the classy finish.

16 RED £5.99

DFJ Touriga Franca/Touriga Nacional 2003 PORTUGAL
Ripe, but has savoury depth and tannic presence.

16 RED £4.99

Finest Pinotage Reserve 2003 SOUTH AFRICA
Very rich and generous, this wine's full of dry ripe
fruit, really expressive of old boots, leather belts and,
as such, wears well with casseroles.

16 RED £5.99

Finest Touriga Nacional 2003 PORTUGAL
Delicious plump cherries with earthy tannins. A
cracking red.

16 RED £4.99

Finest Aglianico Basilicata 2002 ITALY
Screwcap. Earthy, minerally fruit of great class and
volcanic clout.

WHITE £4.99

Finest Australian Reserve AUSTRALIA
Chardonnay 2004

Screwcap. I love its chutzpah. Dry peach and citrus,
elegant and finely tailored.

WHITE £4.99

Finest Sicilian Grillo 2003 ITALY

Stunning! Why can't all Tesco's Italian £5 and under
whites be this individual? This stylish? This dry yet
so stylishly tailored?

Additives in Wine (3)

The additive debate became heated last year as a result of
the discovery that flavorants were being introduced into
South African Sauvignon Blanc. The wines were destroyed,
however, before they could reach the consumer. Additives
can, though, make a wine more palatable. The Greeks bung
in resin, for example, and, to my palate at least, the results
are companionable. This is not always so with the most
widely employed additive of all: cork bark. No wine sealed
with cork can escape the effects of it, either in the form of
taint, a degree of oxidation, or tannin and acid dissipation.

In some wines, of course, these effects may, for a short
while, improve the palatability of the liquid. Grapes may be
grown. But wine is made. The human factor with all wine is
easily the most crucial. It towers above the nonsense of
terroir for example. Human manipulation in wine is
inevitable and makes the liquid what it is.

16

WHITE £6.99

H de l'Hospitalet White, Vin de Pays d'Oc 2003   FRANCE
Dry, slightly creamy lemon and melon with a hint of
raspberry.

16

RED SPARKLING £9.99

Hardy's Crest Sparkling Shiraz NV   AUSTRALIA
Fabulous spicy prunes and custard. Great with game
dishes.

16

WHITE SPARKLING £19.99

Jacquart Champagne NV   FRANCE
Very elegant – with that impish touch of
melon/raspberry-edged fruit to lift its finish.

16

WHITE £5.79

La Forêt Hilaire Entre-Deux-Mers 2003   FRANCE
Fine waxy fruit, very dry, extremely stylish in a very
old-fashioned way.

16

WHITE £5.99

Lindemans Bin 65 Chardonnay 2004   AUSTRALIA
Screwcap. The height of elegance and double-layered
rich yet neat fruit.
Also at Sainsbury.

16

ROSÉ £5.99

Montana East Coast Rosé 2004   NEW ZEALAND
Screwcap. One of the most attractively cherryish, dry,
pert, elegant rosés to pass these tired old lips all year.

16   RED £6.99
Premius Bordeaux Merlot/Cabernet 2002   FRANCE
A most agreeably gruff-voiced claret of depth,
breadth and rich tannicity.

16   WHITE £3.12
Tesco Moscatel de Valencia NV   SPAIN
Screwcap. One of the most deft pudding wines on
the planet. Has complex richness – not just honey
but a suggestion of peach – and with fresh fruit at
the end of a meal it's a treat.

16   FORTIFIED £5.94
Tesco Finest Special Reserve Port NV   PORTUGAL
Bargain richness here which manages that trick, for
an astonishingly low sum, to offer sweet romance
with hard, sexy tannins (soft and short-lived, but at
least they exist).

16   RED £4.48
Tesco Finest Chilean Merlot 2004   CHILE
Screwcap. Scrumptious cocoa-edged tannins, dry,
firmly allied to cherry fruit. The balance is just great.
A hugely generous quaffing specimen.

16   RED £4.99
Tesco Finest Australian Reserve Merlot 2004   AUSTRALIA
Screwcap. Sheer chunky plums, pears, blackberries
and ripe tannins. A terrific mouthful of sunshine.

16

Tesco Finest St-Emilion 2003 FRANCE

So good, it can compete with Aussie Cabs, Merlots
and even a few Shirazes. Has presence, vivaciousness,
and real tannic oomph.

16

WHITE SPARKLING £13.99

Tesco Blanc de Noirs Champagne NV FRANCE

This is one of the most complete of supermarket
own-label champagnes – a wild raspberry undertone
mingles with a subtle citrussiness.

16

WHITE £4.99

Tesco Finest Chilean Sauvignon Blanc 2004 CHILE

Screwcap. Light dusting of chalky gooseberry to dry
citrus. Very firm and rich.

16

WHITE £7.99

Tesco Finest Kenton Valley Estate AUSTRALIA
Reserve Sauvignon Blanc 2004

Screwcap. Rich, Thai-food friendly fruit of great
charm and persistence.

16

WHITE £6.99

Tesco Finest Pinot Grigio 2004 ITALY

Pinot Grigio bland? Not this dry, elegant specimen.
Try it and swallow your prejudice.

16

WHITE £4.99

Tesco Finest South African   SOUTH AFRICA
Chenin Blanc 2004
Demure, elegant, simple, unpretentiously friendly.

16

WHITE £9.99

Tesco Finest Chablis Premier Cru 2001   FRANCE
A real classy white Burgundy of length and savour.
Starts lean and crisp and expands on the palate to
reveal peach and melon.

16

WHITE £18.99

Tesco Finest Meursault 2001   FRANCE
Wow! A real mature white Burgundy with gamy
citrus and earthy minerals with a sleek wood
coating.

16

WHITE £5.99

Tesco Finest Great Southern Riesling 2003   AUSTRALIA
18 points in 2009–10. Screwcap. Creamy, strawberry-
edged citrus with a touch of zesty melon. Will go
funkier and more sensual as it matures in bottle.
Shows just what a great place to grow grapes is
Mount Barker in Western Australia.

16

WHITE £6.99

Tesco Finest Alsace Gewürztraminer 2003   FRANCE
Superb with Thai fish cakes, Peking duck, and a blue
mood – it raises spirits as it enhances oriental
tucker. A spicy, warm, utterly delicious white wine.

16

RED **£4.99**

Tesco Finest Argentinian Malbec Reserve 2004 ARGENTINA
Screwcap. A big juicy casserole red on one hand.
A glugging masterpiece on the other (if you like
tannins you can lick off a spoon).

16

WHITE **£2.99**

Tesco Australian Colombard NV AUSTRALIA
Screwcap. What a stunning, smoky, waxy white wine
of class, elegance and vigour.

16

WHITE **£2.86**

Tesco Chilean White NV CHILE
Screwcap. Wonderful rich melon. Hint of mango to
the citrus finish. Soft, hugely gluggable.

16

RED **£2.99**

Tesco Chilean Cabernet Sauvignon NV CHILE
Screwcap. Superb soft, plump pillows of plummy
ripeness folded around toasty tannins.

16

RED **£2.99**

Tesco Chilean Merlot NV CHILE
Screwcap. Delightfully classy, incisive, no-nonsense
leathery plums with cocoa-edged tannins.

16

WHITE **£3.99**

Tesco Grecanico Chardonnay 2003 ITALY
Interesting bony fruit, hint of wax, touch of subtle
lanolin. Dry but perky.

16

RED £3.99

Tesco Nero d'Avola/Sangiovese Sicilia 2003 ITALY
Screwcap. Sticky cherries with ripe plums and
roasted tannins.

16

WHITE (3 litre box) £18.96

Tesco Finest Australian Chardonnay NV AUSTRALIA
Very elegant, well-textured fruit, hint of oil to it as it
finishes. Very stylish and firmly modulated.

16

RED £2.58

FRANCE

Tesco Claret NV
Good, earthy berries and fine tannins make this a
mouthful of real claret. Dry, a touch austere, and it
takes no prisoners, but a competitively drinkable
Bordeaux under three quid is surely a miracle.

16

RED £9.99

AUSTRALIA

Tim Adams Shiraz 2003
Screwcap. Dark chocolate berries with cherries and
plums mitigated by chewy tannins.

Chardonnay is a village in Burgundy, and for many years it
was the white wines from that region which were
considered the exemplary expression of the grape. But
whilst a few white Burgundies are marvellous (though often
hugely expensive), the grape can express itself more fully
elsewhere – in Australia, New Zealand, South Africa, Chile,
California and a few other hot spots.

16

WHITE £4.99
CHILE

Valdivieso Chardonnay 2004
Elegant, dry, hint of peach to the citrus.

16

RED £4.99
CHILE

Valdivieso Merlot 2003
Mouth-filling yet slow-to-evolve. Most charming
relaxed style of burned berries and chewy tannins.

16

WHITE SPARKLING £3.68
SPAIN

Tesco Brut Cava NV
A bargain dry bubbly. Real class for the dosh.

16

FORTIFIED £10.00
PORTUGAL

Croft Indulgence Port NV
Rich, plummy, chocolate-edged fruit with tannins to
raise it above the general run of sloppy sweetness
which cheap ports can exhibit.

16

RED £4.99
ARGENTINA

Argento Malbec 2004
Screwcap. A very cool, classy customer. Supremely
confident yet not arrogant. Offers lightly burned
blackberries and smooth tannins.
Also at Budgens, Majestic, Sainsbury.

16

WHITE £6.48
NEW ZEALAND

**Montana Marlborough
Sauvignon Blanc 2004**
Screwcap. Bargain gooseberry fruit. Real finesse here.
Also at Budgens, Majestic, Threshers.

OTHER WINES 15.5 AND UNDER

15.5

RED £9.99
Amarone della Valpolicella 'Rocca Alata' 2001   ITALY

WHITE £5.99
Brown Brothers Moscato 2004   AUSTRALIA

WHITE £4.97
Brown Brothers Dry Muscat NV   AUSTRALIA
Screwcap.

RED £12.99
Castillo de San Lorenzo Rioja Reserva 1999   SPAIN

WHITE £7.03
Chapel Hill Unwooded Chardonnay 2004   AUSTRALIA
Screwcap.

RED £9.99
Chapel Hill Cabernet Sauvignon 2001   AUSTRALIA

WHITE £4.99
Da Luca Grillo Chardonnay NV   ITALY

WHITE £4.53
Frontera Chardonnay 2004   CHILE
Screwcap.

WHITE £4.99
Finest Australian Sauvignon Blanc 2004   AUSTRALIA
Screwcap.

RED £7.99
Finest Viña Mara Rioja Reserva 2001   SPAIN

RED £5.99

Finest Viña Mara Gran Reserva Rioja 1998 SPAIN

RED £4.99

Finest Argentinian Malbec Reserve 2003 ARGENTINA

WHITE £4.99

Finest Californian Chardonnay Reserve 2003 USA
Screwcap.

RED £4.99

Leopards Leap Lookout Red 2003 SOUTH AFRICA
Screwcap.

RED £5.99

Leopards Leap Cabernet Sauvignon/ SOUTH AFRICA
Merlot 2003

RED £4.99

Tesco Viña Mara Rioja Crianza 1999 SPAIN

WHITE (3 litre box) £21.99

Tesco New Zealand Marlborough NEW ZEALAND
Sauvignon Blanc

RED £7.99

Tesco Finest Howcroft Estate Reserve AUSTRALIA
Merlot 2004
Screwcap.

WHITE £2.98

Tesco Chilean Sauvignon Blanc NV CHILE
Screwcap.

WHITE £2.86

Tesco Californian Dry White NV   USA
Screwcap.

WHITE £3.48

Tesco Californian Chardonnay NV   USA
Screwcap.

RED £2.86

Tesco Californian Red NV   USA
Screwcap.

RED £4.99

Tesco Finest Reserve Californian Merlot 2003   USA
Screwcap.

FORTIFIED £10.99

Tesco Finest 10-year-old Tawny Port NV   PORTUGAL

FORTIFIED £8.44

Tesco Finest Madeira NV   PORTUGAL

WHITE £6.99

Thandi Chardonnay 2004   SOUTH AFRICA

WHITE £5.99

Veo Grande Chardonnay/Viognier NV   CHILE

WHITE £6.99

Wolf Blass Yellow Label Chardonnay 2004   AUSTRALIA
Screwcap. Also at Budgens.

RED £7.98
Wolf Blass Yellow Label   AUSTRALIA
Cabernet Sauvignon 2003
Also at Somerfield.

WHITE £6.99
Nobilo Marlborough   NEW ZEALAND
Sauvignon Blanc 2004
Screwcap. Also at Somerfield, Threshers.

15

WHITE £7.99
Blason de Bourgogne St-Véran 2003   FRANCE

RED £5.99
Brown Brothers Cienna 2004   AUSTRALIA

RED £5.99
Coteau Brûlé Cairanne,   FRANCE
Côtes du Rhône-Villages 2003

RED £9.99
Château Martin Graves 2001   FRANCE

RED £6.49
Château La Forêt St-Hilaire Bordeaux 2002   FRANCE

RED £4.99
Douglas Green Merlot 2003   SOUTH AFRICA

WHITE £4.99
Finest Chilean Chardonnay Reserve 2003   CHILE
Screwcap.

RED £4.99

Finest Vintage Claret 2002 FRANCE

RED £6.99

Graham Beck Pinotage 2003 SOUTH AFRICA

WHITE £5.56

Jacob's Creek Dry Riesling 2003 AUSTRALIA
Screwcap. Also at Sainsbury, Waitrose.

WHITE £4.99

Leopards Leap Lookout White 2003 SOUTH AFRICA
Screwcap.

WHITE £5.99

La Cité de Foncalieu Grande Réserve FRANCE
Chardonnay 2003

RED £5.99

Luis Felipe Edwards Carmenere 2003 CHILE

RED £5.99

Luis Felipe Edwards Cabernet Sauvignon 2003 CHILE

WHITE £5.99

McGuigan Gold Chardonnay 2004 AUSTRALIA
Screwcap.

WHITE £5.49

Oxford Landing Sauvignon Blanc 2004 AUSTRALIA
Screwcap. Also at Budgens, Sainsbury.

RED £10.29

Penfolds Bin 28 Kalimna Shiraz 2001 AUSTRALIA

WHITE £6.99	
Ravenswood Vintners Blend Chardonnay 2003	USA

RED £7.52	
Rosemount Estate Shiraz 2003	AUSTRALIA

RED £7.99	
St Hallett Faith Shiraz 2003	AUSTRALIA
Screwcap.	

WHITE £4.38	
Torres Viña Sol 2004	SPAIN
Screwcap. Also at Budgens.	

WHITE SPARKLING £2.98	
Tesco Moscato Spumante NV	ITALY

The seductiveness created by the many wine brands on offer, manufactured by colossal wine and spirit combines, is that it makes the wine buyer's job easier. The planet's largest booze conglomerate, Constellation, which has 37 wineries worldwide including Ravenswood, Hardy's, Banrock, Stowells, Nobilo, Paul Masson and Echo Falls (not to mention Blackthorn cider, Stone's Ginger Wine and Babycham), last year gobbled up the Robert Mondavi wine empire of California (and was happy to pay $1.3-billion for it). The only bulwark against such giant wine corporations dominating the wine market and making redundant both skilled wine buyers and enquiring wine critics are brands developed by the supermarkets and high street wine chains in concert with their suppliers (which one hopes are not owned by one or other of those giant wine corps).

RED £3.99
Tesco Californian Cabernet Sauvignon NV USA
Screwcap.

RED £3.99
Tesco Argentinian Shiraz NV ARGENTINA
Screwcap.

FORTIFIED £4.99
Tesco Finest Fino NV SPAIN

WHITE £5.99
Tesco Finest Vouvray Demi-Sec 2003 FRANCE

WHITE (half bottle) £11.99
Tesco Finest Sauternes 2002 FRANCE

FORTIFIED £4.99
Tesco Finest Manzanilla Sherry NV SPAIN

RED £9.99
Tesco's Finest Marlborough NEW ZEALAND
Pinot Noir 2003

WHITE £2.97
Tesco Chilean Chardonnay NV CHILE

WHITE £3.29
Tesco South African Chenin NV SOUTH AFRICA
Screwcap.

WHITE £4.49
NXG Australian Sémillon/Chardonnay 2003 AUSTRALIA

WHITE £4.99

Tesco Finest Chilean Chardonnay Reserve 2004   CHILE

RED £4.99

Trulli Zinfandel 2003   ITALY

RED £2.99

Tesco Sicilian Red 2003   ITALY

RED £3.99

Tesco Claret Reserve 2002   FRANCE
Screwcap.

RED £5.99

**Wyndham Estate Bin 444 Cabernet
Sauvignon 2003**   AUSTRALIA

RED £6.99

Wyndham Estate Bin 555 Shiraz 2002   AUSTRALIA

WHITE SPARKLING £7.99

**Jacob's Creek Sparkling Chardonnay/
Pinot Noir Brut Cuvée NV**   AUSTRALIA
Also at Asda, Sainsbury, Waitrose.

RED £6.98

Ravenswood Vintners Blend Zinfandel 2002   USA
Also at Booths, Budgens, Waitrose.

WHITE £5.49

Oxford Landing Chardonnay 2004   AUSTRALIA
Screwcap. Also at Budgens, Sainsbury.

14.5

ROSÉ £5.98

Fetzer Syrah Rosé 2003 USA
Screwcap.

WHITE £7.99

Finest Chablis 2002 FRANCE

WHITE £4.99

Finest Picpoul de Pinet 2003 FRANCE
Screwcap.

WHITE £3.68

Finest Soave Classico 2004 ITALY

RED £6.98

Gallo Turning Leaf Zinfandel 2002 USA
Screwcap.

RED £4.99

Kumala Cabernet Sauvignon/Shiraz 2004 SOUTH AFRICA
Also at Sainsbury.

ROSÉ £4.48

Kumala Rosé 2004 SOUTH AFRICA

RED £6.49

McWilliams Hanwood Estate Shiraz 2003 AUSTRALIA
Also at Budgens.

WHITE SPARKLING £19.99

Paul Boutet Champagne NV FRANCE

RED £15.03

Penfolds Bin 389 Cabernet/Shiraz 2001 AUSTRALIA

RED £5.03

Peter Lehmann Grenache 2002   AUSTRALIA
Screwcap. Also at Morrison's.

RED £4.99

Tesco Finest Argentinian Shiraz Reserve 2004 ARGENTINA
Screwcap.

RED £4.99

Tesco Finest Australian   AUSTRALIA
Cabernet Sauvignon 2003
Screwcap.

RED £9.99

Tesco Finest Barossa Old Vines Shiraz 2003   AUSTRALIA
Screwcap.

WHITE £4.99

Tesco Organic Australian Chardonnay 2004   AUSTRALIA
Screwcap.

WHITE £4.49

Tesco New Zealand Dry White NV   NEW ZEALAND
Screwcap.

WHITE £3.99

Tesco Australian Sémillon/Chardonnay NV   AUSTRALIA
Screwcap.

WHITE SPARKLING £5.93

Tesco Finest Vintage Cava 2000   SPAIN

RED £3.99
Tesco Californian Merlot NV   USA
Screwcap.

RED £3.48
Tesco Chilean Carmenere NV   CHILE
Screwcap.

WHITE SPARKLING £5.49
Tesco Cava Reserve NV   SPAIN

ROSÉ SPARKLING £3.82
Tesco Rosé Cava NV   SPAIN

FORTIFIED £6.57
Tesco LBV Port 1998   PORTUGAL

WHITE (3 litre box) £9.87
Tesco Soave NV   ITALY

WHITE £3.99
Veo Chardonnay 2003   CHILE

RED £5.49
Yalumba Oxford Landing Shiraz 2002   AUSTRALIA
Screwcap.

WHITE SPARKLING £4.99
The Lakes Reserve Brut NV   AUSTRALIA

WHITE £6.49
Wolf Blass Red Label Chardonnay/   AUSTRALIA
Sémillon 2004
Screwcap. Also at Budgens.

14

ROSÉ £4.98

Arniston Bay Rosé 2004   SOUTH AFRICA

RED £5.99

Blossom Hill Reserve Cabernet Sauvignon 2002   USA

RED £9.99

Badia a Coltibuono Chianti Classico 2002   ITALY

WHITE SPARKLING £8.99

Blason de Bourgogne Crémant de   FRANCE
Bourgogne NV

RED £4.79

Banrock Station Shiraz/Mataro 2003   AUSTRALIA

WHITE £5.87

Cottesbrook Sauvignon Blanc 2004   NEW ZEALAND
Screwcap.

RED £19.99

Errazuriz Estate Don Maximiano Founders   CHILE
Reserve 2000

RED £5.49

Freixenet Ash Tree Estate Monastrell 2003   SPAIN

WHITE £6.49

Faustion V White Rioja NV   SPAIN

WHITE £5.99

Finest Alsace Riesling 2003   FRANCE

WHITE £4.99
Finest Californian Pinot Grigio Reserve 2003 USA
Screwcap.

RED £4.79
Hardy's Voyage Cabernet Sauvignon/ AUSTRALIA
Petit Verdot/Ruby Cabernet 2003
Screwcap. Also at Waitrose.

WHITE £4.79
Hardy's Voyage Colombard/Verdelho/ AUSTRALIA
Chenin Blanc 2004

RED £3.99
Goiya DM Shiraz/Pinotage 2004 SOUTH AFRICA

WHITE £3.99
Goiya Kgeisje Sauvignon/ SOUTH AFRICA
Chardonnay 2004

WHITE £4.99
Glen Ellen Chardonnay 2002 USA

WHITE £6.99
Giesen Marlborough NEW ZEALAND
Sauvignon Blanc 2004
Screwcap.

WHITE £5.99
Kumala Reserve Sauvignon Blanc 2004 SOUTH AFRICA
Screwcap.

WHITE £4.48
Kumala Chardonnay/Sémillon 2004 SOUTH AFRICA

Louis Jadot Pouilly-Fuissé 2002

WHITE £10.99
FRANCE

Montana Marlborough Riesling 2003

WHITE £5.99
NEW ZEALAND

Matua Valley Sauvignon Blanc 2004
Screwcap.

WHITE £6.99
NEW ZEALAND

Montana Reserve Merlot 2003

RED £8.99
NEW ZEALAND

Nicolas Feuillatte Champagne 1997

WHITE SPARKLING £19.99
FRANCE

**Oxford Landing Cabernet Sauvignon/
Shiraz 2002**
Screwcap.

RED £5.49
AUSTRALIA

**Penfolds Koonunga Hill Shiraz/
Cabernet 2002**

RED £6.99
AUSTRALIA

Penfolds Grange 1998

RED £109.99
AUSTRALIA

St Hallett Old Block Shiraz 2001

RED £16.99
AUSTRALIA

Torres Viña Esmeralda 2004
Screwcap.

WHITE £5.49
SPAIN

WHITE £3.29
Tesco South African Colombard/ SOUTH AFRICA
Sauvignon NV
Screwcap.

WHITE (3 litre box) £10.99
Tesco Muscadet NV FRANCE

WHITE £4.99
Tesco Finest Reserve Californian Viognier 2003 USA
Screwcap.

WHITE SPARKLING £14.79
Tesco Champagne Premier Cru NV FRANCE

WHITE SPARKLING £16.94
Tesco Finest Vintage Champagne 2000 FRANCE

RED £7.99
Tesco Finest Howcroft Estate Reserve AUSTRALIA
Shiraz 2003
Screwcap.

RED £5.49
Tesco Finest Fitou Varon de la Tour 2003 FRANCE

RED £3.78
Tesco Californian Zinfandel NV USA
Screwcap.

RED £3.78
Tesco Australian Shiraz/ AUSTRALIA
Cabernet Sauvignon NV
Screwcap.

Tesco Australian Cabernet/Merlot NV
Screwcap.

RED £3.99
AUSTRALIA

Tesco Organic Red NV
Screwcap.

RED £4.99
AUSTRALIA

Tesco Californian Viognier NV
Screwcap.

WHITE £3.99
USA

Tesco Australian Dry White NV
Screwcap.

WHITE £2.80
AUSTRALIA

Tesco Australian Chardonnay NV
Screwcap.

WHITE £3.48
AUSTRALIA

Tesco Argentinian Bonarda NV
Screwcap.

RED £3.99
ARGENTINA

Tesco Argentinian Malbec 2003
Screwcap.

RED £3.99
ARGENTINA

Tesco Bergerac Rouge NV

RED £3.99
FRANCE

Tesco Côtes du Rhône-Villages 2002

RED £3.98
FRANCE

RED **£3.27**

Tesco Marqués de Chive NV   SPAIN

FORTIFIED **£13.99**

Tesco Vintage Port 1995   PORTUGAL

WHITE **£4.29**

Tesco Premières Côtes de Bordeaux NV   FRANCE

WHITE **£4.79**

Van Loveren Sauvignon Blanc 2004   SOUTH AFRICA

RED **£3.99**

Veo Cabernet/Merlot 2003   CHILE

WHITE **£4.99**

Yali Sauvignon Blanc Reserve 2004   CHILE

WHITE SPARKLING **£5.99**

**Hardy's Stamp of Australia Sparkling
Pinot Noir/Chardonnay Brut NV**   AUSTRALIA
Also at Asda, Sainsbury, Somerfield.

THRESHERS

Enjoyment Hall,
Bessemer Road,
Welwyn Garden City,
Hertfordshire AL7 1BL

Tel: (01707) 387200
Fax: (01707) 387416

For tasting notes of Threshers' wines scoring less
than 16 points, and ratings of wines less than
14 points, visit www.superplonk.com

IMPORTANT NOTE RE THRESHERS' PRICING

Unique amongst retailers in this book, this one
offers permanent discounts on all the wines in all its
stores. If you buy two bottles of a wine you get a
third free. There are, as a result, two prices given for
each wine below: the price for a single bottle, and
the price per bottle when you acquire three bottles
of the same wine yet only pay for two. If you wanted
three bottles of different wines, you would get the
cheapest bottle free. Unless otherwise stated, each
wine is rated on its single bottle price.

17.5   WHITE £7.99 (3 x £5.33)
Cazal Viel Viognier Grande Réserve 2004   FRANCE
Buttery apricot, layered pear and citrus – a white
wine of class and uncluttered finesse.

17.5   WHITE £5.99 (3 x £3.99)
Errazuriz Estate Unoaked Chardonnay 2004   CHILE
Big, rich and creamy, wonderful with a seafood salad.
This is an oily, complete, sublimely unhurried wine
of such an absurd price that one rubs one's eyes in
disbelief. If you do get red-eyed from drinking this
wine, now you know why.

17.5   RED £8.99 (3 x £5.99)
Flinders McLaren Vale Terra Nova   AUSTRALIA
Grenache/Shiraz/Viognier 2003
Screwcap. Stunning! How can this opulent wine be
reduced to £5.99!? It's wonderfully loquacious (it
talks sense, what's more), fresh, unpretentious-yet-
serious, and warm-hearted. It has fresh cherries and
berries, couth tannins, and a fine feel to the texture.

17.5   RED £6.99 (3 x £4.66)
Zenato Valpolicella Classico Superiore 2001   ITALY
Bewilderingly delicious roasted plums, grilled nuts,
licorice – and fresh-cut tannins. It is a superb food
wine: risottos, pastas, complex salads with pine nuts
and chicken bits, and will even take to a little gentle
spicing.

17

RED £6.99 (3 x £4.66)

Casillero del Diablo Concha y Toro   CHILE
Carmenere 2003

Simply stupendous charred berries with chocolate
and roasted almonds. It has no sense of urgency. It
simply flops all over the taste-buds and makes itself
deliciously at home.

17

WHITE £5.99 (3 x £3.99)

Errazuriz Estate Sauvignon Blanc 2004   CHILE

A lovely textured rich gooseberry/melon wine. It
competes with Sauvignons costing a great deal more.
Also at E-tailers (Everywine), Oddbins.

17

RED £5.99 (3 x £3.99)

Errazuriz Estate Merlot 2003   CHILE

Melted chocolate dripped over grilled plums.
Also at E-tailers (Everywine), Oddbins, Sainsbury,
Tesco.

17

WHITE £8.99 (3 x £5.99)

Radcliffes Gewürztraminer 2003   FRANCE

Utterly captivating, subtly spicy, beautifully unfussy,
multi-layered, very classy and superbly textured.

17

RED £5.99 (3 x £3.99)

Trivento Shiraz/Malbec Reserve 2004   ARGENTINA

Ripely incisive, rich and very deep, hugely soft
yet characterful, impressively textured (like
taffeta).

17

WHITE £8.99 (3 x £5.99)

Villa Maria Marlborough Sauvignon   NEW ZEALAND
Blanc 2004

Screwcap. Wonderful! One of the classiest Sauvignon Blancs on the planet. It'll age with distinction over a few years and not get crusty or bad tempered.

16.5

WHITE £8.99 (3 x £5.99)

Brampton Estate Sauvignon   SOUTH AFRICA
Blanc 2004

Screwcap. Beautiful dry, very classy, very purposeful, demurely rich.

How is it possible for a wine financially to accommodate all the parties concerned in the growing, making, bottling, transportation and marketing of it and yet be priced at an everyday undiscounted £2.99? A £2.99 bottle yields six glasses of wine at just under 50p a glass. Of that the voracious Exchequer demands at least 27p (duty and VAT), the bottling and shipping costs are around 5p, the production costs and wine producers' profit is 7p, leaving the retailer with 11p income from which to fund sales costs, wine department and marketing overheads, and to make a profit. How much profit? No retailer will tell me.

16.5   RED £10.99 (3 x £7.33)

Cordier Collection Privée 2001   FRANCE

A truly sensual claret with throat-clogging fruit of
purity and roasted richness.

16.5   RED £4.99 (3 x £3.33)

Casillero del Diablo Concha y Toro   CHILE
Carmenere 2004

Simply stunningly deft berries and softly savoury
tannins. If you can say that quickly and with utter
fluency after a bottle of this wine, congratulations.
Also at Majestic, Sainsbury, Tesco.

16.5   WHITE £4.99 (3 x £3.33)

Casillero del Diablo Concha y Toro   CHILE
Sauvignon Blanc 2004

A crisp classic Sauvignon Blanc of length and
crunchy concentration.
Also at Asda, Majestic, Oddbins, Somerfield, Tesco.

16.5   RED £9.99 (3 x £6.66)

Errazuriz Estate Max Reserva Shiraz 2002   CHILE

Catering chocolate softened with milk, slightly
burned with the skin on top! Wow!

16.5   WHITE £8.49 (3 x £5.66)

Huntaway Marlborough   NEW ZEALAND
Sauvignon Blanc 2004

Screwcap. Adds to the conventional gooseberry
recipe a touch of plump apricot.

16.5   RED £6.99 (3 x £4.66)

La Forge Syrah 2003   FRANCE

Sweet plums balanced by cocoa tannins.
Also at Somerfield.

16.5   WHITE £6.99 (3 x £4.66)

McWilliams Hanwood Estate   AUSTRALIA
Chardonnay 2003

Unites a delicious ripe citricity with slightly smoky
apricot and melon.
Also at Budgens.

16.5   RED £11.99 (3 x £7.99)

Monteguelfo Chianti Classico Reserva 2003   ITALY

Tannins, hint of tobacco, beautifully structured.

16.5   RED £7.99 (3 x £5.33)

Penfolds Winemakers Shiraz/   AUSTRALIA
Cabernet 2004

A classic Aussie blend of grapes providing superbly
well-textured depth and assured delivery. Smooth as
the inside of a Gucci slipper.

16.5   WHITE £7.99 (3 x £5.33)

Penfolds Winemakers Chardonnay 2003   AUSTRALIA

Quite gorgeously dry yet plumply self-satisfied
apricot, melon, and pineapple/citrus
complexities.

16.5   WHITE £4.99 (3 x £3.33)

Casillero del Diablo Concha y Toro   CHILE
Chardonnay 2004

Delicious, delicate, elegant. Has a subdued richness
giving this vintage a distinctive classiness.
Also at Asda, Majestic, Oddbins.

16.5   RED £3.49 (3 x £2.33)

Vineyard X Garnacha 2003   SPAIN

At £2.33 it has to be one of the red wines of the
year. Fantastic plummy richness with tannins.
Red wine for peanuts! The 2004 vintage of this
absurdly inexpensive red, tasted literally as this
book waited to go to the printer, rates 16. It has
more spice but it is a touch less tannically
concentrated.

16   RED £5.99 (3 x £3.99)

Cono Sur Pinot Noir 2004   CHILE

Stunningly complete – the tobacco-edged, gamy
cherries linger for ages in the throat.
Also at Majestic, Somerfield, Waitrose.

16   WHITE £7.99 (3 x £5.33)

Anakena Viognier Reserve 2004   CHILE

Very attractively textured with a peachy/apricot
richness the Viognier grape bequeaths to wine (or
does so in good examples).

Tim Dowling, in the *Guardian* of 3 September 2004, reported that
there 'was now a genetic marker for gullibility...they can find out
exactly how gullible you are just by testing...your spit.' Why is it that
spitting and gullibility go together? Come with me to a wine tasting
sometime, Tim, and you'll see gullible folk spitting all over the place.
No analysis of saliva is necessary to see how fantastically suggestible
these people are. Let me give you an example. At a recent tasting of
wines from Spain I was given the opportunity to taste and
expectorate two red wines which together beautifully illustrate the
two dimensions of the gullibility to which wine drinkers are prone.
The first wine was Vega Sicilia Unico 1987. This is a wine from Spain's
most legendary estate. Collectors compete at auctions to acquire
older vintages. The specimen I tasted was of the 1987 vintage and it's
on sale at a few Waitrose branches for £135 the bottle. God, what a
ghastly wine it is. I was grateful the spittoon was so close. The liquid
was stewed and sere, brittle and unlovely; in short, a joke of a wine
outrageously priced. And then there was Vineyard X Garnacha 2003
(from Threshers): brash, modern, unpretentiously plummy and
savoury, alive and kicking, and offering a deep mouthful of rustic yet
polished fruit with firm, gently yielding tannins. It is a terrific little
wine. How much is it? Unbelievably, you can acquire 58 bottles of it
for the same price as one bottle of the dotty Vega Sicilia (to save you
the sweat of working it out, that equals £2.33). Now being a
generous fellow I awarded the first wine 10 points out of 20. I
should, thinking about it now, have given it 5. Vineyard X rates
16.5 points. I have no doubt that Waitrose has customers who
cheerfully fork out £135 for the Vega Sicilia and Threshers has
customers who will turn up their noses at a Spanish red for £2.33.
Saliva testing? Who needs it? Let me know if you want to come to a
wine tasting, Tim, and I'll sort something out. Don't forget to bring a
mac. Some tasters, especially the gullible ones, are not just wayward
in their judgements but equally hit and miss around a spittoon.

16

RED £8.99 (3 x £5.99)

Brampton Estate Shiraz/ NEW ZEALAND
Viognier 2003
Screwcap. Juicy yet has face-and-flavour-saving,
genteel, svelte tannins.

16

WHITE £5.99 (3 x £3.99)

Cono Sur Viognier 2004 CHILE
Unfussy apricot with a hint of macadamia nut.
Delicious? That's an understatement.
Also at Majestic, Somerfield, Waitrose.

16

RED £6.99 (3 x £4.66)

Flinders Realm Shiraz 2002 AUSTRALIA
Screwcap. Mightily jammy but well-balanced tannins
even out its temperament and the result is superior
quaffing.

16

WHITE £5.49 (3 x £3.66)

Flinders Realm Verdelho/Chardonnay 2004 AUSTRALIA
Screwcap. Lovely ripe edge to spicy peach. Would be
great with Thai food.

16

WHITE £6.99 (3 x £4.66)

Flinders Realm Chardonnay 2004 AUSTRALIA
Screwcap. Layers of citrus, pear and pineapple –
tangy and bright.

16

WHITE £6.99 (3 x £4.66)

Hidden Hill Chardonnay/Viognier, FRANCE
Vin de Pays d'Oc 2004
Screwcap. Hint of grilled nut to the melon/lemon
fruit. Excellent style here.

16

RED £5.99 (3 x £3.99)

La Riada Old Vines Garnacha 2004 SPAIN
Fresh and very perky, plummy yet not imbalanced or
flashy.

16

ROSÉ SPARKLING £8.99 (3 x £5.99)

Lindauer Rosé NV NEW ZEALAND
Lovely dry raspberry edge to the crisp fruit.

16

WHITE £7.49 (3 x £4.99)

Montana Marlborough Sauvignon NEW ZEALAND
Blanc 2004
Screwcap. Bargain gooseberry fruit. Real finesse here.
Also at Budgens, Majestic, Tesco.

16

WHITE £9.49 (3 x £6.33)

Montana Reserve East Coast NEW ZEALAND
Gewürztraminer 2004
Has that impish touch of ripe lychee controlled by
dry peach. A terrific aperitif.

16

RED £9.99 (3 x £6.66)

Monteguelfo Chianti Classico 2003 ITALY
Earthy yet full of plummy richness and depth.

16

RED £12.99 (3 x £8.66)

Monteguelfo Chianti Classico Reserva 2001   ITALY

Lovely mature, tightly focussed, rich, classy.

16

RED £7.99 (3 x £5.33)

Nobilo East Coast Merlot 2003   NEW ZEALAND

Screwcap. Terrific curry red – rated on that basis and
at £5.33 only (otherwise 14 points).

16

WHITE £4.99 (3 x £3.33)

Origin Chardonnay 2004   ARGENTINA

Screwcap. Smoky, ripe, hugely quaffable.

16

ROSÉ £4.99 (3 x £3.33)

Origin Garnacha Rosé 2004   SPAIN

Screwcap. A superb cherry-rich rosé of real class and
style. Dry, yet wonderfully refreshing. Rated on its
£3.33 price.

16

WHITE £4.99 (3 x £3.33)

Origin Chenin/Chardonnay 2004   ARGENTINA

Screwcap. Most unusual grapefruit/citrus edge to the
melon fruit. Delicious. Rated on its £3.33 price.

16

RED £3.99 (3 x £2.66)

Riverview Merlot/Cabernet Sauvignon 2001   HUNGARY

Hint of green pepper to the ripe blackberries, warm
tannins, and it's also handsomely textured. A
stunning 16-point mouthful for a modest sum (rated
at £2.66).

16

WHITE £5.99 (3 x £3.99)

Radcliffes Muscadet Sur Lie 2004　　　FRANCE

Wow! A real old-style Muscadet: clean and fresh, with
some modernist, very subtle funky touches. Has
Muscadet caught up with the Third Millennium?

16

WHITE £11.99 (3 x £7.99)

Sacred Hill Marlborough Sauvignon　　NEW ZEALAND
Blanc 2004

Screwcap. Very elegant citrus with a hint of dry
peach.

16

WHITE £6.99 (3 x £4.66)

Saints Marlborough Sauvignon　　　NEW ZEALAND
Blanc 2004

Screwcap. Classic. Extruded gooseberry – well, you'd
expect that – with fine lemon. Rated at £4.66, this
wine would notch up a further half a point.

16

RED £5.99 (3 x £3.99)

35 South Cabernet Sauvignon 2004　　　CHILE

That lovely fresh coal undertone. Odd? Delicious
though.
Also at Asda (15.5 in 3 litre box).

16

RED £7.49 (3 x £4.99)

Vereto Salice Salentino 2001　　　ITALY

Remarkably characterful, rugged-yet-lithe fruit with
grilled tannins on the finish.

OTHER WINES 15.5 AND UNDER

15.5 RED £6.99 (3 x £4.66)
Campo Viejo Tempranillo NV SPAIN

WHITE £4.99 (3 x £3.33)
Flinders Realm Colombard/ AUSTRALIA
Chardonnay 2004
Screwcap.

WHITE £7.99 (3 x £5.33)
Nobilo Marlborough Sauvignon NEW ZEALAND
Blanc 2004
Screwcap. Also at Somerfield, Tesco.

15 WHITE SPARKLING £22.49 (3 x £14.99)
Louis de Brissar Brut Champagne NV FRANCE

ROSÉ £5.99 (3 x £3.99)
Masterpeace Sangiovese/Shiraz Rosé 2004 AUSTRALIA

RED £9.99 (3 x £6.66)
Montana Reserve Pinot Noir 2003 NEW ZEALAND
Also at Majestic, Oddbins.

WHITE £7.99 (3 x £5.33)
Terrunyo Sauvignon Blanc 2004 CHILE

WHITE £5.99 (3 x £3.99)
Verdicchio dei Castelli di Jesi Classico 2004 ITALY

14.5 WHITE £6.99 (3 x £4.66)
Radcliffes Haut Poitou Sauvignon FRANCE
Blanc 2004

14

RED £6.49 (3 x £4.33)

Anakena Merlot Reserve 2003   CHILE

RED £7.99 (3 x £5.33)

Louis Jadot Beaujolais 2004   FRANCE

WHITE £5.99 (3 x £3.99)

35 South Sauvignon Blanc 2004   CHILE

WHITE £6.99 (3 x £4.66)

Vidal East Coast Sauvignon Blanc 2003   NEW ZEALAND
Screwcap.

WAITROSE

Head Office:
Doncaster Road,
Southern Industrial Area,
Bracknell,
Berkshire RG12 8YA

Tel: (01344) 424680

WAITROSE WINE DIRECT

Freepost SW1647,
Bracknell,
Berkshire RG12 8HX

Tel: (0800) 188881
Fax: (0800) 188888

E-mail: customerservice@waitrose.co.uk
Website: www.waitrose.com

For tasting notes of Waitrose wines scoring less than
16 points, and ratings of wines less than 14 points,
visit www.superplonk.com

17.5

Tokay Pinot Gris Selection de Grains   FRANCE
Nobles Altenbourg 'Le Tri', Albert Mann 2001

19 points in 2012–14. The burned butter edge will deepen in time to become truly magnificent. Wines like this, with complex honied fruit, require time not just for the sugars to relax but for the acids to reveal the minerals buried beneath, and the myriad dimensions of the liquid to become wholly apparent.

17.5

RED £22.00

Carmen Gold Reserve Cabernet Sauvignon 1999   CHILE

A Chilean Cabernet in the Aston Martin class: upholstered like a luxury drawing-room with power in reserve. Shows that the Maipo Valley can grow exemplary fruit which, handled with deftness as here, can produce very fine wines indeed.

17.5

RED £6.99

Cono Sur Merlot Reserve 2003   CHILE

Gorgeous depth of spicy blackberries and tannins drying to reveal chocolate.

17

RED £11.99

Chorey-les-Beune, Domaine Pascal   FRANCE
Maillard 2003

One of the least pugnacious yet tannicly teasing 2003 Burgundies I've tasted. Old-style gamy aroma and wild raspberry tinged richness give it class and a marvellous adhesiveness to the palate, recalling a bygone era.

17

Clos de Los Siete 2003
Rich, inordinately rich and deep. Cocoa-covered
tannins poured over roasted berries.
Also in Majestic.

Do you have any idea what a health hazard this job
represents? Dental and osteopathy bills testify to the fact
that the ritual of wine tasting carries two peculiar perils. The
first and most obvious is represented by the acids in the
wine which course over the teeth (but do not descend to the
stomach). Wine tasters must spit out if they are to maintain
sobriety and judgemental objectivity and over the course of
a working year I grapple with around 10-15,000 wines. That is
a minimum average of 27 wines a day (and I drink and taste
wine every single day of the year), but it is most intense in
March, April, May and June, the last two weeks of
September, October and early November when retailers
organise tastings for journalists and other professionals
where up to 250 wines a day are confronted. Added to this
are the many tastings organised expressly for this book and
those put on by regional and national wine boards of
countries exporting to the UK. I first noticed that I was
losing enamel on my back teeth after six months into the
job. Now I have to have the damage repaired twice a year.
Not for nothing in the Moselle wine-growing area of
Germany, where the wines are noted for their elegant yet
emphatic acidity, is dentistry the busiest line of work after
growing grapes. (*Continued on page 305.*)

17

RED £12.99

Domini Plus 2001   PORTUGAL

Perhaps the most haughty Portuguese red I've tasted:
chocolate, burned berries, grand tannins. It's
intensely firm, nicely potent without being abrasive.

17

RED £14.99

Errazuriz Estate La Cumbre Syrah 2002   CHILE

Pure Green & Black's dark chocolate. A very sinful
red to drink in the bath.

17

WHITE £7.99

Errazuriz Estate Max Reserva Chardonnay 2004   CHILE

Lovely waxy-textured, lanolin-coated, melon/
citrus/dry apricot fruit. Quite gorgeous.

17

RED £5.99

Gracia Merlot/Mourvèdre 2003   CHILE

Chewy, cocoa-edged berries, finely roasted and very
classy.

17

WHITE £5.49

Oxford Landing Viognier 2004   AUSTRALIA

Screwcap. Restrained opulence and fine-grained
apricot-fruited insouciance.

17

WHITE £8.99

Warwick Estate Chardonnay 2004   SOUTH AFRICA

Utterly delicious creamy wood layered under peach/
melon fruit (with citrus).

17

WHITE £9.99
ARGENTINA

Catena Chardonnay 2003
Luxurious woody undertone – for people with
double incomes and double garages (and twin
palates to satisfy).
Also at Majestic.

16.5

WHITE £9.99
SOUTH AFRICA

**Bouchard Finlayson Crocodile's Lair
Chardonnay 2003**
Very ripe and rich vintage this, from one of the
Cape's most firmly expressive Chardonnays.

16.5

RED £6.99
FRANCE

Château Cazal Viel Cuvée des Fées 2001
Wonderful classy, rich, elegant, complex, bold,
sensual, aromatic and very exciting.

16.5

WHITE £17.99
NEW ZEALAND

**Cloudy Bay Te Koko Sauvignon
Blanc 2002**
A very individual Sauvignon Blanc with complex,
under-ripe gooseberry, minerals and herbs.

16.5

WHITE £8.99
CHILE

Carmen Winemakers Chardonnay 2003
Rich, oily, beautifully sleek. Ornate yet not over-
designed.

16.5   RED £5.99

Chilcas Malbec/Syrah 2003   CHILE
Chutzpah liquefied! Gorgeous chocolate fruit and
tannins (from organic grapes).

16.5   RED £6.99

Doña Dominga Carmenere Reserva 2002   CHILE
Pulsates with savoury cherries and chocolate berries.
Also at Sainsbury.

16.5   RED £5.99

Errazuriz Estate Shiraz 2003   CHILE
A relaxed style subtle to open, then it goes
emphatically rich and complex, and then it lingers
with cocoa and nuts and burned berries. It is
wickedly unfair of the Chileans to manufacture
wines like this for this kind of money. The rest of
the winemaking world has a difficult job competing.
Also at Tesco.

16.5   RED £5.99

Errazuriz Estate Cabernet Sauvignon 2003   CHILE
Savoury plums, plump tannins. Effortless feel to the
wine.
Also at Asda, E-tailers (Everywine), Oddbins,
Somerfield.

16.5   RED £5.99

Finca Flichman Shiraz Reserva 2004   ARGENTINA
Chewy as a piece of coal – but far more sensually fruity.

16.5 WHITE £7.49

Gobelsburger Riesling 2003 AUSTRIA

18.5 in 2010–12. Quite superb texture and class.

16.5 RED £19.99

Gevrey-Chambertin Vieilles Vignes, FRANCE
Domaine Heresztyn 2003

Lovely sweet edge to gamy richness, which manages
to be both svelte and characterful.

16.5 WHITE £6.99

La Baume Marsanne/Roussanne/ FRANCE
Chardonnay, Vin de Pays d'Oc 2002

A waxy blend of four grapes: 55% Marsanne, 19%
Roussanne, 16% Chardonnay and 10% Viognier.
Terrific *ménage à quatre*! Really weighty richness and
class – lovely!

16.5 RED £4.55

Saumur Les Nivières 2003 FRANCE

Delicious roast plum and deep tannins give the wine
class and concentration. Wonderful price for such
finesse (you see, France can compete with Chile
outside the fashionable regions – like here in the
Loire and with the Cabernet Franc grape).

16.5 RED £7.99

Seigneurs d'Aiguilhe Côtes de Castillon 2003 FRANCE

The roasted plum is sheer velvet heaven.

16.5

**Paul Mas Sauvignon Blanc,
Vin de Pays d'Oc 2004**
Screwcap. Elegant, rich, complex. A remarkable price
for such finesse and class.
Also at Small Merchants (Unwins).

16.5

Diemersfontein Pinotage 2004
Screwcap. Intense tobacco-rich fruit of great creamy,
toasty individuality.
Also at Asda.

16.5

**Casillero del Diablo Concha y Toro
Cabernet Sauvignon 2004**
Superb tannins bring to a fabulous climax a red of
chocolate roasted nuts and warm berries.
Also at Booths, Budgens.

(Continued from page 300.)
But a bad back to add to the crumbling teeth? It comes from
standing on one's feet, often for 4 and 5 hours without a break,
with the top of the neck bent in order to examine wine and then
to write notes about it. I am now compelled to follow a morning
exercise regime to keep me sufficiently flexible to taste without
pain (cycling to and from tastings encourages the thighs but not
the vertebrae). The irony of all this is that the danger I am least
threatened by is the one most people would consider the
greatest: getting plastered.

16.5   WHITE £7.99

D'Arenberg 'The Hermit Crab' Marsanne/   AUSTRALIA
Viognier 2004
Screwcap. 18 points in 2008-9. Finely textured
apricot, melon, lychee and citrus – subtle yet
decisive.
Also at Booths.

16   RED £7.99

Anjou-Villages Brissac Château La Varière   FRANCE
Cabernet Franc, Cuvée Jacques Beaujeau 2003
Very smooth delivery of ripe plum and charred
cherry.

16   RED £9.99

Bonterra Merlot 2002   USA
Firm yet ripely plummy organic fruit, vivid edge to it
underpinned by full-fat tannins.

16   RED £4.99

Concha y Toro Sunrise Merlot 2004   CHILE
Superbly polished plum and cherry immediacy, and
then leathery tannins strike home.
Also at Budgens.

16   WHITE £8.99

Bonterra Chardonnay 2002   USA
The fruit dominates the wood perfectly.

16

WHITE £7.99

Brampton Viognier 2004 SOUTH AFRICA

Screwcap. It's lovely the way the peach cowers the toasty wood into submission.

16

RED £30.00

Brunello di Montalcino Tenuta Nuova Casanova de Neri 2000 ITALY

Big brute of a prune-rich, tannic soup.

16

WHITE (3 litre box) £15.99

Chileño Chardonnay/Sémillon 2004 CHILE

Touch whacky as the fruit ripens in the throat but the richness is charmingly modern and exotic.

16

WHITE £5.99

Chilcas Chardonnay 2003 CHILE

Rich yet elegant, oily, calm, very classy.

16

WHITE £4.99

Cono Sur Viognier 2004 CHILE

Pineapple and peach delicately assembled. Also at Majestic, Somerfield, Threshers.

16

WHITE £29.99

Chablis Grand Cru Grenouille, Les Viticulteurs de Chablis 2002 FRANCE

Chardonnay as tailored by Coco Chanel. Quite, quite lovely, chic and glowing with hauteur.

16

WHITE £6.49
Cune Monopole Rioja 2003   SPAIN
Catch it whilst it's still young, and its oily richness is
not yet fading and becoming submerged under the
creamy oak.

16

WHITE £4.99
Cono Sur Limited Release Viognier 2004   CHILE
Lovely citrus and apricot.

16

RED £7.99
Château Ségonzac,   FRANCE
Premières Côtes de Blaye 2002
Delicious! What a modern dashing claret! And it's
screwcapped.

16

RED £19.95
Château d'Aiguilhe Comtes de Neipperg,   FRANCE
Côtes de Castillon 2001
Very impressive label. The wine is no less elegant.

16

ROSÉ £6.99
Château de Caraguilhes Corbières Rosé 2004   FRANCE
One of the most elegantly dry, purposeful and pert
of pink liquids.

16

ROSÉ £3.55
Cuvée Fleur Rosé, Vin de Pays de l'Hérault 2004   FRANCE
Delicious dry cherry fruit, lean, elegant, hugely
refreshing. The price is something, don't you think?

16 RED £4.99

Cono Sur Pinot Noir 2004 CHILE

Stunningly complete – the tobacco-edged, gamy
cherries linger for ages in the throat.
Also at Majestic, Somerfield, Threshers.

16 WHITE £4.99

Douglas Green Chardonnay 2004 SOUTH AFRICA

Lovely waxy complexity.

16 WHITE £4.99

Finca Las Higueras Pinot Gris 2004 ARGENTINA

Nice waxy edge to lovely dry peach and pear fruit.

16 WHITE SPARKLING £12.99

Green Point ZD 2001 AUSTRALIA

16 points for the fruit. 20 points for the chutzpah!
The first sparkling wine in the UK to be released
under crown seal. A beer cap, my life! Wonderful!

16 WHITE SPARKLING £11.99

Green Point Vintage Brut 1999 AUSTRALIA

If you love that rich yeasty style, you'll fall for this.

16 WHITE £17.50

Gewürztraminer Grand Cru Furstentum FRANCE
Vieilles Vignes, Albert Mann 2002

19 points in 2010–12. A lovely smoky, stylish, full-on
textured Gewürz of towering, almost disdainful
elegance.

16   RED £30.00

Gevrey-Chambertin Les Evocelles 2003   FRANCE
Intense cherry/plum with relief from savoury
raspberry and beautifully polished tannins.

16   WHITE £5.99

Gobelsburger Grüner Veltliner 2004   AUSTRIA
17.5 points in 2009. Beautiful lithe yet plump melon
and pear.

16   RED £4.99

Inycon Shiraz 2003   ITALY
Lovely suede-textured plums and gently charred
cherries.

16   WHITE £5.99

Lugana Villa Flora Zenato 2004   ITALY
Lovely citrus and dry-to-finish under-ripe gooseberry.

16   WHITE £7.49

La Grille Classic Loire, Vin de Pays   FRANCE
du Jardin de la France, Henri Bourgeois,
Sauvignon Blanc 2004
Screwcap. Beautifully elegant, under-ripe, genteel
fruit. Great finesse.

16   WHITE £4.99

Muscadet Côtes de Grandlieu Sur Lie,   FRANCE
Fief Guérin 2004
Delicious tangy complexity and class.

16

RED £35.00
CHILE

Montes Alpha 'M' 2001
Tannins you can scrape off with a spoon.

16

WHITE £5.99
CHILE

Montes Reserve Sauvignon Blanc 2004
Has a very subtle resin edge – most attractive.

16

RED £7.99
CHILE

**Mont Gras Limited Edition
Cabernet Sauvignon 2001**
Ripe edge of charred plum roughed up nicely by
brocade-textured tannins.

16

RED £6.99
CHILE

Mont Gras Carmenere Reserva 2003
Stunningly well-tailored yet slightly raffish. Sheer
delight.

16

WHITE £4.99
FRANCE

Macon-Villages Cave de Prissé Chardonnay 2004
Screwcap. One of the leanest, most elegant of under-
a-fiver white Burgundies. Lovely crisp melon/lemon
fruit.

16

RED £6.55
SPAIN

Mas Collet Cellar de Capcanes Montsant 2002
A fine marriage of 35% bush-vine Garnacha, 25%
Tempranillo, 25% bush-vine Cariñena and 15%

Cabernet Sauvignon. Bush vines are old-fashioned and rustic. The wine is slightly more modern (but only just).

16

WHITE SPARKLING £19.00
Nyetimber Blanc de Blancs 1996
UK
Perhaps the most elegant bubbly ever produced in the UK. Ironically, the owner of the vineyard used to manage a band called Buck's Fizz.

16

WHITE £6.99
Pinot Grigio Alto Adige San Michele-Appiano 2004   ITALY
Fine apricot fruit of subtlety and class.

16

WHITE £13.15
Pinot Gris Le Fromenteau Josmeyer 2003
FRANCE
Smoky apricot with subtle citrus.

16

WHITE £5.99
Porcupine Ridge Sauvignon Blanc 2004   SOUTH AFRICA
Screwcap. Very complete, dry, smooth delivery.

Port growers must look forward to Christmas as it's the one time of the year when sale aren't sluggish. 'The heavy port drinker must be prepared to make some sacrifice of personal beauty and agility,' pointed out Evelyn Waugh. Being a fortified wine of up to 20% alcohol, over-indulgence in port is lethal, but the odd glass is most enjoyable with a rich blue cheese now and then.

16

RED £6.99
SOUTH AFRICA

Porcupine Ridge Syrah 2004
Screwcap. One of the Cape's sassiest Syrahs – ripe,
individual, deeply tannic, sensual.

16

RED £6.99
PORTUGAL

Palha-Canas Casa Santos Lima 2003
Vibrant burned berries and a hint of mocha coffee.

16

RED £4.49
ARGENTINA

Santa Julia Bonarda/Sangiovese 2004
Nicely controlled exuberant berries, subtly charred
with firm tannins.
Also at Morrison's.

16

WHITE £7.99
FRANCE

St-Véran Blason de Bourgogne 2004
Fine chalky edge to the chewy fruit. Real class here.

16

RED £7.55
FRANCE

Saumur-Champigny Château de Targé 2003
Gorgeous smoky fruit with firm tannins. Great
finish of roasted cherry.

16

RED £7.99
SOUTH AFRICA

Spice Route Pinotage 2003
Combines black-cherry/black-olive richness with
tannins like tar. Gorgeous.

WHITE £16.50
FRANCE

**Tokay Pinot Gris Grand Cru
Hengst Albert Mann 2002**
20 points in 2010–12. Rich, luxurious, very subtly
spicy apricot. Its tendency to thrilling funkiness will
develop over time and become perfection (its cork
permitting).

WHITE £5.99
CHILE

**Villa Montes Reserve Sauvignon
Blanc 2003**
Very classy amalgam of under-ripe melon, pineapple
and citrus.
Also at Morrison's, Sainsbury.

WHITE £8.05
NEW ZEALAND

**Villa Maria Private Bin
Gewürztraminer 2004**
Screwcap. 17.5 points in 2010–12. Spicy, warm but
very elegant. An inspired aperitif – though goes well
with complex fish dishes.
Also at Asda.

RED £14.99
NEW ZEALAND

Wither Hills Pinot Noir 2003
Screwcap. 16.5 points in 2007. Beautiful gamy
cherries and raspberries.
Also at Booths, Oddbins.

16
AUSTRALIA

**Wolf Blass President's Selection
Cabernet Sauvignon 2002**
Big, rich, yet only lightly grilled berries with firm
tannins of velvet with denim patches. Very well
modulated Cabernet of some class.
Also at Majestic, Somerfield.

 16
WHITE £6.99
NEW ZEALAND

**Stoneleigh Vineyards Marlborough
Sauvignon Blanc 2004**
Screwcap. Touches of grapefruit, pear and
gooseberries. Yum!
Also at Sainsbury.

OTHER WINES 15.5 AND UNDER

15.5
WHITE £6.99
AUSTRALIA

Brown Brothers Pinot Grigio 2004
Screwcap.

RED £11.55

Cape Mentelle Trinders Cabernet/Merlot 2002 AUSTRALIA
17 points in 2007–8.

WHITE £9.99
NEW ZEALAND

**Craggy Range Old Renwick Vineyard
Marlborough Sauvignon Blanc 2004**
Screwcap.

RED £10.99

Carpe Diem Shiraz 2003 SOUTH AFRICA

RED £15.99

Chevalier de Lascombes Margaux 2001 FRANCE

WHITE £5.99

Château Saint-Jean-des-Graves 2004 FRANCE
Screwcap. Also at Majestic.

RED £8.99

Dourthe Barrel Select St-Emilion 2003 FRANCE

ROSÉ £5.25

Foncaussade Les Parcelles Bergerac Rosé 2004 FRANCE

WHITE £9.95

Hattenheimer Wisselbrunnen GERMANY
Kabinett Von Simmern 2002
18.5 points in 2010–15.

RED £3.99

Los Andes Carmenere/Cabernet Sauvignon 2004 CHILE

WHITE £13.99

Leeuwin Estate Art Series Riesling 2004 AUSTRALIA
Screwcap. 17.5 points in 2008–12.

RED £6.99

La Baume Shiraz/Cabernet, FRANCE
Vin de Pays d'Oc 2001

WHITE £5.99

Palacio de Bornos Rueda Verdejo 2004 SPAIN

WHITE £7.99

Penfolds Clare Valley Organic   AUSTRALIA
Chardonnay 2003
16.5 points in 2007.

WHITE £9.95

Rudesheimer Berg Rottland Spätlese,   GERMANY
Dr Wegler 2002
18 points in 1010–15.

RED £6.99

Rutherglen Estates Durif 2004   AUSTRALIA
Screwcap.

RED £7.99

Stoneleigh Vineyards Marlborough   NEW ZEALAND
Pinot Noir 2003
Screwcap. Also at Small Merchants (Richard &
Richard Fine Wines, Halifax Wines).

WHITE £4.75

Saint-Pourcain Réserve Spéciale,   FRANCE
Cave de Saint-Pourcain 2004

RED £3.99

Santa Julia Fuzion Shiraz/Malbec 2003   ARGENTINA

RED £14.99

Villa Maria Reserve Merlot 2002   NEW ZEALAND
Screwcap. Also at E-tailers (Everywine).

RED £9.99

Don Reca Limited Release Merlot 2002   CHILE
Also at Sainsbury.

15

WHITE £8.99

Borges Alvarinho Vinho Verde 2004 PORTUGAL

RED (3 litre box) £14.99

Chileño Shiraz/Cabernet Sauvignon 2004 CHILE
Also at Sainsbury, Somerfield (16 in bottle).

WHITE £10.55

Cape Mentelle Sémillon/Sauvignon AUSTRALIA
Blanc 2004
Screwcap.17 points in 2007–8.

WHITE £4.49

Devil's Rock Pinot Grigio 2003 GERMANY
Screwcap. 16.5 in 2008.

WHITE £7.99

Felsner Grüner Veltliner Mossbürgerin 2004 AUSTRIA
16.5 points in 2008.

WHITE £4.99

Gavi La Luciana Araldica 2004 ITALY

WHITE £4.99

Jindalee Sauvignon Blanc 2004 AUSTRALIA
Screwcap.

RED £5.99

Jose de Souza 2001 PORTUGAL

WHITE £5.99

Jacob's Creek Dry Riesling 2003 AUSTRALIA
Screwcap. 16.5 points in 2007–9. Also at Sainsbury,
Tesco.

Kumala Journey's End Shiraz 2003
RED £14.99
SOUTH AFRICA

La Baume Viognier, Vin de Pays d'Oc 2004
17 points in 2008.
WHITE £4.99
FRANCE

Leeuwin Estate Art Series Shiraz 2001
RED £15.00
AUSTRALIA

Meursault Le Limozin Vincent Girradin 2002
WHITE £19.99
FRANCE

Penfolds Clare Valley Organic Cabernet Sauvignon/Merlot/Shiraz 2003
RED £9.49
AUSTRALIA

Pinot Noir d'Alsace Domaine Paul Blanck 2004
17 points in 2008.
RED £8.99
FRANCE

Piedra Feliz Pinot Noir 2001
RED £9.99
CHILE

Rustenberg Chardonnay 2003
WHITE £9.99
SOUTH AFRICA

Sirius Blanc Bordeaux 2003
WHITE £6.99
FRANCE

Sancerre Domaine Naudet 2004
WHITE £9.55
FRANCE

Santa Rita Floresta Sauvignon Blanc 2003
WHITE £9.99
CHILE

Santa Julia Fuzion Chenin Blanc/
Chardonnay 2004

WHITE £3.99
ARGENTINA

Soave Classico, Vigneto Colombara, Zenato 2004

WHITE £4.99
ITALY

Schwarzhofberger Riesling Spätlese,
Von Hovel 2002
17.5 points in 2011.

WHITE £9.99
GERMANY

Trivento Viognier 2004

WHITE £4.99
ARGENTINA

Torres San Medin Cabernet Sauvignon Rosé 2004

ROSÉ £5.49
SPAIN

Viñedo Chadwick 1999

RED £30.00
CHILE

Waitrose Chianti 2003

RED £3.99
ITALY

Waitrose Muscadet de Sèvre et Maine 2004
Screwcap.

WHITE £3.99
FRANCE

Wente Chardonnay 2003

WHITE £6.99
USA

Jacob's Creek Sparkling Chardonnay/
Pinot Noir Brut Cuvée NV
Also at Asda, Sainsbury, Tesco.

WHITE SPARKLING £7.99
AUSTRALIA

RED £6.99

Ravenswood Vintners Blend Zinfandel 2002 USA
Also at Booths, Budgens, Tesco.

14·5

RED £3.99

Arniston Bay Shiraz 2004 SOUTH AFRICA

RED £15.99

Cloudy Bay Pinot Noir 2003 NEW ZEALAND
Selected stores only. Also at Majestic, Small
Merchants (Harrods).

RED £17.99

Château Laroque St-Emilion Grand Cru 2001 FRANCE

WHITE £8.99

Chablis Cave des Vignerons de Chablis 2004 FRANCE

WHITE £3.99

Domaine de Plantieu, Vin de Pays des Côtes FRANCE
de Gascogne 2004

WHITE SPARKLING £19.99

Duval-Leroy Fleur de Champagne FRANCE
Premier Cru NV

WHITE £4.99

Firebird Legend Pinot Grigio 2003 MOLDOVA

RED £14.99

Henschke Henry's Seven Shiraz/ AUSTRALIA
Grenache/Viognier 2003
Screwcap.

WHITE £12.99

Henschke Louis Sémillon 2004   AUSTRALIA
Screwcap. 16.5 points in 2009.

RED £5.35

LA Cetto Petite Syrah 2002   MEXICO

RED £6.99

Montana Pinot Noir 2004   NEW ZEALAND
Screwcap. Also at Small Merchants (Waverly Wines &
Spirits).

ROSÉ £4.99

Moulin des Cailloux Côtes de Duras Rosé 2004   FRANCE

WHITE £4.99

Moulin des Cailloux Côtes de Duras   FRANCE
Sauvignon Blanc 2004
Screwcap.

WHITE £4.99

Palandri Pinnacle Sémillon/Sauvignon   AUSTRALIA
Blanc 2004
Screwcap.

RED £7.99

Oyster Bay Merlot 2004   NEW ZEALAND
Screwcap. Also at Majestic, Sainsbury.

RED £12.49

Savigny-les-Beaune, Bouchard Père et Fils 2003   FRANCE

WHITE £11.25

Vouvray Le Mont Sec Huet 2000   FRANCE
Organic. 18 points in 2010–14.

14

Altno Reserva 2000	RED £7.99 PORTUGAL
Beaune Premier Cru Clos des Mouches, Joseph Drouhin 2002	RED £30.00 FRANCE
Corbières La Forge, Gérard Bertrand 2001	RED £21.99 FRANCE
Château Saint-Maurice Côtes du Rhône 2003	RED £4.99 FRANCE
Crozes-Hermitage Cave des Clairmonts 2003	RED £7.49 FRANCE
Cheverny Le Vieux Clos, Delaille 2004	WHITE £5.99 FRANCE
Château Latour Léognan, Pessac-Léognan 2004 Screwcap.	WHITE £9.99 FRANCE
Dourthe No 1 Sauvignon Blanc Bordeaux 2004 Screwcap.	WHITE £5.99 FRANCE
Domaine de Pellehaut Rosé, Vin de Pays des Côtes de Gascogne 2004 Screwcap. Also at Booths.	ROSÉ £5.15 FRANCE
Esporao Reserva 2001	RED £8.99 PORTUGAL

RED £5.99

Gracia Merlot/Mourvèdre Reserva Superior 2003 CHILE

WHITE £6.99

Gewürztraminer Caves de Turckheim 2004 FRANCE
16.5 points in 2007–8.

WHITE £15.99

Hochheimer Kirchenstück Riesling GERMANY
Spätlese Künstler 2003
17 points in 2010–15.

RED £4.79

Hardy's Voyage Cabernet Sauvignon/ AUSTRALIA
Petit Verdot/Ruby Cabernet 2003
Screwcap. Also at Tesco.

WHITE £12.99

Henschke Coralinga Sauvignon Blanc 2003 AUSTRALIA
Screwcap.

WHITE £4.99

Italia Pinot Grigio 2004 ITALY
Screwcap.

RED £7.99

Julienas Georges Duboeuf 2004 FRANCe
Screwcap.

RED £6.99

Ken Forrester Merlot 2003 SOUTH AFRICA

WHITE £4.99

La Pampa Estate Sauvignon Blanc 2004 ARGENTINA

WHITE SPARKLING £6.99
Lindemans Bin 25 Brut Cuvée NV   AUSTRALIA
Also at Co-op, Budgens, Morrison's.

ROSÉ £5.99
Muga Rioja Rosado 2004   SPAIN

RED £6.99
Montana Merlot/Cabernet   NEW ZEALAND
Sauvignon 2003
Screwcap. Also at Oddbins, Somerfield.

WHITE £3.99
Maison Delor Bordeaux Blanc 2004   FRANCE
Screwcap.

RED £7.29
Nepenthe 'Tryst' Cabernet/Zinfandel/   AUSTRALIA
Tempranillo 2004
Screwcap.

RED £4.99
Norton Barbera 2004   ARGENTINA

RED £4.99
Palandri Pinnacle Shiraz 2002   AUSTRALIA

WHITE £7.99
Petit Chablis Cave de Vignerons de Chablis 2004   FRANCE
Screwcap.

WHITE £29.99
Puligny-Montrachet Clos de la Garenne,   FRANCE
Drouhin 2002

WHITE £3.99
Pujalet Vin de Pays du Gers 2004 FRANCE
Screwcap.

WHITE £7.99
Pazo de Seoane Albarinho 2003 PORTUGAL

ROSÉ £4.15
Rosato Veronese Cantina di Monteforte 2004 ITALY

ROSÉ £6.99
Stoneleigh Vineyards Marlborough NEW ZEALAND
Pinot Noir Rosé 2004
Screwcap.

WHITE £6.99
Sauvignon Blanc, Vin de Pays de l'Yonne 2004 FRANCE
Screwcap.

RED £5.99
St Hallett Gamekeeper's Reserve 2004 AUSTRALIA
Screwcap.

RED £4.99
Saint Riche, Vin de Pays des Bouches FRANCE
du Rhône 2004
Organic.

WHITE £6.49
Terrazas Alto Chardonnay 2003 ARGENTINA

RED £14.99
The Chocolate Block 2003 SOUTH AFRICA

WHITE £5.99

The Naked Grape Riesling 2004 GERMANY
Screwcap. 15 points in 2009.

RED £9.99

Vino Nobile di Montepulciano Carbonaia 2001 ITALY

WHITE £4.29

Verdicchio dei Castelli di Jesi Classico ITALY
Moncaro 2004
Screwcap.

WHITE £3.99

Vignale Pinot Grigio 2004 ITALY

ROSÉ £3.99

Waitrose Rosé d'Anjou 2004 FRANCE

WHITE £4.49

Waitrose Chilean Chardonnay/Sauvignon CHILE
Blanc 2003

RED £5.49

Yellow Tail Cabernet Sauvignon 2004 AUSTRALIA
Also at Asda.

YAPP BROTHERS

Mere,
Wiltshire BA12 6OY

Tel: (01747) 860423
Fax: (01747) 860929

E-mail: sales@yapp.co.uk
Website: www.yapp.co.uk

For tasting notes of Yapp wines scoring less than
16 points, and ratings of wines less than 14 points,
visit www.superplonk.com

17.5

RED £11.50
FRANCE

Collioure La Pinède, Domaine de la Tour Vieille 2003
Chocolate and bitter almond. Brilliantly textured thickness and richness.

17.5

RED £8.25
FRANCE

Saumur Champigny, Domaine Filliatreau 2003
Young (will cellar well 3–5 years) and finishes with crumbly dark cocoa (yet is an immediate charmer) and seems eager at first but chocolate and nuts spread slowly as the tannins melt in the throat. Immaculate texture to it. I am often charged to answer the question 'What is your favourite red wine?' and the difficulties of answering this truthfully, since situations where you drink wine change and make one wine less companionable one day than it would be another, force me to remark that if I am sitting by myself reading a book then a chilled bottle of wine like this is wonderful (oh, and you might add a bowl of almonds to that as well).

17

RED £8.25
FRANCE

Côtes du Roussillon 'Tradition', Ferrer-Ribière 2001
Deep velvety yet characterful richness with black olive boosted by handsome tannins (with accompanying perfect weight of 13.5% alcohol). Lively, herby, lengthy, very satisfying.

17

RED £7.50
FRANCE

Côtes du Ventoux, Château Valcombe 2001
Terrific meaty, rich, thick clotted berries and tannins.

17

WHITE £7.95
FRANCE

**Montlouis Sur Loire, Domaine
Les Liards Sec 2003**
That wet wood lanolin tang, leading to dry, and
curiously herby, dry honey edge is typical of the
grape used here, Chenin Blanc. This specimen is
most individual. Has a slightly acquired taste
perhaps, but goodness is it worth acquiring (a glass
or two should do it).

17

RED £11.75
FRANCE

**Saumur Champigny Vieilles Vignes,
Domaine Filliatreau 2002**
Brilliant! How to seriously quaff serious yet
impishily playful red wine. Lovely blend of grilled
berries and tannins here.

16.5

RED £26.00
FRANCE

Châteauneuf-du-Pape Le Vieux Donjon 2001
Raunchy and ripe. Superior, controlled spice.
Wondrously smooth yet provocative tannins.

16.5

WHITE £10.95
FRANCE

Gewürztraminer Charles Schleret, Alsace 1999
Spicy, ripe, firm, textured, yet astonishingly dry to
finish.

16.5   WHITE £8.95

Jurançon Sec, Domaine Bellegarde 2003   FRANCE

Sheer extruded, under-ripe gooseberry and raspberry
leaf. Wonderful crisp, classic, stony.

16.5   WHITE £8.95

Neagles Rock Riesling 2002   AUSTRALIA

18 points in 2008–12. Screwcap. Lovely petrolly
undertone leads to beautiful under-ripe gooseberry
and grapefruit. Rich yet elegant and understated.

16   WHITE £5.25

Côtes de Gascogne, Domaine de Millet 2004   FRANCE

Has that delicious happy-go-luckiness (thirst-
quenching) yet it is a useful food wine (lightly spicy
fish dishes). Delightful floral perfume.

16   RED £7.50

Lirac La Fermade, Domaine Maby 2002   FRANCE

Sweet black cherry, touch of roasted sage, good brisk
tannins – this is a Rhône red of finesse yet genteel
rustic richness.

16   WHITE £9.50

Pinot Blanc Charles Schleret, Alsace 2002   FRANCE

Wonderful end-of-the-day solvent! One sip and the
cares of the day are washed away by white peach,
acids and subtle pear. This is one of those draughts
which once taken turns the incredible early-evening
sulky hulk into a accommodating, relaxed charmer.

16

WHITE £12.75
FRANCE

Savennières 'Avant'
Château de Chamboureau 2001
Delicate yet assertive crispness and wry citrus fruit.
A very poised wine.

16

WHITE £5.95
FRANCE

Saumur, Les Vignerons de Saumur 2003
A wonderful fresh, gritty white wine with the tell-tale
Chenin Blanc wet-wool undertone (not to be
confused with oak taint), but this dimension dries
out in the throat to reveal melon, gooseberry and
mango (subtle).

OTHER WINES 15.5 AND UNDER

15

RED £7.85
FRANCE

Vin de Pays du Mont Caume Bunan
Mourvèdre 2002

14

RED £7.50
FRANCE

Côtes du Ventoux, Château Valcombe 2002

INDEX OF WINE NAMES

1st Cape Colombard/Chardonnay
2004, **14.5**, *Asda*, white, 20

35 South Cabernet Sauvignon
2003, **16**, *Sainsbury*, red, 182

35 South Cabernet Sauvignon
2004, **15.5**, *Asda*, **16**, *Threshers*,
red, 17, 293

35 South Cabernet Sauvignon/
Merlot 2004, **16**, *Asda*, red, 13

35 South Chardonnay 2004, **16**,
Asda, white, 13

35 South Sauvignon Blanc 2004,
14, *Threshers*, white, 295

A

'A' Limoux Chardonnay 2003, **16.5**,
Asda, white, 3

Adobe Cabernet Sauvignon 2003,
15, *Vintage Roots*, red, 77

Adobe Carmenere 2003, **15**,
Vintage Roots, red, 77

Aglianico Rosso di Sicilia, Cantine
Settesoli 2003, **15**, *Majestic*, red,
100

Agramont Navarra Garnacha
Rosado 2004, **14**, *Sainsbury*,
rosé, 190

Alain Graillot Crozes-Hermitage
2003, **16**, *Sainsbury*, red, 171

Alamos Bonarda Catena Zapata
2003, **16**, *Booths*, red, 32

Albet I Noya Lignum 2004, **15.5**,
Asda, white, 17

Albet I Noya Lignum Negre 2003,
16, *Asda*, red, 8

Aldi Cabernet Sauvignon 2003, **16**,
Aldi, red, 211

Aldi Pinot Blanc 2003, **14**, *Aldi*,
white, 220

Alemena Real Reserva Rioja 1998,
16, *Somerfield*, red, 233

Alsace Gewürztraminer 2003, **15**,
Co-op, white, 65

Alsace Gewürztraminer (M & S)
2004, **14.5**, *Marks & Spencer*,
white, 126

Alsace Riesling (M & S) 2004,
14, *Marks & Spencer*, white,
126

Altno Reserva 2000, **14**, *Waitrose*,
red, 323

Altos de Tamaron Ribera del
Duero 2003, **16**, *Sainsbury*, red,
171

Amanti Rosso, **16**, *Somerfield*, red,
228

Amarone della Valpolicella
Musella 1999, **14**, *Oddbins*, red,
158

Amarone della Valpolicella
'Rocca Alata' 2001, **15.5**, *Tesco*,
red, 264

Amberley Estate Margaret River
    Sauvignon Blanc 2004, **14**,
    Majestic, white, 104
Americana Merlot 2004, **14**, *Co-op*,
    red, 67
Anakena Cabernet Sauvignon
    Reserve 2002, **16**, *Asda*, red, 7
Anakena Chardonnay 2004, **15**,
    Asda, white, 18
Anakena Merlot Reserve 2003, **14**,
    Threshers, red, 295
Anakena Viognier Reserve 2004,
    16, *Threshers*, white, 288
Andrew Makepeace 'Masterpeace'
    Rosé 2004, **14.5**, *Co-op*, *Nisa*,
    Unwins, rosé, 67, 219
Andrew Peace Mighty Murray
    Chardonnay, **14**, *Asda*, white,
    2004
Andrew Peace Mighty Murray
    Malbec 2003, **15.5**, *Asda*, red,
    16
Angas Brut Premium Cuvée Pinot
    Noir/Chardonnay NV, **15**,
    Oddbins, *Unwins*, white
    sparkling, 156, 216
Anjou-Villages Brissac Château La
    Varière Cabernet Franc, Cuvée
    Jacques Beaujeau 2003, **16**,
    Waitrose, red, 306
Antipodean Sangiovese Rosé
    2004, **15**, *Hoults*, *Oddbins*, rosé,
    156, 215
Antiyal 2002, **14.5**, *Adnams*, red,
    217
Araldica Gavi, Piemonte 2004,
    14.5, *Sainsbury*, white, 189
Aramonte Catarratto 2004, **16**,
    Marks & Spencer, white, 117

Archiodamo Primitivo di
    Manduria Pervini 2003, **14**,
    Booths, red, 39
Argento Bonarda 2004, **16**,
    Morrison's, red, 131
Argento Chardonnay 2003, **16.5**,
    Tesco, white, 248
Argento Chardonnay 2004, **16.5**,
    Majestic, *Sainsbury*, white, 83,
    170
Argento Chardonnay Reserva
    2003, **16.5**, *Sainsbury*, white,
    168
Argento Malbec 2004, **16**, *Budgens*,
    Majestic, *Sainsbury*, *Tesco*, red,
    46, 88, 171, 263
Argento Pinot Grigio 2004, **16**,
    Majestic, *Morrison's*, white, 88,
    134
Arniston Bay Rosé 2004, **14**, *Tesco*,
    rosé, 275
Arniston Bay Shiraz 2004, **14.5**,
    Waitrose, red, 321
Arrogant Frog Ribet Red
    (Cabernet/Merlot) 2003, **16.5**,
    Unwins, red, 208
Ascheri Barolo Sorano 1998, **16**,
    Tesco, red, 254
Asda Argentinian Malbec
    Reserve 2002, **14.5**, *Asda*, red,
    19
Asda Argentinian Torrontes 2003,
    15, *Asda*, white, 17
Asda Australian Chardonnay NV,
    14.5, *Asda*, white, 20
Asda Australian Red NV, **14.5**,
    Asda, red, 19
Asda Australian Reserve Shiraz
    2003, **15.5**, *Asda*, red, 15

Asda Cava NV, **16**, *Asda*, white sparkling, 7

Asda Champagne Brut NV, **15**, *Asda*, white sparkling, 17

Asda Chianti Classico 2003, **14.5**, *Asda*, red, 20

Asda Chilean Cabernet Sauvignon 2004, **14**, *Asda*, red, 22

Asda Chilean Carmenere 2004, **14.5**, *Asda*, red, 20

Asda Chilean Chardonnay 2004, **15.5**, *Asda*, white, 15

Asda Chilean Merlot NV, **16.5**, *Asda*, red, xiii, 3

Asda Chilean Red NV, **14**, *Asda*, red, 22

Asda Chilean Sauvignon Blanc 2004, **14**, *Asda*, white, 21

Asda Chilean White NV, **14.5**, *Asda*, white, 20

Asda Claret NV, **14.5**, *Asda*, red, 20

Asda Côtes du Rhône NV, **14**, *Asda*, red, 22

Asda Côtes du Rhône-Villages 2003, **15.5**, *Asda*, red, 16

Asda English Regional Wine 2004, **15**, *Asda*, white, 18

Asda Extra Special Barolo 1999, **14**, *Asda*, red, 22

Asda Extra Special Barossa Shiraz 2002, **15**, *Asda*, red, 18

Asda Extra Special Barossa Valley Sémillon 2003, **14.5**, *Asda*, white, 20

Asda Extra Special Casablanca Sauvignon Blanc 2004, **14**, *Asda*, white, 21

Asda Extra Special Chablis Premier Cru 2002, **14**, *Asda*, white, 21

Asda Extra Special New Zealand Sauvignon Blanc 2004, **15.5**, *Asda*, white, 15

Asda Extra Special Pinot Grigio, Maso Gua 2003, **16.5**, *Asda*, white, 3

Asda Extra Special Stellenbosch Pinotage 2003, **16**, *Asda*, red, 7

Asda Fino Sherry NV, **15**, *Asda*, fortified, 17

Asda Hungarian Chardonnay NV, **14**, *Asda*, white, 21

Asda Manzanilla Sherry NV, **15**, *Asda*, fortified, 17

Asda Moscatel de Valencia NV, **16**, *Asda*, white dessert, 7

Asda New Zealand Sauvignon Blanc 2004, **14.5**, *Asda*, white, 20

Asda Premium Claret 2003, **14.5**, *Asda*, red, 19

Asda South African Chardonnay 2004, **15**, *Asda*, white, 18

Asda South African Chenin Blanc 2004, **16**, *Asda*, white, 7

Asda Vin de Pays Sauvignon Blanc NV, **14**, *Asda*, white, 21

Asda Vintage Cava 2002, **16.5**, *Asda*, white sparkling, 3

Asti NV, **15**, *Marks & Spencer*, white sparkling, 125

Ata Rangi Pinot Noir 2002, **15**, *Harrods, Jeroboams*, red, 215

Atlantique Sauvignon Blanc 2004, **15.5**, *Co-op*, white, 64

Avantegarde Pinot Noir 2002, **14**, *Asda*, red, 22

Avila Cabernet Sauvignon 2002, **16.5**, *Oddbins*, red, 144

Avila Chardonnay 2004, **16**, *Oddbins*, white, 147

Avila Côte d'Avila 2002, **15**, *Oddbins*, red, 156

Avila Pinot Noir 2003, **15.5**, *Oddbins*, red, 154

Avila Syrah 2003, **15.5**, *Oddbins*, red, 154

B

Badia a Coltibuono Chianti Classico 2002, **14**, *Tesco*, red, 275

Banrock Station Red 2003, **14**, *Asda*, red, 22

Banrock Station Shiraz/Mataro 2003, **14**, *Tesco*, red, 275

Banrock Station Sparkling Shiraz NV, **16**, *Asda*, *Sainsbury*, red sparkling, 8, 172

Banrock Station White 2004, **14**, *Asda*, white, 22

Banrock Station White NV, **14**, *Asda*, white, 22

Banrock Station White Shiraz 2003, **15**, *Asda*, rosé, 18

Banwell Farm Barossa Valley Sémillon 2002, **17**, *Marks & Spencer*, white, 112

Banwell Farm Eden Valley Riesling 2004, **17**, *Marks & Spencer*, white, 112

Barbera d'Asti Superiore La Luna e I Falo Terre da Vino 2002, **14**, *Booths*, red, 39

Bardolino Classico Tedeschi 2003, **14**, *Majestic*, red, 104

Barnett Vineyards Sleepy Hollow Vineyard Pinot Noir 2003, **14**, *Oddbins*, red, 159

Bear Crossing Sémillon/ Chardonnay NV, **15**, *Asda*, white, 18

Beaujolais Cuvée Vieilles Vignes Cave de Bully 2004, **14.5**, *Majestic*, red, 101

Beaujolais-Villages, Domaine des Côtes de la Molière 2002, **14**, *Booths*, red, 39

Beaujolais-Villages, Domaine de Nuges 2004, **15**, *Majestic*, red, 100

Beaune Premier Cru Clos des Mouches, Joseph Drouhin 2002, **14**, *Waitrose*, red, 323

Bellingham 'The Maverick' Viognier 2004, **14**, *Majestic*, white, 104

Beringer Appellation Collection Napa Valley Cabernet Sauvignon 1999, **16.5**, *Majestic*, red, 84

Beringer Appellation Collection Napa Valley Chardonnay 2004, **14**, *Majestic*, white, 104

Bernard Germain Anjou, Barrel Fermented Chenin Blanc 2002, **16**, *Sainsbury*, white, 172

Bertie Collection Minervois/Syrah 2002, **15.5**, *Oddbins*, red, 154

Bertie Collection Saint-Chinian Grenache 2002, **16**, *Oddbins*, red, 148

Bethany Cabernet/Merlot 2002,
16, *Co-op*, red, 59–60

Bin 042 Chardonnay/Sauvignon
Blanc 2003, **16**, *Asda*, white, 8

Blason de Bourgogne Côtes
Chalonnaise Chardonnay
2004, **14**, *Budgens*, white, 54

Blason de Bourgogne Crémant de
Bourgogne NV, **14**, *Tesco*, white
sparkling, 275

Blason de Bourgogne Macon
Villages 2002, **16**, *Asda*, white, 8

Blason de Bourgogne St-Véran
2003, **15**, *Tesco*, white, 267

Blason de Bourgogne Villages
2003, **14.5**, *Asda*, white, 20

Bleasdale Shiraz/Cabernet
Sauvignon 2001, **16**, *Oddbins*,
red, 148

Bleasdale Shiraz/Cabernet
Sauvignon 2002, **15.5**, *Booths*,
red, 37

Blind River Sauvignon Blanc
2004, **15.5**, *Oddbins*, white, 154

Blossom Hill Chardonnay/
Viognier NV, **16.5**, *Asda*, white,
4

Blossom Hill Reserve Cabernet
Sauvignon 2002, **14**, *Tesco*, red,
275

Blueridge XR Merlot, **16**,
Somerfield, red, 228

Boland Cellar Sauvignon Blanc
2004, **14.5**, *Somerfield*, white, 240

Bonterra Chardonnay 2002, **16**,
Waitrose, white, 306

Bonterra Chardonnay/Sauvignon/
Muscat 2002, **14**, *Budgens*,
white, 53

Bonterra Merlot 2002, **16**,
Waitrose, red, 306

Bonterra Shiraz/Carignan/
Sangiovese 2003, **16**, *Budgens*,
red, 46

Borges Alvarinho Vinho Verde
2004, **15**, *Waitrose*, white, 318

Boschendal Grande Cuvée
Sauvignon Blanc 2004, **16**,
Tesco, white, 254

Botham/Merrill/Willis
Chardonnay 2002, **16**,
Somerfield, white, 228

Bouchard Finlayson Crocodile's
Lair Chardonnay 2003, **16.5**,
Waitrose, white, 302

Bourgogne Blanc, Domaine de
Montmeix Mestre-Michelot
2003, **14**, *Oddbins*, white, 158

Brampton Estate Sauvignon
Blanc 2004, **17**, *Threshers*, white,
285

Brampton Estate Shiraz/Viognier
2003, **16**, *Threshers*, red, 290

Brampton Viognier 2004, **16**,
Waitrose, white, 307

Brindisi Rosso 2001, **14**, *Morrison's*,
red, 136

Brindisi Rosso Cantine Due
Palme 2003, **16**, *Sainsbury*, red,
172

Brolio Chianti Classico 2002, **16.5**,
Sainsbury, red, 168

Brookland Valley 'Verse 1'
Cabernet Sauvignon/Merlot
2002, **14**, *Oddbins*, red, 158

Brookland Valley 'Verse 1'
Sémillon/Sauvignon Blanc
2004, **14**, *Oddbins*, white, 158

Broquel Malbec 2002, **14**, *Sainsbury*, red, 190

Brown Brothers Chenin Blanc 2004, **14**, *Budgens*, white, 53

Brown Brothers Cienna 2004, **15**, *Tesco*, red, 267

Brown Brothers Dry Muscat 2004, **16**, *Asda*, *Budgens*, *Somerfield* white, 15, 49, 229

Brown Brothers Dry Muscat NV, **15.5**, *Tesco*, white, 264

Brown Brothers Late Harvested Orange and Muscat Flora 2003, **14**, *Sainsbury*, white dessert, 190

Brown Brothers Limited Release Riesling 1999, **15**, *Booths*, white, 37

Brown Brothers Merlot 2002, **14.5**, *Budgens*, red, 52

Brown Brothers Moscato 2004, **15.5**, *Tesco*, white, 264

Brown Brothers Pinot Grigio 2004, **15.5**, *Waitrose*, white, 315

Brown Brothers Pinot Gris 2003, **16.5**, *Asda*, white, 3

Brown Brothers Sauvignon Blanc 2004, **15.5**, *Asda*, white, 16

Brown Brothers Tarrango 2003, **14**, *Somerfield*, red, 240

Brunello di Montalcino Tenuta Nuova Casanova de Neri 2000, **16**, *Waitrose*, red, 307

Burgundy Bourgogne Chardonnay 2004, **16**, *Marks & Spencer*, white, 117

Bush View Margaret River Chardonnay 2003, **16.5**, *Marks & Spencer*, white, 113

Bush View Margaret River Shiraz 2002, **14.5**, *Marks & Spencer*, red, 126

Buzet Rouge Cuvée 44 2003, **14.5**, *Somerfield*, red, 239

C

Cabernet Rosé, Vin de Pays du Jardin de la France 2004, **15.5**, *Sainsbury*, rosé, 186

Caldora Sangiovese 2003, **15.5**, *Co-op*, red, 64

Calvet Limited Release Sauvignon Blanc Bordeaux 2004, **16**, *Sainsbury*, white, 173

Campo Viejo Tempranillo NV, **15.5**, *Threshers*, red, 294

Canaletto Primitivo 2002, **16**, *Somerfield*, red, 230

Cano Cosecha Toro 2003, **15**, *Morrison's*, red, 135

Cape Cinsault Ruby Cabernet 2004, **14**, *Morrison's*, red, 136

Cape Grace Cabernet Sauvignon/Merlot 2003, **16**, *Somerfield*, red, 230

Cape Grace Chardonnay/Sémillon 2004, **14**, *Somerfield*, white, 240

Cape Grace Merlot 2003, **14.5**, *Asda*, red, 20

Cape Grace Pinotage Rosé 2005, **15.5**, *Sainsbury*, rosé, 185

Cape Mentelle Sémillon/ Sauvignon Blanc 2004, **15**, *Waitrose*, white, 318

Cape Mentelle Trinders Cabernet/ Merlot 2002, **15.5**, *Waitrose*, red, 315

Cape Promise Colombard 2004, **14**, *Asda*, white, 22

Cape Soleil Sauvignon Blanc 2004, **14**, *Sainsbury*, white, 190

Carmen Gold Reserve Cabernet Sauvignon 1999, **17.5**, *Waitrose*, red, 299

Carmen Nativa Chardonnay 2004, **16**, *Oddbins*, white, 148

Carmen Reserve Carmenere/Cabernet Sauvignon 2002, **15**, *Booths*, red, 38

Carmen Winemakers Chardonnay 2003, **16.5**, *Waitrose*, white, 302

Carmesi Oak Aged Calatayud Garnacha/Tempranillo 2003, **16**, *Sainsbury*, red, 173

Carpe Diem Shiraz 2003, **15.5**, *Waitrose*, red, 316

Casa Lapostolle Cabernet Sauvignon 2002, **16.5**, *Booths*, red, 30

Casa Lapostolle Cuvée Alexandre Apalta Vineyard Merlot 2002, **18**, *Sainsbury*, red, 165

Casa Lapostolle Cuvée Alexandre Casablanca Valley Chardonnay 2003, **17.5**, *Sainsbury*, white, 165

Casa Lapostolle Cuvée Alexandre Library Cabernet Sauvignon 2000, **17.5**, *Oddbins*, red, 141

Casa Lapostolle Cuvée Alexandre Library Merlot 2000, **17**, *Oddbins*, red, 141

Casa Lapostolle Cuvée Alexandre Merlot 2001, **17**, *Sainsbury*, red, 166

Casa Lapostolle Cuvée Alexandre Merlot 2002, **17.5**, *Booths*, red, 29

Casa Leona Cabernet Sauvignon 2004, **16.5**, *Marks & Spencer*, red, 115

Casa Leona Merlot 2004, **16.5**, *Marks & Spencer*, red, 114

Casa Leona Reserve Cabernet Sauvignon 2003, **17**, *Marks & Spencer*, red, 112

Casa Morena Bodega Felix Solis Vino de la Tierra NV, **16**, *Booths*, red, 32

Casa Rivas Cabernet Sauvignon 2003, **16**, *Adnams*, red, 211

Casa Rivas Cabernet Sauvignon Reserva 2002, **16.5**, *Adnams*, red, 208

Casa Rivas Chardonnay 2004, **15**, *Adnams*, white, 216

Casa Rivas Chardonnay Reserva 2003, **14.5**, *Adnams*, white, 218

Casa Rivas Merlot 2003, **16**, *Adnams*, red, 211

Casa Rivas Merlot Reserva 2002, **16.5**, *Adnams*, *Oddbins*, red, 144, 211

Casa Rivas Rosé 2003, **14**, *Adnams*, rosé, 219

Casa Rivas Sauvignon Blanc 2004, **15.5**, *Adnams*, white, 215

Casillero del Diablo Concha y Toro Cabernet Sauvignon 2003, **16**, *Asda*, *Sainsbury*, *Tesco*, red, 8, 184, 254

Casillero del Diablo Concha y Toro Cabernet Sauvignon 2004, **16.5**, *Booths, Budgens, Tesco, Waitrose*, red, 30, 45, 253, 305

Casillero del Diablo Concha y Toro Carmenere 2003, **17**, *Threshers*, red, 284

Casillero del Diablo Concha y Toro Carmenere 2004, **17**, *Majestic, Sainsbury, Tesco, Threshers*, red, 83, 167, 248, 286

Casillero del Diablo Concha y Toro Chardonnay 2004, **16.5**, *Asda, Majestic, Oddbins, Threshers*, white, 4, 87, 147, 288

Casillero del Diablo Concha y Toro Gewürztraminer 2004, **16**, *Asda*, white, 9

Casillero del Diablo Concha y Toro Malbec 2004, **16**, *Majestic*, red, 88

Casillero del Diablo Concha y Toro Merlot 2004, **16**, *Asda*, red, 9

Casillero del Diablo Concha y Toro Riesling 2004, **14**, *Oddbins*, white, 159

Casillero del Diablo Concha y Toro Sauvignon Blanc 2004, **16.5**, *Asda, Majestic, Oddbins, Somerfield, Tesco, Threshers*, white, 4, 84, 144, 227, 249, 286

Casillero del Diablo Concha y Toro Shiraz 2004, **16.5**, *Majestic, Sainsbury, Somerfield*, red, 87, 168, 225

Casillero del Diablo Concha y Toro Viognier 2004, **16**, *Morrison's*, white, 131

Castillo de Almansa Colección Blanco Bodegas Piqueras 2004, **14.5**, *Booths*, white, 39

Castillo de Molina Reserva Chardonnay 2004, **16**, *Morrison's*, white, 131

Castillo de Molina Reserva Shiraz 2003, **16**, *Morrison's*, red, 131

Castillo de San Lorenzo Rioja Reserva 1999, **15.5**, *Tesco*, red, 264

Catena Cabernet Sauvignon 2002, **16**, *Majestic*, red, 89

Catena Chardonnay 2003, **17**, *Majestic, Waitrose*, white, 83, 302

Cava Cristalino Brut, **14**, *Morrison's*, white sparkling, 136

Cave de Turckheim Alsace Grand Cru Riesling Ollwiller 2002, **15**, *Booths*, white, 38

Cazal Viel Viognier Grande Réserve 2004, **17.5**, *Threshers*, white, 283

Chablis Cave des Vignerons de Chablis 2004, **14.5**, *Waitrose*, white, 321

Chablis Grand Cru Grenouille, Les Viticulteurs de Chablis 2002, **16**, *Waitrose*, white, 307

Chablis La Chablisienne 2002, **16**, *Marks & Spencer*, white, 121

Chain of Ponds Novello Rosso Sangiovese/Grenache Rosé 2003, **14**, *D. & D. Wines*, rosé, 219

Champagne Baron-Fuente NV, **16**, *Booths*, white sparkling, 32

Champagne Baron-Fuente Rosé Dolores NV, **14**, *Booths*, rosé sparkling, 32

Champagne Paul Reisder NV, **14**, *Somerfield*, white sparkling, 240

Champagne Pommery Blanc de Blancs NV, **14**, *Oddbins, Unwins*, white sparkling, 159, 219

Chapel Down Century, Bottle Fermented Extra Dry NV, **14.5**, *Sainsbury*, white sparkling, 189

Chapel Hill Cabernet Sauvignon 2001, **15.5**, *Tesco*, red, 264

Chapel Hill Unwooded Chardonnay 2004, **15.5**, *Tesco*, white, 264

Chardonnay Bianco di Sicilia, Cantine Settesoli 2003, **16**, *Majestic*, white, 89

Château Bel Air Bordeaux 2003, **14**, *Budgens*, red, 54

Château Caronne St Gemme Haut Médoc Cru Bourgeois 1999, **15**, *Budgens*, red, 51

Château Cazal Viel Cuvée des Fées 2001, **16.5**, *Waitrose*, red, 302

Château Corbin St-Emilion Grand Cru Classé 2000, **16**, *Majestic*, white, 88

Château d'Aiguilhe Comtes de Neipperg, Côtes de Castillon 2001, **16**, *Waitrose*, red, 308

Château de Béranger Picpoul de Pinet, Cave Co-op de Pomerols 2004, **16**, *Booths*, white, 32

Château de Caraguilhes Corbières Rosé 2004, **16**, *Waitrose*, rosé, 308

Château de la Garde Ilias Bordeaux Supérieur 2001, **14**, *Sainsbury*, red, 190

Château de l'Abbaye de St-Ferme Bordeaux Supérieur 2002, **14**, *Majestic*, red, 105

Château de Respide Graves 2002, **16**, *Budgens*, red, 46

Château de Sours Rosé 2004, **14**, *Majestic*, rosé, 104

Château de Valcombe 'Prestige', Costières de Nîmes 2003, **17**, *Oddbins*, red, 141

Château des Lanes Corbières 2001, **17.5**, *Marks & Spencer*, red, 111

Château du Bluizard Beaujolais Blanc 2002, **16**, *Co-op*, white, 62

Château Fongaban Puisséguin-St-Emilion 2002, **16**, *Somerfield*, red, 230

Château Guiot, Costières de Nîmes 2004, **16**, *Majestic*, red, 89

Château Guiot Rosé, Costières de Nîmes 2004, **14.5**, *Majestic*, rosé, 102

Château Jouanin, Côtes du Castillon 2003, **17**, *Sainsbury*, red, 165

Château Jupille Carillon St-Emilion 1999, **14**, *Booths*, red, 40

Château La Forêt St-Hilaire Bordeaux 2002, **15**, *Tesco*, red, 267

Château La Vieille Cure Fronsac
2000, **16**, *Sainsbury*, red, 173

Château Laroque St-Emilion
Grand Cru 2001, **14.5**, *Waitrose*,
red, 321

Château Latour Léognan, Pessac-
Léognan 2004, **14**, *Waitrose*,
white, 323

Château Laurençon Bordeaux
2003, **15.5**, *Co-op*, red, 64

Château Le Pin Bordeaux Rouge
2003, **14.5**, *Booths*, red, 39

Château Maris Tradition
Minervois 2003, **16**, *Oddbins*,
red, 148

Château Marquis de la Grange
Bordeaux 2004, **14**, *Sainsbury*,
red, 190

Château Marsau Bordeaux, Côte
de Francs 2001, **15**, *Oddbins*,
red, 156

Château Martin Graves 2001, **15**,
Tesco, red, 267

Château Mouchetière Muscadet
Sur Lie, Gérard Sourice 2003,
14.5, *Budgens*, white, 52

Château Paul Mas, Coteaux de
Languedoc Grenache/Syrah/
Mourvèdre 2003, **17.5**, *Stratford
Wine Agencies*, red, 207

Château Pierrail Bordeaux
Blanc 2004, **14**, *Booths*, white,
40

Château Pierrail Bordeaux
Supérieur 2002, **16.5**, *Booths*,
red, xiv, 30

Château Planèzes, Côtes du
Roussillon-Villages 2001, **14**,
Marks & Spencer, red, 127

Château Plo du Roy Minervois
2000, **16.5**, *Marks & Spencer*, red,
115

Château Prince Noir Bordeaux
2002, **14**, *Asda*, red, 23

Château Saint-Jean-des-Graves
2004, **15.5**, *Majestic, Waitrose*,
white, 99, 316

Château Saint-Maurice Côtes du
Rhône 2003, **14**, *Waitrose*, red,
323

Château Ségonzac, Premières
Côtes de Blaye 2002, **16**,
Waitrose, red, 308

Château Sissan, Premières Côtes
de Bordeaux 2001, **15**, *Co-op*,
red, 65

Château Villerembert-Moureau
Minervois 2004, **16**, *Booths*, red,
32

Château Vonnet Entre-Deux-Mers
2004, **15.5**, *Sainsbury*, white,
186

Château Yon-Figéac, St-Emilion
Grand Cru 2001, **14**, *Oddbins*,
red, 159

Châteauneuf-du-Pape 'La
Bernardine' Chapoutier 2003,
16, *Asda*, red, 9

Châteauneuf-du-Pape La Volonté
des Papes 2001, **16**, *Somerfield*,
red, 230

Châteauneuf-du-Pape Le Vieux
Donjon 2001, **16.5**, *Yapp
Brothers*, red, 332

Chevalier de Lascombes Margaux
2001, **15.5**, *Waitrose*, red, 316

Cheverny Le Vieux Clos, Delaille
2004, **14**, *Waitrose*, white, 323

Chianti Burchino Superiore
2003, **16.5**, *Marks & Spencer*, red,
115

Chianti Cantine Leonardo 2003,
14, *Booths*, red, 40

Chianti Colli Fiorentini Terre
de'Nocenti 2003, **16**, *Marks &
Spencer*, red, 117

Chilcas Chardonnay 2003, **16**,
Waitrose, white, 307

Chilcas Malbec/Syrah 2003, **16.5**,
Waitrose, red, 303

Chileño Chardonnay/Sémillon
2004, **16**, *Waitrose*, white, xiii,
307

Chileño Gold Sauvignon Blanc
2004, **16**, *Somerfield*, white, 230

Chileño Shiraz/Cabernet
Sauvignon 2004, **15**, *Waitrose*,
16, *Sainsbury*, *Somerfield*, red,
172, 229, 318

Chinon Cuvée de Pâques,
Domaine de la Roche
Honneur 2003, **15**, *Booths*, red,
38

Chorey-les-Beune, Domaine
Pascal Maillard 2003, **17**,
Waitrose, red, 299

Churton Pinot Noir 2003, **14**,
Tanners Wines, red, 219

Cielo de Luz Cabernet Sauvignon
2004, **16**, *Morrison's*, red, 131

Cielo de Luz Carmenere 2004, **16**,
Morrison's, red, 131

Cielo de Luz Sauvignon Blanc
2004, **16**, *Morrison's*, white, 133

Clancy's Red Peter Lehmann
2002, **16**, *Booths*, *Budgens*, red,
36, 49

Clocktower Sauvignon Blanc
2004, **16**, *Marks & Spencer*,
white, 117

Clos de Los Siete 2003, **17**,
Majestic, *Waitrose*, red, 83, 300

Clos de Reynard 2004, **14**, *Marks &
Spencer*, red, 126

Clos Petite Bellane 'Les Echalas'
Valréas, Côtes du Rhône-
Villages 2003, **16**, *Oddbins*, red,
148

Clos Roque d'Aspes Faugères
2001, **16**, *Marks & Spencer*, red,
118

Cloudy Bay Pinot Noir 2003, **14.5**,
Harrods, *Majestic*, *Waitrose*, red,
102, 217, 321

Cloudy Bay Sauvignon Blanc
2004, **16.5**, *Tesco*, white, 248

Cloudy Bay Te Koko Sauvignon
Blanc 2002, **16.5**, *Waitrose*,
white, 302

Co-op Adelaide Hills Chardonnay
Reserve 2004, **16.5**, *Co-op*,
white, 59

Co-op Argentinian Malbec 2004,
16, *Co-op*, red, 61

Co-op Australian Lime Tree
Grenache 2004, **15.5**, *Co-op*, red,
64

Co-op Australian Sparkling Brut
NV, **16**, *Co-op*, white sparkling,
60

Co-op Cape Limited Release
Gewürztraminer 2004, **14**,
Co-op, white, 68

Co-op Cape Seal Bay Chardonnay
Reserve 2003, **15**, *Co-op*, white,
65

Co-op Casa del Sol Sauvignon Blanc/Verdejo 2004, **14**, *Co-op*, white, 68

Co-op Centolla Pinot Noir 2003, **16**, *Co-op*, red, 61

Co-op Coonawarra Cabernet Sauvignon Reserve 2003, **16**, *Co-op*, red, 61

Co-op Elephant Trail Pinotage/ Shiraz 2004, **14**, *Co-op*, red, 67

Co-op Explorer's Vineyard Sauvignon Blanc 2004, **14**, *Co-op*, white, 68

Co-op Fair Trade Cape Affinity Red 2004, **14**, *Co-op*, red, 68

Co-op French Organic Chardonnay/Sauvignon Blanc 2004, **15**, *Co-op*, white, 65

Co-op Island Vines Cyprus White 2004, **15**, *Co-op*, white, 65

Co-op Jacaranda Hill Shiraz 2004, **15**, *Co-op*, red, 65

Co-op Moses Lake Cabernet Sauvignon 2003, **16**, *Co-op*, red, 61

Co-op Moses Lake Chardonnay 2004, **15**, *Co-op*, white, 65

Co-op Pinot Grigio 2004, **14**, *Co-op*, white, 68

Co-op Romanian Prairie Merlot 2003, **15**, *Co-op*, red, 65

Co-op Soave Classico 2004, **14**, *Co-op*, white, 68

Co-op Starlight Coast Zinfandel 2003, **14**, *Co-op*, red, 68

Co-op Vin de Pays du Jardin de la France Sauvignon Blanc 2004, **14**, *Co-op*, white, 68

Coldridge Estate Chardonnay 2004, **16**, *Majestic*, white, 88

Coldridge Estate Merlot 2003, **16**, *Majestic*, red, xiv, 89

Collioure La Pinède, Domaine de la Tour Vieille 2003, **17.5**, *Yapp Brothers*, red, 331

Comte Cathare Le Parfait Chardonnay 2003, **14**, *Oddbins*, red, 159

Comte Cathare Le Parfait Syrah 2002, **14**, *Oddbins*, red, 159

Concerto Lambrusco Reggiano Medici Ermete 2003, **16**, *Booths*, red sparkling, 32

Concha y Toro Late Harvest Sauvignon Blanc 2001, **15.5**, *Majestic*, white, 99

Concha y Toro Sauvignon Blanc 2004, **14.5**, *Budgens*, white, 52

Concha y Toro Sunrise Merlot 2004, **16**, *Budgens, Waitrose*, red, 50, 306

Concha y Toro Winemakers Lot 20 Riesling 2004, **15**, *Oddbins*, white, 156

Concha y Toro Winemakers Lot 406 Syrah 2004, **16**, *Majestic*, red, 88

Concha y Toro Winemakers Lot 1006 Merlot 2004, **15.5**, *Majestic*, red, 99

Concha y Toro Winemakers Lot Chardonnay 2002, **16**, *Virgin*, white, 77

Concha y Toro Winemakers Lot Gewürztraminer 2004, **16**, *Oddbins*, white, 148

Concha y Toro Winemakers Lot Merlot/Syrah 2003, **16**, *Majestic*, red, 96

Conde de Siruela Ribera del Duero, Tinto Roble 2003, **17**, *Sainsbury*, red, 166

Cono Sur Cabernet Sauvignon 2004, **16**, *Tesco*, red, 254

Cono Sur Chardonnay 2003, **16**, *Tesco*, white, 255

Cono Sur Chardonnay 2004, **15.5**, *Budgens*, white, 51

Cono Sur Gewürztraminer 2004, **16**, *Majestic*, white, 89

Cono Sur Gewürztraminer 2004, **16**, *Sainsbury*, white, 173

Cono Sur Limited Release Viognier 2004, **16**, *Waitrose*, white, 308

Cono Sur Merlot 2003, **16**, *Tesco*, red, 254

Cono Sur Merlot 2004, **15.5**, *Sainsbury*, red, 185

Cono Sur Merlot Reserve 2003, **17.5**, *Waitrose*, red, 299

Cono Sur Pinot Noir 2004, **16**, *Majestic, Somerfield, Threshers, Waitrose*, red, 98, 236, 288, 309

Cono Sur Pinot Noir Reserve 2002, **16**, *Tesco*, red, 255

Cono Sur Reserve Chardonnay 2004, **16**, *Somerfield*, white, 231

Cono Sur Viognier 2004, **16**, *Majestic, Somerfield, Threshers, Waitrose*, white, 97, 229, 290, 307

Cono Sur Vision Gewürztraminer 2002, **14**, *Sainsbury*, white, 190

Corbières La Forge, Gérard Bertrand 2001, **14**, *Waitrose*, red, 323

Corbières (M & S) 2003, **14**, *Marks & Spencer*, red, 127

Cordier Collection Privée 2001, **16.5**, *Threshers*, red, 286

Coteau Brûlé Cairanne, Côtes du Rhône-Villages 2003, **15**, *Tesco*, red, 267

Côtes de Gascogne, Domaine de Millet 2004, **16**, *Yapp Brothers*, white, 333

Côtes du Roussillon 'Tradition', Ferrer-Ribière 2001, **17**, *Yapp Brothers*, red, 331

Côtes du Ventoux, Château Valcombe 2001, **17**, *Yapp Brothers*, red, 332

Côtes du Ventoux, Château Valcombe 2002, **14**, *Yapp Brothers*, red, 334

Cottesbrook Sauvignon Blanc 2004, **14**, *Tesco*, white, 275

Coulée d'Argent Bourillon d'Orléans Vouvray Sec 2004, **15**, *Majestic*, white, 100

Coyam 2002, **16.5**, *Vintage Roots*, red, 74

Craggy Range Old Renwick Vineyard Marlborough Sauvignon Blanc 2004, **15.5**, *Waitrose*, white, 315

Craggy Range Te Muna Pinot Noir 2003, **14.5**, *Amey's Wines, The Wine Society*, red, 218

Cranswick Reserve Selection Botrytis Sémillon 2002, **16.5**, *Asda*, white dessert, 5

Croft Indulgence Port NV, **16**, *Tesco*, fortified, 263

Crozes-Hermitage Blanc, Domaine Belle Père et Fils 2002, **15**, *Oddbins*, white, 156

Crozes-Hermitage Cave des Clairmonts 2003, **14**, *Waitrose*, red, 323

Cullen Estate Diana Madelaine Cabernet/Merlot 2001, **14**, *Majestic*, red, 105

Cune Monopole Rioja 2003, **16**, *Waitrose*, red, 308

Cusumano Benuara Nero d'Avola/ Syrah 2003, **14**, *Oddbins*, white, 159

Cusumano Nero d'Avola 2003, **14**, *Oddbins*, red, 159

Cuvée de Richard Blanc, Vin de Pays du Comte Tolosan 2004, **14**, *Majestic*, white, 104

Cuvée des Amandiers, Vin de Pays d'Oc 2004, **14**, *Majestic*, red, 104

Cuvée des Amandiers Blanc, Vin de Pays d'Oc 2004, **14.5**, *Majestic*, white, 102

Cuvée des Amandiers Rosé, Vin de Pays d'Oc 2004, **14**, *Majestic*, rosé, 104

Cuvée Fleur Rosé, Vin de Pays de l'Hérault 2004, **16**, *Waitrose*, rosé, xiii, 308

Cuvée Picheral Bin 040, Vin de Pays du Gard 2001, **14**, *Asda*, red, 22

D

Da Luca Grillo Chardonnay NV, **15.5**, *Tesco*, white, 264

Da Luca Primitivo Merlot 2003, **17**, *Co-op*, *Tesco*, red, 59, 246

Da Luca Primitivo Merlot 2004, **14**, *Budgens*, red, 54

Dancing Monkey 'Alpha Series' Cabernet Sauvignon 2003, **15.5**, *Oddbins*, red, 155

Dancing Monkey 'Alpha Series' Chardonnay 2004, **14**, *Oddbins*, white, 159

Dancing Monkey 'Alpha Series' Malbec 2003, **15.5**, *Oddbins*, red, 154

Dancing Monkey 'Alpha Series' Merlot 2003, **16**, *Oddbins*, red, 149

Dancing Monkey Cabernet Sauvignon/Merlot/Malbec 2003, **16**, *Oddbins*, red, 149

Dancing Monkey Chardonnay/ Sémillon 2004, **16**, *Oddbins*, white, 149

Danie de Wet Chardonnay Sur Lie 2004, **17**, *Tesco*, white, 245

Danie de Wet Chardonnay Sur Lie Unoaked 2004, **16**, *Asda*, white, 9

D'Arenberg 'Footbolt' Old Vine Shiraz 2002, **16**, *Oddbins*, red, 147

D'Arenberg 'The Bonsai Vine' Grenache/Shiraz/Mourvèdre 2001, **16.5**, *Oddbins*, red, 145

D'Arenberg 'The Hermit Crab' Marsanne/Viognier 2003, **16.5**, *Booths*, white, 30

D'Arenberg 'The Hermit Crab' Marsanne/Viognier 2004, **16.5**, *Waitrose*, white, 306

D'Arenberg 'The Money Spider' Roussanne 2003, **17**, *Oddbins*, white, 142

D'Arenberg 'The Olive Grove' Chardonnay 2003, **17**, *Oddbins*, white, 142

Darting Estate Michelsberg Riesling 2004, **16**, *Marks & Spencer*, white, 118

Dashwood Sauvignon Blanc 2004, **14**, *Oddbins*, white, 160

De Martino Legado Carmenere Reserva 2003, **14.5**, *Virgin*, red, 78

De Martino Legado Sauvignon Blanc Reserva 2004, **14**, *Virgin*, white, 79

De Martino Single Vineyard Pinot Noir 2002, **14**, *Virgin*, red, 79

De Martino Single Vineyard Syrah 2003, **14**, *Virgin*, red, 80

Deakin Estate Chardonnay/Pinot Noir Brut NV, **15**, *Bibendum*, *Oddbins*, white sparkling, 157, 216

Deakin Estate Colombard/ Chardonnay 2004, **15.5**, *Oddbins*, white, 154

Deakin Estate Rosé 2004, **14**, *Bibendum*, *Oddbins*, rosé, 159, 220

Delegat's Oyster Bay Central Otago Merlot 2004, **16**, *Sainsbury*, red, 174

Delicato Shiraz 2002, **14.5**, *Sainsbury*, red, 189

Delta Vineyards Pinot Noir 2004, **14**, *Liberty Wines*, red, 220

Denis Marchais Hand Picked Vouvray 2003, **14**, *Asda*, white, 23

Desroches Champagne NV, **16**, *Marks & Spencer*, white sparkling, 118

Deux Soleils 'Les Romains' Chardonnay/Viognier, Vin de Pays d'Oc 2003, **16**, *Oddbins*, white, 149

Devil's Rock Pinot Grigio 2003, **15**, *Waitrose*, white, 318

Devil's Rock Riesling 2003, **16**, *Sainsbury*, white, 174

DFJ Touriga Franca/Touriga Nacional 2003, **16**, *Tesco*, red, 255

Diemersfontein Pinotage 2004, **16.5**, *Asda*, *Waitrose*, red, 5, 305

Distinto Catarratto/Chardonnay 2004, **15**, *Morrison's*, white, 135

Divinum Riesling 2004, **15**, *Somerfield*, white, 238

Dogajolo Carpineto Toscana 2003, **14**, *Majestic*, red, 105

Dolphin Bay Shiraz 2004, **15.5**, *Marks & Spencer*, red, 124

Domaine Bégude Sauvignon Blanc, Vin de Pays d'Oc 2004, **16**, *Oddbins*, white, 149

Domaine Borie de Maurel Esprit d'Automne 2003, **16.5**, *Oddbins*, red, 145

Domaine Bunan Bandol 2001, **16.5**, *Marks & Spencer*, red, 115

Domaine Cady Harmonie, Coteaux du Layon 2001, **14**, *Oddbins*, white, 160

Domaine Carrette Pouilly-Fuissé 2003, **15.5**, *Morrison's*, white, 134

Domaine Chaume-Arnaud Côtes du Rhône-Villages Vinsobres 2002, **16**, *Booths*, red, 33

Domaine de la Bastide Viognier, Vin de Pays de l'Hautérive 2004, **16**, *Booths*, white, 33

Domaine de la Janasse Terre de Bussière, Vin de Pays de la Principauté d'Orange 2003, **14**, *Majestic*, red, 105

Domaine de Pellehaut Blanc, Vin de Pays des Côtes de Gascogne 2004, **15.5**, *Booths*, white, 37

Domaine de Pellehaut Rosé, Vin de Pays des Côtes de Gascogne 2004, **14**, *Booths*, *Waitrose*, rosé, 40, 323

Domaine de Piaugier Côtes de Rhône-Villages Sablet 2002, **15.5**, *Majestic*, red, 99

Domaine de Plantieu, Vin de Pays des Côtes de Gascogne 2004 **14.5**, *Waitrose*, white, 321

Domaine de Saint-Antoine 'Selection Coin du Murier', Costières de Nîmes 2003, **16**, *Oddbins*, red, 150

Domaine de Sours Bordeaux Rosé 2004, **14**, *Sainsbury*, rosé, 191

Domaine du Bois Viognier, Vin de Pays d'Oc 2003, **15.5**, *Somerfield*, white, 237

Domaine du Colombier Chinon 2003, **17**, *Sainsbury*, red, 167

Domaine Galatis Chardonnay/ Viognier 2004, **16**, *Marks & Spencer*, white, 118

Domaine La Galine 2003, **15.5**, *Majestic*, red, 99

Domaine Leonce Cuisset, Saussignac 2003, **15.5**, *Sainsbury*, dessert white, 186

Domaine Mandeville Viognier 2004, **14**, *Marks & Spencer*, white, 127

Domaine St-Laurent St-Chinian 2003, **14**, *Booths*, red, 40

Domini Plus 2001, **17**, *Waitrose*, red, 301

Domus Aurea Cabernet Sauvignon 1999, **15**, *Oddbins*, red, 157

Domus Aurea Cabernet Sauvignon 2001, **14**, *Oddbins*, red, 160

Don Reca Limited Release Merlot 2002, **15.5**, *Sainsbury*, *Waitrose*, red, 186, 317

Doña Dominga Cabernet Sauvignon/Carmenere 2003, **15.5**, *Sainsbury*, red, 186

Doña Dominga Carmenere Reserva 2002, **16.5**, *Sainsbury*, *Waitrose*, red, 169, 303

Doña Dominga Chardonnay/Sémillon 2004, **14.5**, *Sainsbury*, white, 189

Dorrien Estate Bin 442 Barossa Shiraz 2003, **17.5**, *Marks & Spencer*, red, 111

Douglas Green Chardonnay 2004, **16**, *Waitrose*, white, 309

Douglas Green Merlot 2003, **15**, *Tesco*, red, 267

Douglas Green Sauvignon Blanc 2004, **14.5**, *Asda*, white, 20

Dourthe Barrel Select St-Emilion 2003, **15.5**, *Waitrose*, red, 316

Dourthe No 1 Sauvignon Blanc Bordeaux 2004, **14**, *Waitrose*, white, 323

Dr L Riesling Mosel-Saar-Ruwer 2004, **14**, *Sainsbury*, white, 191

Drappier Carte d'Or Champagne NV, **16**, *Co-op*, white sparkling, 62

Dumisani Chenin/Chardonnay 2004, **14**, *Asda*, white, 23

Durius Arribes del Duero Tempranillo 2003, **15**, *Majestic*, red, 100

Durius Marqués de Griñon Tempranillo 2003, **14**, *Sainsbury*, red, 191

Durius Tempranillo 2003, **16**, *Budgens*, red, 46

Durius Tempranillo Alto Duero 2003, **16**, *Sainsbury*, red, 173

Duval-Leroy Fleur de Champagne Premier Cru NV, **14.5**, *Waitrose*, white sparkling, 321

E

El Dorado Sauvignon Blanc Reserva 2004, **14**, *Sainsbury*, white, 191

El Dueño Chardonnay 2004, **16**, *Marks & Spencer*, white, 119

El Dueño Shiraz 2004, **15**, *Marks & Spencer*, red, 125

El Malbec de Ricardo Santos, La Madras Vineyard 2003, **14.5**, *Majestic*, red, 102

Emiliana Chardonnay 2004, **14**, *Somerfield*, white, 240

Emiliana Syrah 2004, **16**, *Somerfield*, red, 231

English Oak Minervois La Livinière 2002, **17**, *Booths*, red, 29

Ernst Loosen Erdener Treppchen Riesling Kabinett 2004, **14**, *Marks & Spencer*, white, 127

Errazuriz Estate Cabernet Sauvignon 2003, **16.5**, *Asda, Everywine, Oddbins, Somerfield, Waitrose*, red, 6, 75, 147, 225–6, 303

Errazuriz Estate Carmenere 2003, **16.5**, *Asda, D. Byrne & Co., Everywine, Luvians, Vicki's of Chobham, Wimbledon Wine Cellars*, red, 5, 75, 208

Errazuriz Estate Chardonnay 2004, **16.5**, *Budgens, Everywine, Oddbins, Sainsbury, Somerfield, Tesco*, white, 45, 75, 147, 168, 225, 249

Errazuriz Estate Don Maximiano Founders Reserve 2000, **14**, *Tesco*, red, 275

Errazuriz Estate Dos Valles Reserve Syrah 2002, **14**, *Virgin*, red, 79

Errazuriz Estate La Cumbre Syrah 2002, **17**, *Waitrose*, red, 301

Errazuriz Estate Max Reserva Cabernet Sauvignon 2001, **17**, *Tesco*, red, 246

Errazuriz Estate Max Reserva Cabernet Sauvignon 2002, **17.5**, *Budgens*, red, 45

Errazuriz Estate Max Reserva Chardonnay 2004, **17**, *Waitrose*, white, 301

Errazuriz Estate Max Reserva Shiraz 2002, **16.5**, *Threshers*, red, 286

Errazuriz Estate Max Reserva Syrah 2002, **16.5**, *Majestic*, red, 84

Errazuriz Estate Merlot 2003, **17**, *Everywine, Oddbins, Sainsbury, Tesco, Threshers*, red, 73–4, 144, 167, 247, 284

Errazuriz Estate Merlot 2004, **15.5**, *Sainsbury*, red, 186

Errazuriz Estate Sangiovese 2003, **17.5**, *D.Byrne & Co., Everywine, Luvians, Vicki's of Chobham, Wimbledon Wine Cellars*, red, 73, 207

Errazuriz Estate Sauvignon Blanc 2004, **17**, *Everywine, Oddbins, Threshers*, white, 73, 143, 284

Errazuriz Estate Shiraz 2003, **16.5**, *Tesco, Waitrose*, red, 248, 303

Errazuriz Estate Syrah 2003, **16**, *Sainsbury*, red, 175

Errazuriz Estate Unoaked Chardonnay 2004, **17.5**, *Threshers*, white, 283

Esk Valley Reserve Merlot/Malbec/ Cabernet Sauvignon 2002, **15**, *Everywine, Vicki's of Chobham, Wimbledon Wine Cellars*, red, 78, 216

Esperanza Merlot 2004, **16**, *Majestic*, red, 90

Esperanza Sauvignon Blanc 2004, **14**, *Majestic*, white, 105

Esporao Reserva 2001, **14**, *Waitrose*, red, 323

Evans & Tate Classic White 2004, **15.5**, *Asda*, white, 16

Evans & Tate Langhorne Creek Shiraz 2003, **16**, *Asda*, red, 9

Evans & Tate Shiraz/Cabernet 2003, **15.5**, *Asda*, red, 16

Excelsior Estate Merlot 2003, **14**, *Sainsbury*, red, 191

Excelsior Estate Special Reserve Cabernet Sauvignon 2002, **14**, *Sainsbury*, red, 191

Excelsior Paddock Shiraz 2004, **16**, *Sainsbury, Somerfield*, red, 175, 236

Fagus de Loto de Hayas 2002, **14**, *Asda*, red, 23

Fairleigh Estate Riesling 2004, **14**, *Majestic*, white, 105

Fairleigh Estate Single Vineyard Marlborough Chardonnay 2003, **16**, *Majestic*, white, 90

Fairleigh Estate Single Vineyard Marlborough Sauvignon Blanc 2004, **15**, *Majestic*, white, 100

Fairview 'Peg Leg' Carignan 2003, **16**, *Majestic*, red, 90

Falanghina Feudi di San Gregorio 2003, **16**, *Oddbins*, white, 150

Falasco Garganega Vendemmia Tardiva Valpantena 2004, **15**, *Booths*, white, 38

Familia Zuccardi 'Q' Tempranillo 2002, **17.5**, *Tesco*, red, 245

Faustion V White Rioja NV, **14**, *Tesco*, white, 275

Felsner Grüner Veltliner Mossbürgerin 2004, **15**, *Waitrose*, white, 318

Ferrari Brut NV, **16.5**, *Oddbins*, white sparkling, 145

Ferrari Brut Perle NV, **14**, *Oddbins*, white sparkling, 160

Fetzer Chardonnay/Viognier 2003, **14.5**, *Budgens*, white, 52

Fetzer Eagle Peak Merlot 2003, **14**, *Budgens*, red, 54

Fetzer Syrah Rosé 2003, **14.5**, *Tesco*, rosé, 272

Fetzer Syrah Rosé 2004, **14**, *Budgens*, rosé, 54

Fetzer Valley Oaks Syrah Rosé 2004, **15.5**, *Asda*, rosé, 16

Fetzer Zinfandel/Shiraz 2003, **15**, *Budgens*, *Co-op*, red, 52, 65

Feudi di Santa Teresa 'Nivuro' Nero d'Avola/Cabernet 2001, **16**, *Oddbins*, red, 151

Finca Flichman Shiraz Reserva 2004, **16.5**, *Waitrose*, red, 303

Finca Las Higueras Pinot Gris 2004, **16**, *Waitrose*, white, 309

Finca Las Moras Viognier 2004, **16.5**, *Majestic*, white, 84

Finca Les Moras Shiraz Rosé 2004, **14.5**, *Majestic*, rosé, 102

Finest Aglianico Basilicata 2002, **16**, *Tesco*, red, 255

Finest Alsace Riesling 2003, **14**, *Tesco*, white, 275

Finest Argentinian Malbec Reserve 2003, **15.5**, *Tesco*, red, 265

Finest Australian Reserve Chardonnay 2004, **16**, *Tesco*, white, 256

Finest Australian Sauvignon Blanc 2004, **15.5**, *Tesco*, white, 264

Finest Californian Chardonnay Reserve 2003, **15.5**, *Tesco*, white, 265

Finest Californian Pinot Grigio Reserve 2003, **14**, *Tesco*, white, 276

Finest Chablis 2002, **14.5**, *Tesco*, white, 272

Finest Chilean Chardonnay Reserve 2003, **15**, *Tesco*, white, 267

Finest New Zealand Hawkes Bay Chardonnay 2002, **16.5**, *Tesco*, white, 249

Finest Picpoul de Pinet 2003, **14.5**, *Tesco*, white, 272

Finest Pinotage Reserve 2003, **16**, *Tesco*, red, 255

Finest Sicilian Grillo 2003, **16**, *Tesco*, white, 256

Finest Soave Classico 2004, **14.5**, *Tesco*, white, 272

Finest Touriga Nacional 2003, **16**, *Tesco*, red, 255

Finest Viña Mara Gran Reserva Rioja 1998, **15.5**, *Tesco*, red, 265

Finest Viña Mara Rioja Reserva 2001, **15.5**, *Tesco*, red, 264

Finest Vintage Claret 2002, **15**, *Tesco*, red, 268

Firebird Legend Pinot Grigio 2003, **14.5**, *Waitrose*, white, 321

Firefinch Colombard/
Chardonnay, Springfield
Estate 2004, **16**, *Booths*, white,
33

Fitou 2002, **16**, *Marks & Spencer*,
red, 119

Flagstone Fish Hoek Rosé 2004,
15, *Oddbins*, rosé, 157

Flagstone Noon Gun 2004, **15.5**,
Oddbins, white, 155

Flagstone Semaphore Rosé 2004,
14.5, *Oddbins*, rosé, 158

Flagstone The Berrio Cabernet
Sauvignon 2004, **15**, *Oddbins*,
red, 157

Flagstone The Berrio Sauvignon
Blanc 2004, **14**, *Oddbins*, white,
160

Flagstone Two Roads 2004, **15.5**,
Oddbins, white, 155

Fleur du Cap Sauvignon Blanc
2004, **14**, *Oddbins*, white, 160

Fleurie Domaine Fonfotin 2002,
14, *Budgens*, red, 54

Flinders McLaren Vale Terra
Nova Grenache/Shiraz/
Viognier 2003, **17.5**, *Threshers*,
red, 283

Flinders Realm Chardonnay 2004,
16, *Threshers*, white, 290

Flinders Realm Colombard/
Chardonnay 2004, **15.5**,
Threshers, white, 294

Flinders Realm Shiraz 2002, **16**,
Threshers, red, 290

Flinders Realm Verdelho/
Chardonnay 2004, **16**,
Threshers, white, 290

Foncaussade Les Parcelles
Bergerac Rosé 2004, **15.5**,
Waitrose, rosé, 316

Forrest Estate Pinot Noir 2003, **15**,
Adnams, red, 216

Freixenet Ash Tree Estate
Monastrell 2003, **14**, *Tesco*, red,
275

French Connection Reserve
Chardonnay 2004, **14.5**, *Co-op*,
white, 66

French Connection Reserve
Merlot 2004, **14.5**, *Co-op*, red,
66

Friuli Sauvignon Blanc 2004, **16**,
Marks & Spencer, white, 119

Frontera Cabernet Sauvignon/
Chardonnay 2004, **16**,
Sainsbury, white, 175

Frontera Cabernet Sauvignon/
Merlot 2004, **17**, *Sainsbury*, *Spar*,
red, 167, 207

Frontera Chardonnay 2004, **15.5**,
Tesco, white, 264

Frontera Sauvignon/Chardonnay
2004, **16**, *Spar*, white, 212

Funky Llama Cabernet
Sauvignon 2004, **16**, *Asda*, red,
10

Gallo Turning Leaf Zinfandel
2002, **14.5**, *Tesco*, red, 272

Gavi Brico Battistina 2004, **15.5**,
Majestic, white, 99

Gavi del Commune di Gavi
Masseria dei Carmelitani 2004,
15, *Booths*, white, 38

Gavi di Gavi La Tolcadana Raccolto Tardivo 2004, **16**, *Majestic*, white, 90

Gavi La Luciana Araldica 2004, **15**, *Waitrose*, white, 318

Gavi Terredavino 2004, **16**, *Majestic*, white, 90

Geoff Merrill Grenache Rosé 2004, **14.5**, *Amey's Wines, Charles Hennings, Christopher Piper Wine*, rosé, 218

Gérard Bertrand Classic Fitou 2002, **16**, *Asda*, red, 10

Gérard Bertrand Collection Pinot Noir, Vin de Pays d'Oc 2001, **15.5**, *Asda*, red, 16

Gérard Bertrand Terroir, Coteaux du Languedoc 2001, **16**, *Asda*, red, 10

Gevrey-Chambertin Les Evocelles 2003, **16**, *Waitrose*, red, 310

Gevrey-Chambertin Vieilles Vignes, Domaine Heresztyn 2003, **16.5**, *Waitrose*, red, 304

Gewürztraminer Caves de Turckheim 2004, **14**, *Waitrose*, white, 324

Gewürztraminer Charles Schleret, Alsace 1999, **16.5**, *Yapp Brothers*, white, 332

Gewürztraminer d'Alsace Preiss Zimmer 2003, **14**, *Morrison's*, white, 136

Gewürztraminer Grand Cru Eichberg Zinck 2002, **16.5**, *Majestic*, white, 85

Gewürztraminer Grand Cru Furstentum Vieilles Vignes,

Albert Mann 2002, **16**, *Waitrose*, white, 309

Giesen Marlborough Sauvignon Blanc 2004, **14**, *Tesco*, white, 276

Gladstone Vineyards Pinot Noir 2004, **14**, *James Nicholson Wine Merchants*, red, 220

Glen Ellen Chardonnay 2002, **14**, *Tesco*, white, 276

Gobelsburger Grüner Veltliner 2004, **16**, *Waitrose*, white, 310

Gobelsburger Riesling 2003, **16.5**, *Waitrose*, white, 304

Goiya DM Shiraz/Pinotage 2004, **14**, *Tesco*, red, 276

Goiya Kgeisje Sauvignon/ Chardonnay 2004, **14**, *Tesco*, white, 276

Gold Label Cabernet Sauvignon, Vin de Pays d'Oc 2004, **14**, *Marks & Spencer*, red, 127

Gold Label Cabernet Sauvignon/ Merlot, Vin de Pays d'Oc 2002, **16.5**, *Marks & Spencer*, red, 116

Gold Label Chardonnay, Vin de Pays d'Oc 2004, **16**, *Marks & Spencer*, white, 119

Gold Label Rosé, Vin de Pays d'Oc 2004, **14**, *Marks & Spencer*, rosé, 127

Goldwater 'Goldie' Cabernet Sauvignon/Merlot/Cabernet Franc 2002, **16**, *Avery's of Bristol*, red, 212–13

Goundrey Cabernet/Merlot 2003, **15.5**, *Somerfield*, red, 237

Goundrey Unwooded
   Chardonnay 2004, **16**,
   Somerfield, white, 231
Gracia Merlot/Mourvèdre 2003,
   17, *Waitrose*, red, 301
Gracia Merlot/Mourvèdre Reserva
   Superior 2003, **14**, *Waitrose*, red,
   324
Graffigna Shiraz/Cabernet
   Sauvignon 2003, **16.5**, *Co-op*,
   red, xiv, 59
Graham Beck Pinotage 2003, **15**,
   Tesco, red, 268
Graham Beck Sauvignon Blanc
   2004, **14**, *Asda*, white, 23
Graham Beck Shiraz 2003, **16**,
   Asda, red, 11
Graham Beck Viognier 2004, **15**,
   Sainsbury, white, 187
Gran'Arte Trincadeira 2003, **16**,
   Booths, red, 33
Green Point Chardonnay/Pinot
   Noir Brut 1999, **16**, *Oddbins*,
   white sparkling, 151
Green Point Vintage Brut 1999,
   16, *Waitrose*, white sparkling,
   309
Green Point ZD 2001, **16**,
   Waitrose, white sparkling, xiv,
   309
Greenfield Winery Chardonnay
   2003, **15**, *Asda*, white, 18
Griffin Vineyards Verdelho 2003,
   16, *Majestic*, white, 91
Grüner Veltliner Atrium 2004,
   16, *Marks & Spencer*, white,
   120

H

H. Blin & Co. Brut Tradition NV,
   15.5, *Oddbins*, white sparkling,
   154
H de l'Hospitalet White, Vin de
   Pays d'Oc 2003, **16**, *Tesco*, white,
   257
Hanging Rock 'Amaroo Farm'
   Mourvèdre 2004, **14**, *Asda*, red,
   23
Hanging Rock Sauvignon Blanc
   2004, **14**, *Asda*, white, 23
Hardy's Crest Sparkling Shiraz
   NV, **16**, *Tesco*, red sparkling, 257
Hardy's Nottage Hill Sparkling
   Chardonnay 2004, **15.5**,
   Sainsbury, *Somerfield*, white
   sparkling, 186, 237
Hardy's Stamp of Australia
   Grenache/Shiraz Rosé 2004, **14**,
   Morrison's, rosé, 136
Hardy's Stamp of Australia
   Sparkling Pinot Noir/
   Chardonnay Brut NV, **14**, *Asda*,
   Sainsbury, *Somerfield*, *Tesco*,
   white sparkling, 23, 191, 240,
   280
Hardy's Tintara Cabernet
   Sauvignon 1999, **15**, *Budgens*,
   red, 51
Hardy's Voyage Cabernet
   Sauvignon/Petit Verdot/Ruby
   Cabernet 2003, **14**, *Tesco*,
   Waitrose, red, 276, 324
Hardy's Voyage Colombard/
   Verdelho/Chenin Blanc 2004,
   14, *Tesco*, white, 276

Hardy's Wayfarer Chardonnay 2004, **15.5**, *Asda*, white, 16

Harrowgate Shiraz 2003, **17**, *Marks & Spencer*, red, 113

Hattenheimer Wisselbrunnen Kabinett Von Simmern 2002, **15.5**, *Waitrose*, white, 316

Heathcote Cambrian Rise Shiraz 2002, **14**, *Asda*, red, 23

Henri Harlin Champagne NV, **16**, *Oddbins*, white sparkling, 151

Henschke Coralinga Sauvignon Blanc 2003, **14**, *Waitrose*, white, 324

Henschke Henry's Seven Shiraz/Grenache/Viognier 2003, **14.5**, *Waitrose*, red, 321

Henschke Louis Sémillon 2004, **14.5**, *Waitrose*, white, 322

Herrick Merlot, Vin de Pays d'Oc 2003, **16**, *Budgens*, red, 47

Herrick Syrah, Vin de Pays d'Oc 2002, **16**, *Budgens*, red, 47

Hidden Hill Chardonnay/ Viognier, Vin de Pays d'Oc 2004, **16**, *Threshers*, white, 291

Hidden Hill Sauvignon Blanc 2004, **16**, *Stratford Wine Agencies*, white, 213

Hochheimer Kirchenstück Riesling Spätlese Künstler 2003, **14**, *Waitrose*, white, 324

Honey Tree Reserve Chardonnay 2004, **16**, *Marks & Spencer*, white, 120

Honey Tree Shiraz/Cabernet Sauvignon 2004, **14**, *Marks & Spencer*, red, 127

Houdamond Pinotage 2004, **14**, *Marks & Spencer*, red, 127

Huia Pinot Noir 2003, **16**, *Bibendum*, red, 213

Huntaway Marlborough Sauvignon Blanc 2004, **16.5**, *Threshers*, white, 286

Ile La Forge Cabernet Sauvignon 2003, **16**, *Aldi*, red, 213

Initial de Desmirail Margaux 2002, **15**, *Marks & Spencer*, red, 125

Inspire Sauvignon Blanc 2004, **15.5**, *Morrison's*, white, 134

Inti Reserve Chardonnay 2004, **15**, *Somerfield*, white, 238

Inti Reserve Shiraz 2004, **15.5**, *Somerfield*, red, 237

Inycon Cabernet Sauvignon Rosé 2003, **16**, *Morrison's*, rosé, 133

Inycon Chardonnay 2004, **16**, *Morrison's, Tesco*, white, 133, 253

Inycon Fiano 2004, **16**, *Booths*, white, 33

Inycon Merlot 2003, **16.5**, *Tesco*, red, 249

Inycon Nero d'Avola 2003, **16**, *Booths*, red, 34

Inycon Shiraz 2003, **16**, *Waitrose*, red, 310

Iona Sauvignon Blanc 2003, **17**, *Booths*, white, 29–30

Ironstone Cabernet Franc 2002, **16**, *Somerfield*, red, 231

Ironstone Viognier 2003, **15**, *Somerfield*, white, 238
Italia Pinot Grigio 2004, **14**, *Waitrose*, white, 324

Jackson Estate Marlborough Pinot Noir 2003, **14**, *Somerfield*, red, 241
Jackson Estate Marlborough Sauvignon Blanc 2004, **16**, *Booths, Sainsbury, Somerfield*, white, 36, 185, 231
Jacob's Creek Chardonnay 2004, **15.5**, *Asda*, white, 16
Jacob's Creek Dry Riesling 2003, **15**, *Sainsbury, Tesco, Waitrose*, white, 187, 268, 318
Jacob's Creek Reserve Chardonnay 2002, **16.5**, *Asda*, white, 6
Jacob's Creek Reserve Riesling 2003, **16**, *Asda*, white, 11
Jacob's Creek Shiraz/Cabernet Sauvignon 2003, **15**, *Asda*, white, 18
Jacob's Creek Sparkling Chardonnay/Pinot Noir Brut Cuvée NV, **15**, *Asda, Sainsbury, Tesco, Waitrose*, white sparkling, 18, 187, 271, 320
Jacob's Creek Sparkling Rosé NV, **15**, *Asda*, rosé, 18
Jacquart Champagne NV, **16**, *Tesco*, white sparkling, 257
Jaime Rioja 2003, **11**, *Asda*, red, 11
Jamiesons Run Chardonnay 2002, **16**, *Asda*, white, 11

Jansz Premium Cuvée NV, **16**, *Oddbins, Selfridges, Noel Young Wines*, white sparkling, 151, 213
Jindalee Chardonnay 2003, **15**, *Morrison's*, white, 135
Jindalee Sauvignon Blanc 2004, **15**, *Waitrose*, white, 318
Jindalee Shiraz 2003, **14**, *Morrison's*, red, 136
JJ McWilliams Sémillon/Chardonnay 2004, **16**, *Asda*, white, 11
JJ McWilliams Sémillon/Sauvignon 2004, **14**, *Asda*, white, 24
JJ McWilliams Shiraz/Cabernet 2004, **14**, *Asda*, red, 24
Jon Josh Estate Chardonnay 2003, **14**, *Co-op*, white, 68
Jose de Souza 2001, **15**, *Waitrose*, red, 318
JP Chenet Colombard/Chardonnay NV, **14**, *Asda*, white, 23
Julienas Georges Duboeuf 2004, **14**, *Waitrose*, red, 324
Jurançon Sec, Domaine Bellegarde 2003, **16.5**, *Yapp Brothers*, white, 333

Kaituna Blue Sauvignon Blanc/Sémillon 2004, **15**, *Marks & Spencer*, white, 125
Kaituna Hills Chardonnay 2004, **14**, *Marks & Spencer*, white, 127

Kaituna Hills East Coast Riesling 2004, **16**, *Marks & Spencer*, white, 120

Kaituna Hills Merlot/Cabernet Sauvignon 2003, **15**, *Marks & Spencer*, red, 125

Kaituna Hills Reserve Pinot Noir 2003, **15**, *Marks & Spencer*, red, 125

Kaituna Hills Reserve Sauvignon Blanc 2004, **14.5**, *Marks & Spencer*, white, 126

Kangarilla Road McLaren Vale Cabernet Sauvignon 2002, **16**, *Majestic*, red, 92

Kangarilla Road McLaren Vale Chardonnay 2004, **16**, *Majestic*, red, 92

Kangarilla Road McLaren Vale Shiraz 2003, **16**, *Majestic*, red, 92

Katnook Founders Block Cabernet Sauvignon 2002, **15**, *Oddbins*, red, 157

Katnook Founders Block Sauvignon Blanc 2004, **14**, *Oddbins*, white, 160

Ken Forrester Chenin Blanc 2004, **15**, *Sainsbury*, white, 187

Ken Forrester Merlot 2003, **14**, *Waitrose*, red, 324

Ken Forrester Petit Pinotage 2004, **14**, *Asda*, **16.5**, *Somerfield*, red, 24, 226

Kendall-Jackson Vintners Reserve Cabernet Sauvignon 2001, **14**, *Morrison's*, red, 136

Kendall-Jackson Vintners Reserve Chardonnay 2003, **14**, *Morrison's*, white, 137

Kendermanns Pinot Grigio 2004, **15**, *Sainsbury*, white, 187

Kim Crawford Pinot Noir 2004, **15**, *Amps Fine Wines, Bacchus Fine Wines, Beaconsfield Wine Cellars*, red, 216

Kingston Empiric Selection Durif 2001, **14**, *Morrison's*, red, 137

Kingston Empiric Selection Viognier 2002, **15.5**, *Morrison's*, white, 134

Knappstein Hand Picked Clare Valley Riesling 2003, **16**, *Majestic*, white, 91

Knappstein Shiraz 2001, **16**, *Oddbins*, red, 151

Kumala Cabernet Sauvignon/ Shiraz 2004, **14.5**, *Sainsbury, Tesco*, red, 189, 272

Kumala Chardonnay/Sémillon 2004, **14**, *Tesco*, white, 276

Kumala Journey's End Shiraz 2003, **15**, *Waitrose*, red, 319

Kumala Reserve Sauvignon Blanc 2004, **14**, *Tesco*, white, 276

Kumala Rosé 2004, **14.5**, *Tesco*, rosé, 272

Kumala Sauvignon Blanc/ Sémillon 2004, **14**, *Sainsbury*, white, 191

Kuyen 2002, **15**, *Adnams*, red, 217

La Basca Uvas Blancas 2004, **16**, *Marks & Spencer*, white, 121

La Basca Uvas Tintas 2004, **16**, *Marks & Spencer*, red, 120

La Baume Marsanne/Roussanne/ Chardonnay, Vin de Pays d'Oc 2002, **16.5**, *Waitrose*, white, 304

La Baume Sauvignon Blanc, Vin de Pays d'Oc 2004, **15**, *Sainsbury*, white, 187

La Baume Shiraz/Cabernet, Vin de Pays d'Oc 2001, **15.5**, *Waitrose*, red, 316

La Baume Viognier, Vin de Pays d'Oc 2004, **15**, *Waitrose*, white, 319

La Capitana Merlot Barrel Reserve Viña La Rosa 2002, **16**, *Somerfield*, red, 232

LA Cetto Petite Syrah 2002, **14.5**, *Waitrose*, red, 322

La Chasse du Pape Grande Réserve, Côtes du Rhône 2003, **16**, *Asda*, red, 12

La Chasse du Pape Syrah, Vin de Pays d'Oc 2004, **16**, *Sainsbury*, red, 175

La Cité de Foncalieu Grande Réserve Chardonnay 2003, **15**, *Tesco*, white, 268

La Cuvée Mythique, Vin de Pays d'Oc 2001, **15.5**, *Co-op*, red, 64

La Finca Cabernet Sauvignon 2004, **16**, *Co-op*, red, 62

La Forêt Hilaire Entre-Deux-Mers 2003, **16**, *Tesco*, white, 257

La Forge Syrah 2003, **16.5**, *Somerfield*, *Threshers*, red, 227, 287

La Forge Viognier 2004, **16.5**, *Stratford Wine Agencies*, white, 209

La Grille Classic Loire, Vin de Pays du Jardin de la France, Henri Bourgeois, Sauvignon Blanc 2004, **16**, *Waitrose*, white, 310

La Marca Madrid Tempranillo 2003, **14**, *Morrison's*, red, 137

La Palmeria Huachitos Estate Carmenere/Cabernet Sauvignon 2001, **14**, *Oddbins*, red, 160

La Pampa Estate Sauvignon Blanc 2004, **14**, *Waitrose*, white, 324

La Prendina Estate Pinot Grigio 2004, **17**, *Marks & Spencer*, white, 113

La Rectorie Côtes du Rhône-Villages 2004, **14.5**, *Majestic*, red, 102

La Remonta Malbec 2003, **17**, *Booths*, red, 29

La Réserve de Léoville-Barton, St-Julien 2000, **14**, *Majestic*, red, 106

La Riada Old Vines Garnacha 2004, **16**, *Threshers*, red, 291

L'Angélique de Montbusquet St-Emilion 2001, **16**, *Booths*, red, 34

Langenbach Spätlese 2003, **14**, *Budgens*, white, 54

Langhorne Creek Estate Pinot Grigio 2004, **14**, *Marks & Spencer*, white, 127

Lanson Rosé NV, **14**, *Majestic*, rosé sparkling, 105

Las Almenas Bobal Crianza 2002, **16**, *Marks & Spencer*, red, 120

Las Brisas Estate Chardonnay Reserve 2002, **14.5**, *Co-op*, white, 67

Las Brisas Estate Pinot Noir Reserve 2003, **16**, *Sainsbury*, red, 175–6

Las Brisas Estate Pinot Noir Reserve 2004, **14**, *Co-op*, red, 68

Las Moras Bonarda 2004, **15**, *Co-op*, red, 66

Laurent Perrier Ultra Brut NV, **14**, *Majestic*, white sparkling, 105

Le Big Macon, Jean-Luc Terrier 2001, **15.5**, *Oddbins*, white, 155

Leaping Horse Chardonnay 2003, **14**, *Somerfield*, white, 241

Leasingham Bin 61 Shiraz 2002, **16.5**, *Budgens*, red, 45

Leeuwin Estate Art Series Riesling 2004, **15.5**, *Waitrose*, white, 316

Leeuwin Estate Art Series Shiraz 2001, **15**, *Waitrose*, red, 319

Lenbridge Forge Yarra Valley Chardonnay 2003, **18**, *Marks & Spencer*, white, 111

Leon de Oro Merlot/Cabernet Sauvignon 2003, **17.5**, *Marks & Spencer*, red, 112

Leopards Leap Cabernet Sauvignon/Merlot 2003, **15.5**, *Tesco*, red, 265

Leopards Leap Lookout Red 2003, **15.5**, *Tesco*, red, 265

Leopards Leap Lookout White 2003, **15**, *Tesco*, white, 268

Leopards Leap Sauvignon Blanc 2004, **14**, *Co-op*, white, 69

Leopards Leap Shiraz 2002, **15.5**, *Co-op*, red, 64

Les Argelières Chardonnay, Vin de Pays d'Oc 2004, **15**, *Majestic*, white, 100

Les Crouzels Fitou 2003, **16**, *Sainsbury*, red, 176

Les Deux Colombard/ Chardonnay, Vin de Pays des Côtes de Gascogne 2004, **15**, *Booths*, white, 38

Les Deux Grenache/Syrah, Vin de Pays de Vaucluse 2004, **14**, *Booths*, red, 40

Les Faisses Grenache/Syrah 2003, **17**, *Stratford Wine Agencies*, red, 208

Les Jamelles Syrah, Vin de Pays d'Oc 2003, **16**, *Co-op*, red, 62

Les Jamelles Viognier, Vin de Pays d'Oc 2004, **14.5**, *Co-op*, white, 67

Les Marionettes Ancient Vines Carignan 2002, **15.5**, *Morrison's*, red, 135

Les Marquières, Vin de Pays des Coteaux de Fontcaude 2004, **14.5**, *Majestic*, red, 102

Les Marquières, Vin de Pays du Comte Tolosan 2004, **14**, *Majestic*, white, 105

Les Ruffes La Sauvageonne, Coteaux de Languedoc 2003, **15**, *Booths*, red, 38

L'Hospitalet 2002, **16.5**, *Somerfield*, red, 227

L'Hospitalet White 2002, **16**, *Somerfield*, white, 232

Lily Red, Côtes de Gascogne 2004, **14**, *Co-op*, red, 69

Lily White, Vin de Pays des Côtes de Gascogne 2002, **14**, *Co-op*, white, 69

Lily White, Côtes de Gascogne 2004, **15**, *Co-op*, white, 66

Lindauer Brut NV, **14**, *Budgens*, white sparkling, 54

Lindauer Rosé NV, **16**, *Threshers*, rosé sparkling, 291

Lindemans Bin 25 Brut Cuvée NV, **14**, *Budgens, Co-op, Morrison's, Waitrose*, white sparkling, 55, 69, 137, 325

Lindemans Bin 35 Rosé 2004, **15**, *Budgens*, rosé, 51

Lindemans Bin 50 Shiraz 2004, **14**, *Sainsbury*, red, 191

Lindemans Bin 55 Shiraz/Cabernet 2004, **16**, *Asda*, red, 12

Lindemans Bin 65 Chardonnay 2004, **16**, *Sainsbury, Tesco*, white, 176, 257

Lindemans Bin 77 Sémillon/Chardonnay 2004, **16.5**, *Asda*, white, 6

Lindemans Cawarra Merlot 2004, **14**, *Asda*, red, 24

Lindemans Reserve Merlot 2002, **15.5**, *Asda*, red, 16

Lindemans Reserve Merlot 2003, **14**, *Asda*, red, 24

Lingenfelder Bee Label Morio Muskat 2003, **16**, *Oddbins*, white, 152

Lingenfelder Bird Label Riesling 2003, **15.5**, *Oddbins*, white, 155

Lingenfelder Fish Label Riesling 2003, **15**, *Oddbins*, white, 157

Lingenfelder Hare Label Gerwürtztraminer 2003, **16.5**, *Oddbins*, white, 145

Lingenfelder Owl Label Pinot Grigio 2003, **16.5**, *Oddbins*, white, 145

Lirac La Fermade, Domaine Maby 2002, **16**, *Yapp Brothers*, red, 333

Lizards of Oz Reserve Malbec 2002, **14**, *Asda*, red, 24

Lizards of Oz Reserve Viognier 2004, **15**, *Asda*, white, 18

Los Andes Carmenere/Cabernet Sauvignon 2004, **15.5**, *Waitrose*, red, 316

Los Monteros Valencia 2003, **16**, *Sainsbury*, red, 176

Los Robles 'Fairtrade' Carmenere 2004, **14.5**, *Sainsbury*, red, 189

Lost Valley Cortese 2004, **14**, *Oddbins*, white, 160

Lost Valley Hazy Mountain Merlot 2003, **15**, *Oddbins*, red, 157

Louis Chatel, Vin de Pays d'Oc Listel NV **15**, *Booths*, red, 38

Louis de Brissar Brut Champagne NV, **15**, *Threshers*, white sparkling, 294

Louis Eschenauer Merlot, Vin de Pays d'Oc 2003, **15**, *Budgens*, red, 51

Louis Jadot Beaujolais 2004, **14**, *Threshers*, red, 295

Louis Jadot Beaujolais-Villages 2004, **14**, *Somerfield*, red, 241

Louis Jadot Macon Blanc Villages 2004, **16**, *Budgens*, white, 48

Louis Jadot Pouilly-Fuissé 2002, **14**, *Tesco*, white, 277

Lugana Villa Flora Zenato 2004, **16**, *Waitrose*, white, 310

Luis Felipe Edwards Cabernet Sauvignon 2003, **15**, *Tesco*, red, 268

Luis Felipe Edwards Carmenere 2003, **15**, *Tesco*, red, 268

M

McGuigan Gold Chardonnay 2004, **15**, *Tesco*, white, 268

Macon-Villages 2004, **14**, *Marks & Spencer*, white, 127

Macon-Villages Teissèdre 2003, **14.5**, *Morrison's*, white, 136

Macon-Prissé Cave Co-op de Prissé 2004, **16**, *Majestic*, white, 92

Macon-Villages Cave de Prissé Chardonnay 2004, **16**, *Waitrose*, white, 311

McWilliams Hanwood Estate Chardonnay 2003, **16.5**, *Budgens, Threshers*, white, 46, 287

McWilliams Hanwood Estate Shiraz 2003, **14.5**, *Budgens, Tesco*, red, 53, 272

Maison Delor Bordeaux Blanc 2004, **14**, *Waitrose*, white, 325

Mandorla Syrah Sicilia 2003, **16.5**, *Marks & Spencer*, red, 116

Marbore Bodega Pirineos Somontano 2000, **14.5**, *Sainsbury*, red, 189

Marc Ducourneau, Vin de Pays des Côtes de Gascogne 2002, **15.5**, *Majestic*, white, 99

Marin Ridge Lodi Malbec 2002, **15**, *Marks & Spencer*, red, 125

Marqués de Casa Concha Cabernet Sauvignon 2003, **15.5**, *Morrison's*, red, 135

Marqués de Casa Concha Merlot 2003, **15**, *Sainsbury*, red, 188

Marqués de Griñon Reserva Rioja 2000, **16.5**, *Tesco*, red, 250

Marqués de Griñon Rioja 2003, **14**, *Budgens*, red, 54

Marqués de Monistrol Rosé Cava NV, **15**, *Budgens*, rosé, 51

Marqués de Monistrol Vintage Cava 2000, **14**, *Budgens*, white sparkling, 54

Martin Estate Riesling 2004, **16**, *Marks & Spencer*, white, 121

Mas Collet Cellar de Capcanes Montsant 2002, **16**, *Waitrose*, red, 311

Mas de Guiot Cabernet/Syrah, Vin de Pays du Gard 2003, **16.5**, *Majestic*, red, 85

Mas Las Cabes, Jean Gardies, Côtes du Roussillon 2003, **16**, *Majestic*, red, 93

Mas Las Cabes, Jean Gardies, Vin de Pays des Côtes Catalanes Muscat Sec 2004, **14**, *Majestic*, white, 106

Masterpeace Cabernet Sauvignon/ Merlot 2004, **14**, *Somerfield*, red, 241

Masterpeace Chardonnay 2004, **16**, *Somerfield*, white, 232

Masterpeace Rosé 2004, **14.5**, *Co-op*, rosé, 67

Masterpeace Sangiovese/Shiraz Rosé 2004, **15**, *Threshers*, rosé, 294

Masterpeace Shiraz 2004, **15**, *Co-op*, red, 66

Matahiwi Estate Pinot Noir 2004, **14**, *Oddbins*, red, 161

Matua Paretai Sauvignon Blanc 2004, **14**, *Asda*, white, 24

Matua Valley Pinot Noir 2004, **14**, *Cockburn & Campbell*, red, 220

Matua Valley Sauvignon Blanc 2004, **14**, *Tesco*, white, 277

Mercurey 1er Cru 'Clos des Barrault' Domaine Juillot 2000, **15**, *Majestic*, white, 101

Merloblu Castello di Luzzano 2003, **15.5**, *Booths*, white, 37

Metala Shiraz/Cabernet Sauvignon 2002, **14**, *Asda*, red, 25

Meursault 2003, **16**, *Marks & Spencer*, white, 121

Meursault Le Limozin Vincent Girardin 2002, **15**, *Waitrose*, white, 319

Mezzomondo Montepulciano d'Abruzzo 2003, **14.5**, *Budgens*, red, 52

Mineralstein Riesling 2004, **16**, *Marks & Spencer*, white, 122

Minervois 2003, **16**, *Marks & Spencer*, red, 121

Misiónes de Rengo Cabernet Rosé 2004, **15.5**, *Somerfield*, rosé, 237

Misiónes de Rengo Carmenere 2003, **15.5**, *Morrison's*, red, 135

Misiónes de Rengo Chardonnay 2004, **15**, *Asda*, *Somerfield*, white, 19, 238

Misiónes de Rengo Chardonnay Reserve 2003, **15**, *Asda*, white, 19

Misiónes de Rengo Merlot 2003, **16**, *Asda*, red, 12

Misiónes de Rengo Sauvignon Blanc 2004, **16**, *Asda*, red, 12

Moët & Chandon 1999, **16**, *Budgens*, white sparkling, 48

Monastier Cabernet Franc, Vin de Pays d'Oc 2004, **16**, *Majestic*, red, 93

Mondiale Sauvignon Blanc NV, **14**, *Aldi*, white, 220

Monferrato Bianco 'Alteserre' Bava 2000, **16.5**, *Oddbins*, white, 146

Monferrato Rosso 'Le Monache' Michele Chiarlo 2003, **15.5**, *Oddbins*, red, 155

Monkey Puzzle Cabernet Sauvignon/Merlot 2004, **14**, *Asda*, red, 24

Monos Locos Cabernet Sauvignon 2001, **14**, *Virgin*, red, 80

Monos Locos Chardonnay 2004, **14**, *Virgin*, white, 79

Monos Locos Sauvignon Blanc 2004, **14**, *Virgin*, white, 79

Mont Gras Carmenere Reserva 2003, **16**, *Waitrose*, red, 311

Mont Gras Limited Edition Cabernet Sauvignon 2001, **16**, *Waitrose*, red, 311

Mont Gras Quatro Reserva 2002, **16.5**, *Everywine*, *Unwins*, red, 76, 209

Mont Tauch Fitou 2003, **16**, *Somerfield*, red, 232

Montana Brancott Estate Sauvignon Blanc 2002, **14**, *Oddbins*, white, 161

Montana East Coast Rosé 2004, **16**, *Tesco*, rosé, 257

Montana East Coast Unoaked Chardonnay 2004, **16**, *Budgens, Majestic*, white, 50, 92

Montana Marlborough Riesling 2003, **14**, *Tesco*, white, 277

Montana Marlborough Sauvignon Blanc 2004, **16**, *Budgens, Majestic, Tesco, Threshers*, white, 50, 98, 263, 291

Montana Merlot/Cabernet Sauvignon 2003, **14**, *Oddbins, Somerfield, Waitrose*, red, 161, 241, 325

Montana Pinot Noir 2004, **14.5**, *Waitrose, Waverly Wines & Spirits*, red, 218, 322

Montana Reserve East Coast Gewürztraminer 2004, **16**, *Threshers*, white, 291

Montana Reserve Merlot 2003, **14**, *Tesco*, red, 277

Montana Reserve Pinot Noir 2003, **15**, *Majestic, Oddbins, Threshers*, red, 101, 157, 294

Monteguelfo Chianti Classico 2003, **16**, *Threshers*, red, 291

Monteguelfo Chianti Classico Reserva 2001, **16**, *Threshers*, red, 292

Monteguelfo Chianti Classico Reserva 2003 NV, **16.5**, *Threshers*, red, 287

Montes Alpha 'M' 2001, **16**, *Waitrose*, red, 311

Montes 'Limited Selection' Cabernet/Carmenere 2004, **16**, *Majestic*, red, 93

Montes 'Limited Selection' Pinot Noir 2004, **16**, *Majestic*, red, 93

Montes Reserve Sauvignon Blanc 2004, **16**, *Majestic, Waitrose*, white, 93, 311

Montlouis Sur Loire, Domaine Les Liards Sec 2003, **17**, *Yapp Brothers*, white, 332

Morgon Les Charmes Domaine Brisson 2003, **14**, *Co-op*, red, 69

Moulin des Cailloux Côtes de Duras Rosé 2004, **14.5**, *Waitrose*, rosé, 322

Moulin des Cailloux Côtes de Duras Sauvignon Blanc 2004, **14.5**, *Waitrose*, white, 322

Moulin-à-Vent Les Michelons, Louis Latour 2003, **14.5**, *Majestic*, red, 102

Mount Difficulty Central Otago Pinot Noir 2002, **14**, *Sainsbury*, red, 191

Mud House Riesling 2004, **14**, *Everywine*, white, 80

Mud House Sauvignon Blanc 2004, **15**, *Bentalls, Booths, Harrods, Harvey Nichols, Selfridges*, white, 39, 217

Muga Rioja Rosado 2004, **14**, *Waitrose*, rosé, 325

Muruve Roble Toro 2003, **16**, *Sainsbury*, red, 177

Muscadet Côtes de Grandlieu Sur Lie, Fief Guérin 2004, **16**, *Waitrose*, white, 310

Muscadet La Régate 2004, **16**, *Sainsbury*, white, xiv, 176

Muscat de Saint Jean de Minervois 2002, **16**, *Oddbins*, white, 152

Myrtle Grove Shiraz 2001, **14.5**, *Morrison's*, red, 135

N

Nagyrede Estate Cabernet Sauvignon Rosé 2004, **16**, *Booths, Budgens*, rosé, 35, 48

Nautilus Estate Pinot Noir 2002, **16**, *Christopher Piper Wines, Majestic, Thomas Panton Wine Merchants*, red, 94, 214

Navasques Tempranillo Navarra 2003, **14.5**, *Morrison's*, red, 136

Navigators' LBV Port 1999, **16**, *Somerfield*, fortified, 232

Neagles Rock Riesling 2002, **16.5**, *Yapp Brothers*, white, 333

Neblina Merlot 2004, **16**, *Majestic*, red, 95

Neblina Sauvignon Blanc 2004, **16**, *Majestic*, white, 94

Neil Ellis Stellenbosch Chardonnay 2003, **17**, *Tesco*, white, 246

Nepenthe 'Tryst' 2003, **14**, *Booths, Oddbins*, red, 40, 152

Nepenthe 'Tryst' Cabernet/ Zinfandel/Tempranillo 2003, **16**, *Oddbins, Somerfield*, red, 152, 236

Nepenthe 'Tryst' Cabernet/ Zinfandel/Tempranillo 2004, **14**, *Waitrose*, red, 325

Nepenthe 'Tryst' Sauvignon Blanc/Sémillon 2004, **15**, *Somerfield*, white, 238

Nepenthe 'Tryst' White 2004, **14**, *Booths*, white, 40

Nicolas Feuillatte Champagne 1997, **14**, *Tesco*, white sparkling, 277

Nicole d'Aurigny Brut Champagne, **14**, *Morrison's*, white sparkling, 137

Nivole Moscato d'Asti Michele Chiarlo 2004, **16**, *Booths*, dessert white, 35

No 2 French Merlot NV, **16**, *Asda*, red, xiii, 12

No 4 Chardonnay NV, **15**, *Asda*, white, 19

Nobilo East Coast Merlot 2003, **16**, *Threshers*, red, 292

Nobilo Marlborough Sauvignon Blanc 2004, **15.5**, *Somerfield, Tesco, Threshers*, white, 238, 267, 294

Norton Barbera 2004, **14**, *Waitrose*, red, 325

Novas Cabernet Sauvignon/ Merlot 2003, **16.5**, *Vintage Roots*, red, 76

Novas Carmenere/Cabernet Sauvignon 2002, **16.5**, *Asda, Vintage Roots*, red, 6, 76

Novas Chardonnay/Marsanne/ Viognier 2004, **14.5**, *Vintage Roots*, white, 78

Novas Sauvignon Blanc 2004, **14.5**, *Vintage Roots*, white, 78

Novas Syrah/Mourvèdre 2003, **16**, *Vintage Roots*, red, 76

Nuits-St-Georges 1er Cru Les Chaignots, Robert Chévillon 2002, **14**, *Majestic*, red, 106

NXG Australian Sémillon/ Chardonnay 2003, **15**, *Tesco*, white, 270

Nyetimber Blanc de Blancs 1996, **16**, *Waitrose*, white sparkling, 312

Old Coach Road Pinot Noir 2003, **14**, *Peter Watts Wines, F. L. Dickins, Flagship Wines*, red, 220

Old Vines Grenache Noir, Vin de Pays des Côtes Catalanes 2004, **14**, *Marks & Spencer*, red, 128

Oracle Sauvignon Blanc 2004, **14**, *Oddbins*, white, 161

Organic Villa Masera 2004, **15.5**, *Marks & Spencer*, white, 124

Origin Chardonnay 2004, **16**, *Threshers*, white, 292

Origin Chenin/Chardonnay 2004, **16**, *Threshers*, white, 292

Origin Garnacha Rosé 2004, **16**, *Threshers*, rosé, 292

Orobio Rioja Artadi 2003, **14**, *Oddbins*, red, 161

Oudinot Brut 2000, **16.5**, *Marks & Spencer*, white sparkling, 116

Oudinot Cuvée Brut NV, **16**, *Marks & Spencer*, white sparkling, 122

Oudinot Rosé Champagne NV, **14**, *Marks & Spencer*, rosé sparkling, 128

Oxford Landing Cabernet Sauvignon/Shiraz 2002, **14**, *Tesco*, red, 277

Oxford Landing Cabernet Sauvignon/Shiraz 2003, **14.5**, *Budgens, Co-op*, red, 53, 67

Oxford Landing Chardonnay 2004, **15**, *Budgens, Sainsbury, Tesco*, white, 51, 189, 271

Oxford Landing Merlot 2003, **14**, *Budgens*, red, 54

Oxford Landing Sauvignon Blanc 2004, **15**, *Budgens, Sainsbury, Tesco*, white, 52, 189, 268

Oxford Landing Viògnier 2004, **17**, *Waitrose*, white, 301

Oyster Bay Chardonnay 2003, **15.5**, *Morrison's*, white, 135

Oyster Bay Merlot 2004, **14.5**, *Majestic, Sainsbury, Waitrose*, red, 103, 190, 322

Oyster Bay Pinot Noir 2004, **15**, *Wimbledon Wine Cellars*, red, 217

Oyster Bay Sauvignon Blanc 2004, **16**, *Co-op, Morrison's, Sainsbury*, white, 62, 134, 185

Pago Real Rioja 2002, **15.5**, *Marks & Spencer*, red, 125

Palacio de Bornos Rueda Verdejo 2004, **15.5**, *Waitrose*, white, 316

Palacio de la Vega Cabernet
    Sauvignon/Tempranillo
    Crianza Navarra 2000, **16**,
    Budgens, red, 49
Palandri Pinnacle Sémillon/
    Sauvignon Blanc 2004, **14.5**,
    Waitrose, white, 322
Palandri Pinnacle Shiraz 2002, **14**,
    Waitrose, red, 325
Palha-Canas Casa Santos Lima
    2003, **16**, *Waitrose*, red, 313
Pasqua Sagramosa Soave 2003,
    14.5, *Asda*, white, 21
Paul Boutet Champagne NV,
    14.5, *Tesco*, white sparkling,
    272
Paul Mas Cabernet Sauvignon,
    Vin de Pays d'Oc 2004, **16.5**,
    Unwins, red, 210
Paul Mas Rosé de Syrah, Vin de
    Pays d'Oc 2004, **15.5**, *Stratford
    Wine Agencies*, rosé, 215
Paul Mas Sauvignon Blanc, Vin de
    Pays d'Oc 2003, **16**, *Asda*, white,
    13
Paul Mas Sauvignon Blanc, Vin de
    Pays d'Oc 2004, **16.5**, *Waitrose*,
    white, 305
Paul Mas Viognier, Vin de Pays
    d'Oc 2004, **16**, *Stratford Wine
    Agencies*, white, 214
Pazo de Seoane Albarinho 2003,
    14, *Waitrose*, white, 326
Pazo Serantellos Albarino 2004,
    16.5, *Tesco*, white, 250
Peaks View Sauvignon Blanc 2004,
    14.5, *Booths*, white, 39
Peñalolen Cabernet Sauvignon
    2002, **15**, *Oddbins*, red, 157

Penfolds Bin 28 Kalimna Shiraz
    2001, **15**, *Tesco*, red, 268
Penfolds Bin 389 Cabernet/Shiraz
    2001, **14.5**, *Tesco*, red, 272
Penfolds Clare Valley Organic
    Cabernet Sauvignon/Merlot/
    Shiraz 2003, **15**, *Waitrose*, red,
    319
Penfolds Clare Valley Organic
    Chardonnay 2003, **15.5**,
    Waitrose, white, 317
Penfolds Grange 1998, **14**, *Tesco*,
    red, 277
Penfolds Koonunga Hill Shiraz/
    Cabernet 2002, **14**, *Tesco*, red, 277
Penfolds Thomas Hyland
    Chardonnay 2003, **16**, *Asda*,
    white, 13
Penfolds Winemakers
    Chardonnay 2003, **16.5**,
    Threshers, white, 287
Penfolds Winemakers
    Shiraz/Cabernet 2004, **16.5**,
    Threshers, red, 287
Peregrine Pinot Noir 2003, **15.5**,
    Oddbins, red, 155
Perrin & Fils Rasteau 'L'Andeol',
    Côtes du Rhône 2003, **14**,
    Majestic, red, 106
Perrin Cairanne 'Peyre Blanche',
    Côtes du Rhône-Villages 2003,
    14.5, *Majestic*, red, 103
Peter Lehmann Barossa Cabernet
    Sauvignon 2001, **16**, *Oddbins*,
    red, 152
Peter Lehmann Barossa Sémillon
    2003, **16**, *Asda, Booths,
    Morrison's, Sainsbury*, white, 13,
    37, 134, 184

Peter Lehmann Barossa Shiraz 2002, **16.5**, *Asda*, red, 6

Peter Lehmann Chenin Blanc 2004, **16**, *Budgens*, white, 48

Peter Lehmann Grenache 2002, **14.5**, *Morrison's, Tesco*, red, 136, 273

Peter Lehmann Sémillon 2002, **16.5**, *Tesco*, white, 250

Peter Lehmann Wildcard Chardonnay 2004, **16**, *Budgens*, white, 48

Peter Lehmann Wildcard Shiraz 2003, **15**, *Budgens, Co-op*, red, 52, 66

Petit Chablis Cave de Vignerons de Chablis 2004, **14**, *Waitrose*, white, 325

Petite Ruche Crozes-Hermitage Chapoutier 2002, **16**, *Asda*, red, 13

Pheasant Gully Sémillon/ Sauvignon Blanc 2004, **14.5**, *Marks & Spencer*, white, 126

Pica Broca La Sauvageonne, Coteaux de Languedoc 2002, **16**, *Booths*, red, 35

Piedra Feliz Pinot Noir 2001, **15**, *Waitrose*, red, 319

Pierre Gimonnet & Fils Premier Cru Cuvée Gastronome NV, **14**, *Oddbins*, white sparkling, 161

Pink Pink Fizz Cava, **14.5**, *Morrison's*, rosé sparkling, 136

Pinot Blanc Charles Schleret, Alsace 2002, **16**, *Yapp Brothers*, white, 333

Pinot d'Alsace Domaine Bott-Geyl 2002, **15**, *Majestic*, white, 101

Pinot Grigio 2004, **15**, *Marks & Spencer*, white, 125

Pinot Grigio Alto Adige San Michele-Appiano 2004, **16**, *Waitrose*, white, 312

Pinot Grigio NV, **16**, *Marks & Spencer*, white sparkling, 122

Pinot Gris Le Fromenteau Josmeyer 2003, **16**, *Waitrose*, white, 312

Pinot Noir d'Alsace Domaine Paul Blanck 2004, **15**, *Waitrose*, red, 319

Pinot Noir Valmoissine Louis Latour, Vin de Pays des Coteaux du Verdon 2002, **14**, *Majestic*, red, 106

Pirramimma McLaren Vale Petit Verdot 2001, **16.5**, *Majestic*, red, 85

PKNY Carmenere 2003, **14**, *Asda*, red, 25

PKNY Chardonnay 2003, **14**, *Asda*, white, 25

Polizano Rosso di Montepulciano 2004, **16**, *Sainsbury*, red, 177

Porcupine Ridge Sauvignon Blanc 2004, **16**, *Waitrose*, white, 312

Porcupine Ridge Syrah 2004, **16**, *Waitrose*, red, 313

Pouilly-Fuissé Bouchard 2003, **14**, *Budgens*, white, 55

Pouilly-Fumé Fouassier Père et Fils 2004, **15**, *Budgens*, white, 52

Prahova Valley Pinot Noir Reserve 2000, **16**, *Asda*, red, 12

Premier Vin du Château de Pitray, Côtes de Castillon 2001, **14.5**, *Majestic*, red, 103

Premius Bordeaux Merlot/ Cabernet 2002, **16**, *Tesco*, red, 258

Prestige du Roc Sauvignon Blanc Bordeaux 2004, **16**, *Sainsbury*, white, 177

Prosecco NV, **14.5**, *Marks & Spencer*, white sparkling, 126

Pujalet Vin de Pays du Gers 2004, **14**, *Waitrose*, white, 326

Puligny-Montrachet Clos de la Garenne, Drouhin 2002, **14**, *Waitrose*, white, 325

Quartz Reef Pinot Noir 2003, **14.5**, *Majestic*, red, 103

Quincy Jean-Charles Borgnat 2004, **15**, *Majestic*, white, 101

Quinta de Fafide 2003, **15**, *Marks & Spencer*, red, 125

Quinta de la Rosa 2002, **16**, *Booths*, red, 35

Quinta des Setencostas Alenquer 2003, **14**, *Sainsbury*, red, 192

Quintis Amarone della Valpolicella Valpantena 2001, **16**, *Booths*, red, 35

Radcliffes Gewürztraminer 2003, **17**, *Threshers*, white, 284

Radcliffes Haut Poitou Sauvignon Blanc 2004, **14.5**, *Threshers*, white, 294

Radcliffes Muscadet Sur Lie 2004, **16**, *Threshers*, white, 293

Railroad Red Cabernet Sauvignon/Shiraz 2003, **16.5**, *Asda*, *Tesco*, red, 7, 250

Rapido Rosso Beneventano 2004, **14**, *Booths*, red, 41

Rasteau Cuvée Chambert, Côtes du Rhône-Villages 2003, **16**, *Marks & Spencer*, red, 123

Rasteau Prestige Domaine des Coteaux de Travers 2003, **15**, *Booths*, red, 38

Ravenswood Lodi Old Vine Zinfandel 2002, **16**, *Sainsbury*, red, 177

Ravenswood Vintners Blend Chardonnay 2003, **15**, *Tesco*, white, 269

Ravenswood Vintners Blend Zinfandel 2002, **15**, *Booths*, *Budgens*, *Tesco*, *Waitrose*, red, 39, 51, 271, 321

Rawnsley Estate Chardonnay 2003, **16.5**, *Tesco*, white, 250

Réserve des Tuileries, Côtes du Roussillon 2004, **16**, *Sainsbury*, red, 177

Réserve St Marc Sauvignon Blanc, Vin de Pays d'Oc 2004, **16**, *Sainsbury*, white, 178

Reuilly 'Les Bouchauds' Gerard Bigonneau 2004, **14**, *Majestic*, white, 106

Rex Goliath Giant 47-Pound Rooster Cabernet Sauvignon NV, **16**, *Majestic*, red, 95

Riesling Burgreben de Zelenberg Domaine Bott-Geyl 2001, **16.5**, *Majestic*, white, 85

Riesling Kabinett Josef Leitz 2003, **14**, *Booths*, white, 41

Riesling Paul Blanck Alsace 2003, **16**, *Oddbins*, white, 153

Riff Pinot Grigio delle Venezie, Alois Lageder 2004, **16.5**, *Majestic*, white, 85–6

Riverview Cabernet Sauvignon 2000, **16**, *Somerfield*, red, 233

Riverview Gewürztraminer 2002, **14**, *Asda*, white, 25

Riverview Kekfrankos Merlot NV, **15.5**, *Somerfield*, red, 237

Riverview Merlot/Cabernet Sauvignon 2001, **16**, *Threshers*, red, 292

Robert's Rock Chardonnay/Sémillon 2004, **14**, *Co-op*, white, 69

Robert's Rock Pinotage/Pinot Noir 2004, **14**, *Co-op*, red, 69

Robertson Winery Sauvignon Blanc 2004, **14**, *Majestic*, white, 106

Rock Red Shiraz/Grenache/Pinot Noir 2003, **15**, *Asda*, red, 19

Roero Arneis Cantine Ascheri 2003, **15.5**, *Booths*, white, 37

Roero Arneis Terre da Vino 2004, **16**, *Majestic*, white, 95

Rosado Cava NV, **14.5**, *Marks & Spencer*, rosé sparkling, 126

Rosato Veronese Cantina di Monteforte 2004, **14**, *Waitrose*, rosé, 326

Rosemount Estate Sémillon/Chardonnay 2004, **14**, *Sainsbury*, white, 192

Rosemount Estate Shiraz 2003, **15**, *Tesco*, red, 269

Rosso di Montepulciano Azienda Agricola Poliziano 2003, **16.5**, *Booths*, red, 31

Rudesheimer Berg Rottland Spätlese, Dr Wegler 2002, **15.5**, *Waitrose*, white, 317

Rully 1er Cru Vieilles Vignes, Vincent Girardin 2003, **16.5**, *Majestic*, white, 86

Ruppertsberger Riesling Eiswein 2001, **16**, *Sainsbury*, white, 178

Rustenberg Chardonnay 2003, **15**, *Waitrose*, white, 319

Rutherglen Estates Durif 2004, **15.5**, *Waitrose*, red, 317

Rutherglen Estates Grenache/Shiraz/Mourvèdre 2004, **15**, *Somerfield*, red, 239

Rutherglen Estates Marsanne/Chardonnay 2004, **16**, *Somerfield*, white, 233

RWC Shiraz Reserve 2003, **15**, *Asda*, red, 19

S

Sablet Côtes du Rhône-Villages, Château de Rignon 2003, **14.5**, *Booths*, red, 39

Sacred Hill Marlborough Sauvignon Blanc 2004, **16**, *Threshers*, white, 293

Sagramoso Valpolicella Superiore 2002, **14**, *Asda*, red, 25

Sainsbury's Argentinian Bonarda NV, **16**, *Sainsbury*, red, 180

Sainsbury's Argentinian Malbec NV, **16**, *Sainsbury*, red, 179

Sainsbury's Argentinian Torrontes NV, **15**, *Sainsbury*, red, 188

Sainsbury's Australian Ruby Cabernet Sauvignon/Shiraz 2004, **15**, *Sainsbury*, red, 188

Sainsbury's Australian Shiraz 2004, **14**, *Sainsbury*, red, 193

Sainsbury's Bin 20 Australian Chardonnay 2004, **14**, *Sainsbury*, white, 192

Sainsbury's Bin 60 Australian Cabernet Sauvignon/Shiraz 2004, **16.5**, *Sainsbury*, red, 169

Sainsbury's Chilean Reserve Chardonnay 2002, **16**, *Sainsbury*, white, 182

Sainsbury's Classic Selection Alsace Gewürztraminer 2003, **16**, *Sainsbury*, white, 182

Sainsbury's Classic Selection Amarone della Valpolicella Valpentena 2002, **16**, *Sainsbury*, red, 178

Sainsbury's Classic Selection Barossa Shiraz 2003, **16**, *Sainsbury*, red, 178

Sainsbury's Classic Selection Muscadet Sèvre et Maine Sur Lie 2004, **16.5**, *Sainsbury*, white, 169

Sainsbury's Classic Selection Padthaway Chardonnay 2004, **16**, *Sainsbury*, white, 182

Sainsbury's Classic Selection Pinot Grigio 2004, **15.5**, *Sainsbury*, white, 187

Sainsbury's Classic Selection Pouilly-Fumé 2004, **14**, *Sainsbury*, white, 192

Sainsbury's Classic Selection South African Cabernet Sauvignon/Merlot 2002, **16**, *Sainsbury*, red, 180

Sainsbury's Classic Selection South African Chardonnay 2003, **14**, *Sainsbury*, white, 192

Sainsbury's Classic Selection St-Emilion 2002, **14**, *Sainsbury*, red, 192

Sainsbury's Classic Selection Vintage Claret 2004, **14**, *Sainsbury*, red, 192

Sainsbury's Classic Selection Vouvray 2004, **14**, *Sainsbury*, white, 192

Sainsbury's Classic Selection Western Australia Cabernet Sauvignon/Merlot 2003, **16**, *Sainsbury*, red, 179

Sainsbury's Classic Selection Western Australia Sauvignon Blanc/Sémillion 2004, **15**, *Sainsbury*, white, 188

Sainsbury's Medium Dry Amontillado Sherry NV, **16.5**, *Sainsbury*, fortified, 169

Sainsbury's Medium Sweet Oloroso Sherry NV, **16**, *Sainsbury*, fortified, 179

Sainsbury's New Zealand Sauvignon Blanc 2004, **15**, *Sainsbury*, white, 188

Sainsbury's Pale Dry Manzanilla Sherry NV, **16**, *Sainsbury*, fortified, 179

Sainsbury's Premier Cru Extra Dry Champagne NV, **16.5**, *Sainsbury*, white sparkling, 168

Sainsbury's Reserve Selection Argentinian Malbec 2003, **14.5**, *Sainsbury*, red, 189

Sainsbury's Reserve Selection Chilean Cabernet Sauvignon 2004, **16.5**, *Sainsbury*, red, 170

Sainsbury's Reserve Selection Chilean Carmenere 2003, **16**, *Sainsbury*, red, 178

Sainsbury's Reserve Selection Chilean Merlot 2004, **16**, *Sainsbury*, red, 182

Sainsbury's Reserve Selection Corbières 2002, **14**, *Sainsbury*, red, 192

Sainsbury's Reserve Selection Minervois 2002, **15**, *Sainsbury*, red, 188

Sainsbury's Rosé Brut Champagne NV, **16**, *Sainsbury*, rosé spakling, 171

St Gall Brut Premier Cru NV, **14.5**, *Marks & Spencer*, white sparkling, 126

St Gall Grand Cru 2000, **15.5**, *Marks & Spencer*, white sparkling, 125

St Hallett Faith Shiraz 2003, **15**, *Tesco*, red, 269

St Hallett Gamekeeper's Reserve 2004, **14**, *Waitrose*, red, 326

St Hallett Gamekeeper's Reserve Shiraz/Grenache 2004, **15**, *Co-op*, red, 66

St Hallett Old Block Shiraz 2001, **14**, *Tesco*, red, 277

St Hallett Poacher's Blend Sémillon/Sauvignon Blanc 2004, **16**, *Co-op*, white, 63

Saint Riche, Vin de Pays des Bouches du Rhône 2004, **14**, *Waitrose*, red, 326

Saint-Pourcain Réserve Spéciale, Cave de Saint-Pourcain 2004, **15.5**, *Waitrose*, white, 317

Saints Marlborough Sauvignon Blanc 2004, **16**, *Threshers*, white, 293

Sancerre Domaine Gerard Fiou 2004, **15**, *Majestic*, white, 101

Sancerre Domaine Naudet 2004, **15**, *Waitrose*, white, 319

Sancerre Les Chasseignes Fouassier Père et Fils 2004, **14**, *Budgens*, white, 55

Sanctuary Marlborough Pinot Gris 2004, **16.5**, *Sainsbury*, white, 170

Sanctuary Marlborough Sauvignon Blanc 2004, **15.5**, *Sainsbury*, white, 187

Santa Clara Chilean Red Viña Requinqua NV, **16**, *Booths*, red, 36

Santa Julia Bonarda/Sangiovese 2004, **16**, *Morrison's*, *Waitrose*, red, 133, 313

Santa Julia Fuzion Chenin Blanc/Chardonnay 2004, **15**, *Waitrose*, white, 320

Santa Julia Fuzion Shiraz/Malbec 2003, **15.5**, *Waitrose*, red, 317

Santa Julia Tempranillo 2004, **16.5**, *Somerfield*, *Tesco*, red, 227, 252

Santa Julia Viognier 2004, **16**, *Sainsbury*, white, 179

Santa Rita 120 Merlot 2003, **15.5**, *Oddbins*, red, 155

Santa Rita Cabernet Sauvignon Reserva 2002, **15**, *Sainsbury*, red, 188

Santa Rita Cabernet Sauvignon Reserva 2003, **16**, *Sainsbury*, red, 180

Santa Rita Cabernet Sauvignon Rosé 2004, **15**, *Majestic*, rosé, 101

Santa Rita Chardonnay 2004, **14.5**, *Sainsbury*, white, 190

Santa Rita Floresta Sauvignon Blanc 2003, **15**, *Waitrose*, white, 319

Santa Rita Reserva Merlot 2003, **15.5**, *Majestic*, red, 99

Santa Rita Reserva Sauvignon Blanc 2004, **16**, *Majestic*, white, 96

Santerra Dry Muscat 2004, **15.5**, *Asda*, white, 17

Santerra Tempranillo 2003, **14**, *Asda*, red, 25

Saumur, Les Vignerons de Saumur 2003, **16**, *Yapp Brothers*, white, 334

Saumur Blanc Reserve des Vignerons 2004, **14.5**, *Majestic*, white, 103

Saumur Champigny, Domaine Filliatreau 2003, **17**, *Yapp Brothers*, red, 331

Saumur Champigny 'Les Tuffeaux', Château de Targe 2003, **16**, *Majestic*, red, 95

Saumur Champigny Vieilles Vignes, Domaine Filliatreau 2002, **17**, *Yapp Brothers*, red, 332

Saumur Les Nivières 2003, **16.5**, *Waitrose*, red, 304

Saumur-Champigny Château de Targé 2003, **16**, *Waitrose*, red, 313

Sauvignon Blanc, Vin de Pays de l'Yonne 2004, **14**, *Waitrose*, white, 326

Sauvignon Blanc, Vin de Pays du Jardin de la France 2004, **14**, *Marks & Spencer, Sainsbury*, white, 128, 192

Sauvignon de Touraine, Domaine de la Prévote 2004, **16**, *Majestic*, white, 95

Savennières 'Avant' Château de Chamboureau 2001, **16**, *Yapp Brothers*, white, 334

Savigny 1er Cru La Bataillière aux Vergelesses Albert Morot 2001, **14**, *Majestic*, red, 107

Savigny-les-Beaune, Bouchard Père et Fils 2003, **14.5**, *Waitrose*, red, 322

Scaranto Rosso 1999, **15**, *Oddbins*, red, 158

Scarbolo Sauvignon Blanc 2003, **14**, *Oddbins*, white, 161

Schwarzhofberger Riesling Spätlese, Von Hovel 2002, **15**, *Waitrose*, white, 320

Scotchmans Hill Geelong Chardonnay 2003, **16**, *Oddbins*, white, 153

Scotchmans Hill Swan Bay Pinot Noir Rosé 2004, **14.5**, *Oddbins*, rosé, 158

Scotchmans Hill Swan Bay Shiraz 2003, **14**, *Oddbins*, red, 161

Secano Estate Pinot Noir 2004, **16**, *Marks & Spencer*, red, 123

Secano Estate Sauvignon Blanc 2004, **14**, *Marks & Spencer*, white, 128

Seifried Pinot Noir 2003, **15**, *Peter Watts Wines, F.L. Dickins, Flagship Wines*, red, 217

Seigneurs d'Aiguilhe Côtes de Castillon 2003, **16.5**, *Waitrose*, red, 304

Selva d'Oro Falchini Bianco di Toscana 2004, **14**, *Booths*, white, 41

Septembre Minervois 2002, **16**, *Oddbins*, red, 153

Serafino Cabernet Sauvignon Reserve 2002, **15.5**, *Asda*, red, 17

Serafino Shiraz Reserve 2002, **15**, *Asda*, red, 19

Seresin Pinot Noir 2003, **15**, *Selfridges, Handford Wines*, red, 217

Shady Grove Cabernet Sauvignon 2001, **17**, *Marks & Spencer*, red, 113

Shaw & Smith Sauvignon Blanc 2004, **14**, *Booths*, white, 41

Shepherds Ridge Marlborough Sauvignon Blanc 2004, **16.5**, *Marks & Spencer*, white, 116

Sherwood Estate Pinot Noir 2004, **15.5**, *I Vini*, red, 215

Shingle Peak Pinot Noir 2004, **15**, *Sainsbury*, red, 188

Sincerely Sauvignon Blanc 2004, **16**, *Sainsbury*, white, 180

Sirius Blanc Bordeaux 2003, **15**, *Waitrose*, white, 319

Skillogalee Riesling 2003, **14**, *Booths*, white, 41

Skuttlebutt Shiraz/Merlot Rosé 2004, **15.5**, *Sainsbury*, rosé, 186

Snake Creek Marsanne 2002, **16.5**, *Oddbins*, white, 146

Soave Classico, Vigneto Colombara, Zenato 2004, **15**, *Waitrose*, white, 320

Somerfield Argentine Chardonnay NV, **16.5**, *Somerfield*, white, 227

Somerfield Chablis 2003, **14**, *Somerfield*, white, 241

Somerfield First Flight Reserve Chardonnay 2003, **15**, *Somerfield*, red, 239

Somerfield First Flight Reserve Shiraz 2003, **16**, *Somerfield*, red, 234

Somerfield First Flight Shiraz/ Cabernet 2003, **16**, *Somerfield*, red, 234

Somerfield First Flight Unoaked Chardonnay 2004, **14.5**, *Somerfield*, white, 240

Somerfield Pale Cream Sherry, **16**, *Somerfield*, fortified, 233

Somerfield Vintage Cava Brut 2000, **17.5**, *Somerfield*, white sparkling, xiii, 225

Sonoma Creek Chardonnay 2001, **14**, *Majestic*, white, 106

Sonoma Creek Merlot 2000, **14**, *Majestic*, red, 107

Southbank Estate Sauvignon Blanc 2004, **14**, *Majestic*, white, 106

Spice Route Pinotage 2003, **16**, *Waitrose*, red, 313

Spier Inspire Cabernet Sauvignon 2003, **15**, *Somerfield*, red, 239

Spier Private Collection Malbec 2004, **15.5**, *Asda*, red, 17

Spier Private Collection Pinotage 2004, **14**, *Asda*, red, 25

Springfield Estate Cabernet Sauvignon 2002, **15.5**, *Booths*, red, 37

Springfield Estate 'Life from Stone' Sauvignon Blanc 2004, **17**, *Booths*, white, 29

Springfield Estate Special Cuvée Sauvignon Blanc 2004, **15**, *Sainsbury*, white, 188

Spy Valley Pinot Noir 2003, **14.5**, *Bibendum*, red, 218

St-Véran Blason de Bourgogne 2004, **16**, *Waitrose*, white, 313

St-Véran Orchys 2003, **15**, *Majestic*, white, 101

Steenberg Sémillon 2003, **14**, *Booths*, white, 41

Steenberg Sémillon 2004, **14**, *Sainsbury*, white, 193

Stella Aurea Cabernet Sauvignon 2001, **15.5**, *Oddbins*, red, 155

Stella Aurea Cabernet Sauvignon 2002, **15.5**, *Oddbins*, red, 156

Sterling Rocks Sémillon/ Sauvignon Blanc 2004, **14**, *Asda*, white, 25

Sticks Yarra Valley Chardonnay 2003, **16.5**, *Majestic*, white, 87

Sticks Yarra Valley Pinot Noir 2003, **14**, *Majestic*, red, 107

Stoneleigh Vineyards Marlborough Pinot Noir Rosé 2004, **14**, *Waitrose*, rosé, 326

Stoneleigh Vineyards Marlborough Pinot Noir 2003, **15.5**, *R & R Wines*, *Halifax Wines*, *Waitrose*, red, 215, 317

Stoneleigh Vineyards Marlborough Sauvignon Blanc 2004, **16**, *Sainsbury*, *Waitrose*, white, 180, 315

Stoneleigh Vineyards Rapaura Series Pinot Noir 2003, **14**, *Coe Vintners*, red, 221

Stormhoek Cabernet Sauvignon 2003, **16**, *Asda*, red, 14

Stormhoek Pinot Grigio 2004, **15.5**, *Asda*, white, 17

Stormhoek Select Rosé 2004, **14.5**, *Majestic*, rosé, 103

Sutter Home Unoaked Chardonnay 2003, **15**, *Everywine*, white, 78

Sweet Chestnut Chardonnay Limoux 2002, **14**, *Booths*, white, 41

Syrah Domaine du Petit Roubie, Vin de Pays de l'Hérault 2003, **14**, *Booths*, white, 41

Tabali Reserva Cabernet Sauvignon 2002, **14**, *Sainsbury*, red, 193

Tabali Reserva Chardonnay 2003, **16**, *Asda*, white, 14

Tabali Reserva Merlot 2002, **15**, *Asda*, red, 19

Tariquet Famille Grassa Rosé 2004, **14.5**, *Somerfield*, rosé, 240

Tariquet Famille Grassa Sauvignon Blanc 2004, **15**, *Somerfield*, white, 239

Tariquet Vin de Pays des Côtes Gascogne Blanc 2004, **15**, *Somerfield*, white, 239

Te Kairanga Reserve Pinot Noir 2003, **14**, *Bibendum*, red, 221

Tempranillo La Serrana Vino de la Tierra 2003, **15.5**, *Majestic*, red, 100

Terra Organica Bonarda/ Sangiovese 2004, **16**, *Somerfield*, white, 234

Terra Organica Chenin Blanc 2004, **16**, *Somerfield*, white, 234

Terramar Cabernet Sauvignon/Merlot 2002, **14**, *Morrison's*, red, 137

Terrazas Alto Chardonnay 2003, **14**, *Waitrose*, white, 326

Terre du Lion Saint Julien Bordeaux 1999, **16**, *Marks & Spencer*, red, 123

Terrunyo Sauvignon Blanc 2004, **15**, *Threshers*, white, 294

Tesco Argentinian Bonarda NV, **14**, *Tesco*, red, 279

Tesco Argentinian Malbec 2003, **14**, *Tesco*, red, 279

Tesco Argentinian Shiraz NV, **15**, *Tesco*, red, 270

Tesco Australian Cabernet/ Merlot NV, **14**, *Tesco*, red, 279

Tesco Australian Chardonnay NV, **14**, *Tesco*, white, 279

Tesco Australian Colombard NV, **16**, *Tesco*, white, 261

Tesco Australian Dry White NV, **14**, *Tesco*, white, 279

Tesco Australian Sémillon/Chardonnay NV, **14.5**, *Tesco*, white, 273

Tesco Australian Shiraz/Cabernet Sauvignon NV, **14**, *Tesco*, red, 278

Tesco Bergerac Rouge NV, **14**, *Tesco*, red, 279

Tesco Blanc de Noirs Champagne NV, **16**, *Tesco*, white sparkling, 259

Tesco Brut Cava NV, **16**, *Tesco*, white sparkling, 263

Tesco Californian Cabernet Sauvignon NV, **15**, *Tesco*, red, 270

Tesco Californian Chardonnay NV, **15.5**, *Tesco*, white, 266

Tesco Californian Dry White NV, **15.5**, *Tesco*, white, 266

Tesco Californian Merlot NV, **14.5**, *Tesco*, red, 274

Tesco Californian Red NV, **15.5**, *Tesco*, red, 266

Tesco Californian Viognier NV, **14**, *Tesco*, white, 279

Tesco Californian Zinfandel NV, **14**, *Tesco*, red, 278

Tesco Cava Reserve NV, **14.5**, *Tesco*, white sparkling, 274

Tesco Champagne Premier Cru NV, **14**, *Tesco*, white sparkling, 278

Tesco Chilean Cabernet Sauvignon NV, **16**, *Tesco*, red, 261

Tesco Chilean Carmenere NV, **14.5**, *Tesco*, red, 274

Tesco Chilean Chardonnay NV, **15**, *Tesco*, white, 270

Tesco Chilean Merlot NV, **16**, *Tesco*, red, 261

Tesco Chilean Red NV, **16.5**, *Tesco*, red, 252

Tesco Chilean Sauvignon Blanc NV, **15.5**, *Tesco*, white, 265

Tesco Chilean White NV, **16**, *Tesco*, white, xiii, 261

Tesco Claret NV, **16**, *Tesco*, red, 262

Tesco Claret Reserve 2002, **15**, *Tesco*, red, 271

Tesco Côtes du Rhône-Villages 2002, **14**, *Tesco*, red, 279

Tesco Finest 10-year-old Tawny Port NV, **15.5**, *Tesco*, fortified, 266

Tesco Finest Alsace Gewürztraminer 2003, **16**, *Tesco*, white, 260

Tesco Finest Argentinian Malbec Reserve 2004, **16**, *Tesco*, red, 261

Tesco Finest Argentinian Shiraz Reserve 2004, **14.5**, *Tesco*, red, 273

Tesco Finest Australian Cabernet Sauvignon 2003, **14.5**, *Tesco*, red, 273

Tesco Finest Australian Chardonnay NV, **16**, *Tesco*, white, 262

Tesco Finest Australian Reserve Merlot 2004, **16**, *Tesco*, red, 258

Tesco Finest Barossa Old Vines Sémillon 2003, **16.5**, *Tesco*, white, 252

Tesco Finest Barossa Old Vines Shiraz 2003, **14.5**, *Tesco*, red, 273

Tesco Finest Chablis Premier Cru 2001, **16**, *Tesco*, white, 260

Tesco Finest Chilean Chardonnay Reserve 2004, **15**, *Tesco*, white, 271

Tesco Finest Chilean Merlot 2004, **16**, *Tesco*, red, 258

Tesco Finest Chilean Sauvignon Blanc 2004, **16**, *Tesco*, white, 259

Tesco Finest Denman Estate Reserve Sémillon 2002, **17**, *Tesco*, white, 247

Tesco Finest Fino NV, **15**, *Tesco*, fortified, 270

Tesco Finest Fitou Varon de la Tour 2003, **14**, *Tesco*, red, 278

Tesco Finest Gavi 2004, **16.5**, *Tesco*, white, 251

Tesco Finest Great Southern Riesling 2003, **16**, *Tesco*, white, 260

Tesco Finest Howcroft Estate Reserve Cabernet/Merlot 2003, **16.5**, *Tesco*, red, 252

Tesco Finest Howcroft Estate Reserve Merlot 2004, **15.5**, *Tesco*, red, 265

Tesco Finest Howcroft Estate Reserve Shiraz 2003, **14**, *Tesco*, red, 278

Tesco Finest Kenton Valley Estate Reserve Sauvignon Blanc 2004, **16**, *Tesco*, white, 259

Tesco Finest Madeira NV, **15.5**, *Tesco*, fortified, 266

Tesco Finest Manzanilla Sherry NV, **15**, *Tesco*, fortified, 270

Tesco Finest Marlborough Sauvignon Blanc 2004, **17**, *Tesco*, white, 246

Tesco Finest Meursault 2001, **16**, *Tesco*, white, 260

Tesco Finest Oloroso Sherry NV, **16.5**, *Tesco*, fortified, xiv, 251

Tesco Finest Pinot Grigio 2004, **16**, *Tesco*, white, 259

Tesco Finest Reserve Californian Merlot 2003, **15.5**, *Tesco*, red, 266

Tesco Finest Reserve Californian Viognier 2003, **14**, *Tesco*, white, 278

Tesco Finest Sauternes 2002, **15**, *Tesco*, white, 270

Tesco Finest South African Chenin Blanc 2004, **16**, *Tesco*, white, 260

Tesco Finest Special Reserve Port NV, **16**, *Tesco*, fortified, 258

Tesco Finest St-Emilion 2003, **16**, *Tesco*, red, 259

Tesco Finest Vintage Cava 2000, **14.5**, *Tesco*, white sparkling, 273

Tesco Finest Vintage Champagne 2000, **14**, *Tesco*, white sparkling, 278

Tesco Finest Vouvray Demi-Sec 2003, **15**, *Tesco*, white, 270

Tesco Grecanico Chardonnay 2003, **16**, *Tesco*, white, 261

Tesco LBV Port 1998, **14.5**, *Tesco*, fortified, 274

Tesco Marqués de Chive NV, **14**, *Tesco*, red, 280

Tesco Moscatel de Valencia NV, **16**, *Tesco*, white, 258

Tesco Moscato Spumante NV, **15**, *Tesco*, white sparkling, 269

Tesco Muscadet NV, **14**, *Tesco*, white, 278

Tesco Nero d'Avola/Sangiovese Sicilia 2003, **16**, *Tesco*, red, 262

Tesco New Zealand Dry White NV, **14.5**, *Tesco*, white, 273

Tesco New Zealand Marlborough Sauvignon Blanc **15.5**, *Tesco*, white, 265

Tesco Organic Australian Chardonnay 2004, **14.5**, *Tesco*, white, 273

Tesco Organic Red NV, **14**, *Tesco*, red, 279

Tesco Premières Côtes de Bordeaux NV, **14**, *Tesco*, white, 280

Tesco Rosé Cava NV, **14.5**, *Tesco*, rosé sparkling, 274

Tesco Sicilian Red 2003, **15**, *Tesco*, red, 271

Tesco Soave NV, **14.5**, *Tesco*, white, 274

Tesco South African Chenin NV, **15**, *Tesco*, white, 270

Tesco South African Colombard/ Sauvignon NV, **14**, *Tesco*, white, 278

Tesco Viña Mara Rioja Crianza 1999, **15.5**, *Tesco*, red, 265

Tesco Vintage Port 1995, **14**, *Tesco*, fortified, 280

Tesco's Finest Marlborough Pinot Noir 2003, **15**, *Tesco*, red, 270

Thandi Cabernet/Merlot 2004, **15**, *Co-op*, red, 66

Thandi Chardonnay 2004, **15.5**, *Tesco*, white, 266

The Boulders Viognier 2003, **15.5**, *Co-op*, white, 64

The Chocolate Block 2003, **14**, *Waitrose*, red, 326

The Cork Grove Fernao Pires 2004, **16**, *Co-op*, white, 63

The Gables Chardonnay 2004, **14**, *Morrison's*, white, 137

The Lakes Reserve Brut NV, **14.5**, *Tesco*, white sparkling, 274

The Naked Grape Riesling 2004, **14**, *Waitrose*, white, 327

The Reserve Yellow Tail Shiraz 2002, **15.5**, *Somerfield*, red, 237

The Wolftrap Boekenhoutskloof 2004, **16**, *Sainsbury*, red, 183

Thomas Mitchell Marsanne 2003, **17**, *Oddbins*, white, 142

Three Choirs Variations Aromatic 2004, **14**, *Asda*, white, 25

Tim Adams Sémillon 2003, **17.5**, *Tesco*, white, 245

Tim Adams Shiraz 2003, **16**, *Tesco*, red, 262

Timara Sauvignon Blanc/ Sémillon 2003, **14.5**, *Budgens*, white, 53

Tokay Pinot Gris Grand Cru Hengst Albert Mann 2002, **16**, *Waitrose*, white, 314

Tokay Pinot Gris Selection de Grains Nobles Altenbourg 'Le Tri', Albert Mann 2001, **17.5**, *Waitrose*, white, 299

Torres San Medin Cabernet Sauvignon Rosé 2004, **15**, *Waitrose*, rosé, 320

Torres Sangre de Toro 2003, **15.5**, *Budgens*, red, 51

Torres Viña Esmeralda 2004, **14**, *Tesco*, white, 277

Torres Viña Sol 2004, **15**, *Budgens*, *Tesco*, white, 52, 269

Torresoto Rioja 2003, **16**, *Marks & Spencer*, white, 123

Touchstone Cabernet Sauvignon 2003, **14.5**, *Vintage Roots*, red, 79

Touchstone Merlot 2002, **15**, *Vintage Roots*, red, 78

Touchstone Sauvignon Blanc 2004, **15**, *Vintage Roots*, white, 78

Trackers Trail Shiraz 2004, **16**, *Marks & Spencer*, red, 123

Trinity Hill Pinot Noir 2004, **16**, *Selfridges*, red, 214

Trio Chardonnay/Pinot Grigio/Pinot Blanc 2004, **15.5**, *Co-op*, *Somerfield*, white, 65, 237

Trio Merlot/Carmenere/Cabernet Sauvignon 2004, **16**, *Co-op*, *Somerfield*, red, 63, 234

Trio Sauvignon Blanc 2004, **14**,
 Booths, white, 41
Trio Shiraz/Cabernet Sauvignon/
 Cabernet Franc NV, **16.5**, *Tesco*,
 red, 252
Trivento Shiraz/Malbec Reserve
 2004, **17**, *Threshers*, red, 284
Trivento Viognier 2004, **15**,
 Waitrose, white, 320
Trulli Zinfandel 2003, **15**, *Tesco*,
 red, 271
Tuatara Bay Pinot Noir 2004, **14.5**,
 Hallgarten Wines, Selfridges, red,
 218
Tukulu Pinotage 2002, **14**,
 Oddbins, red, 161
Tupagato Chardonnay 2003, **17.5**,
 Marks & Spencer, white, 112
Two Hands Brave Faces Barossa
 Valley Shiraz/Grenache 2002,
 14, *Sainsbury*, red, 193

V

Vacqueyras 2003, **17**, *Somerfield*,
 red, 225
Valdivieso Cabernet Sauvignon
 2003, **16.5**, *Tesco*, red, 253
Valdivieso Cabernet Sauvignon
 2004, **16.5**, *Tesco*, red, 253
Valdivieso Chardonnay 2004, **16**,
 Tesco, white, 263
Valdivieso Merlot 2003, **16**, *Tesco*,
 red, 263
Valdivieso Merlot 2004, **16.5**,
 Tesco, red, 253
Valdivieso Reserve Cabernet
 Sauvignon 2002, **16**, *Sainsbury*,
 red, 183

Valley of the Roses Cabernet
 Sauvignon Rosé 2004, **14.5**,
 Co-op, rosé, 67
Valpolicella Classico Superiore
 Ripasso La Casetta di Ettore
 Righetti 2001, **16**, *Majestic*, red,
 96
Valréas Côtes du Rhône,
 Domaine de la Grande
 Bellance 2003, **15**, *Co-op*, red,
 66
Van Loveren Blanc de Noirs 2003,
 14.5, *Budgens*, rosé, 53
Van Loveren Sauvignon Blanc
 2004, **14**, *Tesco*, white, 280
Vasse Felix 'Adams Road'
 Cabernet/Merlot 2003, **15.5**,
 Majestic, red, 100
Vasse Felix 'Adams Road'
 Chardonnay 2004, **14.5**,
 Majestic, white, 103
Vavasour Sauvignon Blanc 2004,
 14, *Booths*, white, 42
Vega Barcelona Tempranillo/
 Shiraz 2003, **16**, *Asda*, red, 14
Veo Cabernet/Merlot 2003, **14**,
 Tesco, red, 280
Veo Chardonnay 2003, **14.5**, *Tesco*,
 white, 274
Veo Grande Chardonnay/
 Viognier NV, **15.5**, *Tesco*, white,
 266
Veramonte Cabernet Sauvignon
 2001, **16**, *Somerfield*, red, 235
Veramonte Sauvignon Blanc
 2004, **15**, *Somerfield*, white, 239
Verdicchio dei Castelli di Jesi
 Classico 2004, **15**, *Threshers*,
 white, 294

Verdicchio dei Castelli di Jesi
    2004, **16**, *Marks & Spencer*,
    white, 124
Verdicchio dei Castelli di Jesi
    Classico Moncaro 2004, **14**,
    Waitrose, white, 327
Verdicchio dei Castelli di Jesi
    Croce del Moro 2004, **14.5**,
    Majestic, white, 103
Vereto Salice Salentino 2001, **16**,
    Threshers, red, 293
Vergelegen Cabernet Sauvignon
    2001, **17.5**, *Oddbins*, red, 141
Vergelegen Cabernet Sauvignon
    2003, **16**, *Majestic*, red, 96
Vergelegen Chardonnay 2003, **16**,
    Majestic, Oddbins, white, 96,
    153
Vergelegen Merlot 2001, **17**,
    Oddbins, red, 142
Vergelegen Sauvignon Blanc
    2004, **15.5**, *Oddbins*, white, 156
Veuve Clicquot Ponsardin Brut
    NV, **14.5**, *Budgens*, white
    sparkling, 53
Via Leyda Pinot Noir 'Lot 21'
    2002, **14.5**, *Adnams*, red, 219
Via Ulivi Pinot Grigio 2004, **14.5**,
    Marks & Spencer, white, 126
Vidal East Coast Sauvignon
    Blanc 2003, **14**, *Threshers*,
    white, 295
Vieux Château Gaubert 2001, **16**,
    Laithwaites, white, 77
Vignale Pinot Grigio 2004, **14**,
    Waitrose, white, 327
Vigneti di Montegradella
    Valpolicella Classico 2001,
    17.5, *Tesco*, red, 245

Villa Maria Marlborough
    Sauvignon Blanc 2004, **17**,
    Threshers, white, 285
Villa Maria Private Bin
    Gewürztraminer 2004, **16**,
    Asda, Waitrose, white, 14, 314
Villa Maria Private Bin Riesling
    2004, **16**, *Budgens, Majestic*,
    white, 49, 98
Villa Maria Private Bin Sauvignon
    Blanc 2004, **16**, *Asda, Budgens,
    Sainsbury, Somerfield, Tesco*,
    white, 14, 49, 184, 235, 253
Villa Maria Reserve Cabernet
    Sauvignon/Merlot 2002, **14**,
    *Everywine, Vicki's of Chobham,
    Wimbledon Wine Cellars*, red,
    80, 221
Villa Maria Reserve Merlot 2002,
    15.5, *Everywine, Waitrose*, red,
    77, 317
Villa Maria Single Vineyard
    Taylors Pass Pinot Noir 2003,
    14.5, *Everywine, Luvians,
    Wimbledon Wine Cellars*, red,
    79, 218
Villa Montes Reserve Sauvignon
    Blanc 2003, **16**, *Morrison's,
    Sainsbury, Waitrose*, white, 133,
    183, 314
Villalta Amarone della
    Valpolicella Classico 2000, **18**,
    Marks & Spencer, red, 111
Vin de Pays de l'Ardèche Gamay
    2004, **16.5**, *Marks & Spencer*,
    red, 117
Vin de Pays d'Oc Sauvignon
    Blanc 2004, **16**, *Marks &
    Spencer*, white, 124

Vin de Pays du Mont Caume Bunan Mourvèdre 2002, **15**, *Yapp Brothers*, red, 334

Viña Albali Gran Reserva Valdepeñas 1998, **14**, *Sainsbury*, red, 193

Viña Albali Reserva Valdepeñas 2000, **14.5**, *Asda, Budgens*, red, 21, 53

Viña Albali Tinto Reserva 1999, **14.5**, *Co-op*, red, 67

Viña Alta Mar Jumilla Monastrell/Cabernet Sauvignon 2001, **14**, *Majestic*, red, 107

Viña Leyda Chardonnay 2001, **14**, *Adnams*, white, 221

Viña Leyda Pinot Noir 2004, **14**, *Adnams*, red, 221

Viña Misiónes Cabernet Franc Reserve 2003, **16**, *Co-op*, red, 64

Viña Porta Reserva Pinot Noir 2003, **14.5**, *Oddbins*, red, 158

Viña Sardasol Merlot Bodega Virgen Blanca Navarra 2003, **14**, *Booths*, red, 42

Viñas del Vero Chardonnay/ Macabeo 2004, **14**, *Co-op*, white, 69

Viñedo Chadwick 1999, **15**, *Waitrose*, red, 320

Vineyard X Garnacha 2003, **16.5**, *Threshers*, white, 288

Vino Nobile di Montepulciano Carbonaia 2001, **14**, *Waitrose*, red, 327

Vouvray Domaine de la Pouvraie 2003, **16**, *Marks & Spencer*, white, 124

Vouvray La Couronne des Plantagenets 2003, **16**, *Sainsbury*, white, 183

Vouvray Le Mont Sec Huet 2000, **14.5**, *Waitrose*, white, 322

Voyager Estate Cabernet/Merlot 2000, **14**, *Oddbins*, red, 162

Voyager Estate Chardonnay 2003, **14.5**, *Oddbins*, white, 158

Voyager Estate Sauvignon Blanc/ Sémillon 2004, **15.5**, *Oddbins*, white, 156

Voyager Estate Sémillon 2002, **14**, *Oddbins*, white, 161

Voyager Estate Shiraz 2003, **14**, *Oddbins*, red, 162

Waimea Estate Pinot Noir 2003, **15**, *Majestic*, red, 101

Waimea Estate Sauvignon Blanc 2004, **15.5**, *Majestic*, white, 100

Waitrose Chianti 2003, **15**, *Waitrose*, red, 320

Waitrose Chilean Chardonnay/ Sauvignon Blanc 2003, **14**, *Waitrose*, white, 327

Waitrose Muscadet de Sèvre et Maine 2004, **15**, *Waitrose*, white, 320

Waitrose Rosé d'Anjou 2004, **14**, *Waitrose*, rosé, 327

Wakefield Estate Cabernet Sauvignon 2002, **16.5**, *Unwins*, red, 210

Wakefield Estate Riesling 2003, **16**, *Oddbins*, white, 153

Wakefield Estate Shiraz 2003, **16.5**, *Oddbins, Unwins*, red, 146, 210–11

Wakefield Promised Land Cabernet/Merlot 2002, **15.5**, *Somerfield*, red, 238

Warwick Estate Chardonnay 2004, **17**, *Waitrose*, white, 301

Watchpost Bianco di Custoza 2003, **14.5**, *Asda*, white, 21

Weinert Malbec 1999, **16**, *Sainsbury*, red, 183

Wente Chardonnay 2003, **15**, *Waitrose*, white, 320

West Brook Pinot Noir 2004, **14.5**, *Great Western Wines*, red, 219

Windy Peak Cabernet Rosé 2004, **14**, *Amps Fine Wines*, rosé, 221

Wither Hills Pinot Noir 2003, **16**, *Booths, Oddbins, Waitrose*, red, 36, 154, 314

Wolf Blass Cabernet Sauvignon/Merlot 2004, **14.5**, *Asda*, red, 21

Wolf Blass Eagle Hawk Chardonnay 2004, **16**, *Asda, Sainsbury, Somerfield*, white, 15, 183, 235

Wolf Blass Eagle Hawk Rosé 2004, **14.5**, *Asda, Sainsbury*, rosé, 21, 190

Wolf Blass Eagle Hawk Shiraz/Merlot/Cabernet 2003, **14.5**, *Somerfield*, red, 240

Wolf Blass President's Selection Cabernet Sauvignon 2002, **16**, *Majestic, Somerfield, Waitrose*, red, 98, 228, 315

Wolf Blass President's Selection Chardonnay 2003, **15**, *Somerfield*, white, 239

Wolf Blass Red Label Cabernet Sauvignon/Shiraz 2003, **14**, *Budgens*, red, 55

Wolf Blass Red Label Chardonnay 2004, **15.5**, *Asda*, white, 17

Wolf Blass Red Label Chardonnay/Sémillon 2004, **14.5**, *Budgens, Tesco*, white, 53, 274

Wolf Blass Red Label Sparkling Chardonnay/Pinot Noir NV, **14**, *Asda, Sainsbury*, white sparkling, 26, 193

Wolf Blass Yellow Label Cabernet Sauvignon 2002, **15**, *Somerfield*, red, 239

Wolf Blass Yellow Label Cabernet Sauvignon 2003, **15.5**, *Somerfield, Tesco*, red, 238, 267

Wolf Blass Yellow Label Cabernet Sauvignon/Shiraz 2003, **15.5**, *Budgens*, red, 51

Wolf Blass Yellow Label Chardonnay 2004, **15.5**, *Budgens, Tesco*, white, 50, 265

Wontanella Colombard/Viognier 2004, **15**, *Asda*, white, 19

Wontanella Sangiovese/Petit Verdot, 2004, **14**, *Asda*, red, 25

Wontanella Tempranillo 2004, **14**, *Asda*, red, 26

Woodhaven Shiraz 2004, **16**, *Marks & Spencer*, red, 124

Woolpunda Cabernet Sauvignon, **15**, *Morrison's*, white, 135

Woolpunda Chardonnay 2002, **15**, *Morrison's*, white, 135

Wyndham Estate Bin 555 Sparkling Shiraz NV, **16**, *Morrison's*, red sparkling, 1133

Wyndham Estate Bin 444 Cabernet Sauvignon 2003, **15**, *Tesco*, red, 271

Wyndham Estate Bin 555 Shiraz 2002, **15**, *Tesco*, red, 271

Yali Sauvignon Blanc Reserve 2004, **14**, *Tesco*, white, 280

Yalumba Oxford Landing Shiraz 2002, **14.5**, *Tesco*, red, 274

Yellow Tail Cabernet Sauvignon 2004, **14**, *Asda*, *Waitrose*, red, 26, 327

Yellow Tail Merlot 2004, **15**, *Co-op*, red, 66

Yering Frog Yarra Valley Chardonnay 2003, **16**, *Majestic*, white, 96

Yering Station 'ED' Pinot Noir Rosé 2003, **14.5**, *Philglas & Swiggot*, rosé, 219

Yering Station Yarra Valley Chardonnay 2003, **16**, *Majestic*, white, 97

Yering Station Yarra Valley Marsanne/Roussanne/ Viognier 2004, **16.5**, *Majestic*, white, 87

Yering Station Yarra Valley Pinot Noir 2002, **14.5**, *Majestic*, red, 13

Yering Station Yarra Valley Pinot Noir Rosé 2004, **16**, *Majestic*, rosé, 97

Yering Station Yarrabank Cuvée Pinot Noir/Chardonnay 2000, **16**, *Philglas & Swiggot*, *Wine Cellars*, white sparkling, 214

Zamora Zinfandel 2003, **14.5**, *Marks & Spencer*, red, 126

Zenato Valpolicella Classico Superiore 2001, **17.5**, *Threshers*, red, 283

Zilzie Estate Chardonnay 2004, **16**, *Asda*, white, 15

Zondernaam Sauvignon Blanc 2004, **15**, *Majestic*, white, 101

Zonte's Footsteps Langhorne Creek Cabernet/Petit Verdot Rosé 2004, **16**, *Sainsbury*, *Unwins*, rosé, 184, 214

Zonte's Footsteps Langhorne Creek Shiraz/Viognier 2004, **15.5**, *Sainsbury*, *Somerfield*, red, 187, 237

Zonte's Footsteps Langhorne Creek Verdelho 2004, **16**, *Somerfield*, white, 236

The *Guardian*'s Superplonk column appeared between March 1989 and December 2004. When it ceased, I received a torrent of letters and e-mails, unanimously kind. To all those hundreds of readers who wrote, I extend my heartfelt gratitude. Especial thanks, for the richness of their correspondence, are due to Ian Evans, David Armitage, Jacqui Worsley, Ross Kightly, Margaret Williams, George McRobie, Malcolm Swire, Peter Richards, Graham Starmer, Alan Tice, Michael Carradice, Simon Roberts, Fred Bleasdale, Alun J. Carr, Toni King, John Winterton, Geoff Hill, John Archer, John Gooch, FG7AUD, Martin McNicol, Andy Stobbie, Robert Polfreman, Bryan Rippin, Jane Clucas, Matt Smith, Patrick Macartney, Chris Spicer, Valerie Kirkham, John Boardman, Sean Clarke, Peter Barnes, Chris Peel, Jim Helling, Jacqui Dally, Kay Steward, Mike Barnes, Patsy and Alan Aplin, Elizabeth Keeble, Kern Brown, John Gooch, John Speller, Mike Barnes, George Smith, Kenneth Brown, Colin Ibbotson, Jill Thorne, Brian Mulligan, Denis Keane, Lesley Saltmarsh, Heidi and Mayer Hillman, Barry Catchpole, David Little, Denis Keane, Robert Saunders, Richard Trussell, Jeff Allinson, Donald King, and Peter Mounfield.